INTRODUCTION TO
ESTATE PLANNING

IN A NUTSHELL

By

ROBERT J. LYNN
Professor of Law Emeritus
Ohio State University

FOURTH EDITION

ST. PAUL, MINN.
WEST PUBLISHING CO.
1992

COPYRIGHT © 1975, 1978, 1983 WEST PUBLISHING CO.
COPYRIGHT © 1992 By WEST PUBLISHING CO.
                          610 Opperman Drive
                          P.O. Box 64526
                          St. Paul, MN 55164–0526

Library of Congress Cataloging-in-Publication Data

Lynn, Robert J.
    Introduction to estate planning in a nutshell / by Robert J. Lynn.
— 4th ed.
        p.   cm. — (Nutshell series)
    Includes index.
    ISBN 0–314–00809–8
    1. Estate planning—United States. I. Title. II. Series.
KF750.L9 1992
346.7305'2—dc20
[347.30652]   92–15358
                                                               CIP

ISBN 0–314–00809–8

        Lynn, Est.Planning, 4th Ed. NS
        2nd Reprint—1997

PREFACE

This book is a third revision of *An Introduction to Estate Planning* (1975). It is intended for law students, lawyers, and non-lawyers interested in wills, trusts, future interests, insurance, pensions, federal estate and gift taxation, and fiduciary administration.

Because each chapter stands as much as possible as a separate unit, I have included no internal references, and I have occasionally repeated material. Successive chapters do, however, tend to build on preceding chapters. Therefore, one ought not to read (say) chapter 8 on Trusts unless he has knowledge of the information in chapters 1 through 5.

Citations are few. Citations sufficient to satisfy a specialist distract and discourage the non-specialist. There are numerous excellent publications directed to the former, and I have therefore chosen to try to assist the latter.

David A. Paxton, Esq., now of the Colorado bar, assisted in the preparation of the earlier ver-

sion of this book. This revision still carries the
mark of his conscientious work.

ROBERT J. LYNN

Columbus, Ohio

OUTLINE

		Page
PREFACE		III
TABLE OF CASES		XIII

Chapter 1. The Estate and Estate Planning 1

§ 1.1	Estate Planning and This Book	1
§ 1.2	Lifetime Gifts	4
§ 1.3	"Simple" (Non–Trust) Inter Vivos Gifts of Personal Property	5
§ 1.4	"Estate" in the Largest Sense	10
§ 1.5	Administration of the Estate	13
§ 1.6	Responsibility of the Executor or Administrator	15
§ 1.7	Settling "Small" Estates	16
§ 1.8	Property "Outside" the Probate Estate	18
§ 1.9	The Importance of State Law	19
§ 1.10	The Importance of Federal Law	20
§ 1.11	Community Property	22
§ 1.12	"Foreign" Assets	23

Chapter 2. The Transfer of Property at Death by Will and Under the Intestate Law 25

§ 2.1	The Probate Estate	25
§ 2.2	Testacy and Intestacy	25

Page

§ 2.3   Those Who Take the Net Probate
        Estate 26
§ 2.4   Executor and Administrator 27
§ 2.5   Intestacy: Estate Planning "By Op-
        eration of Law" 27
§ 2.6   Lapse 30
§ 2.7   Ademption 31
§ 2.8   Codicil 32
§ 2.9   "Provision" for the Surviving Spouse   32
§ 2.10 The Right of Election of the Surviv-
        ing Spouse 33
§ 2.11 Freedom of Testation 34
§ 2.12 Revocation 35
§ 2.13 Survivorship: What Is Required? .. 36
§ 2.14 Advancement 38
§ 2.15 Satisfaction 38
§ 2.16 Abatement 38
§ 2.17 Per Capita and Per Stirpes 39
§ 2.18 From Whom Property Is Acquired.. 41
§ 2.19 Adoption 42
§ 2.20 Illegitimacy 43
§ 2.21 Disclaimer 43

Chapter 3. Survivorship Interests 45
§ 3.1   What Motivates the Creation of Sur-
        vivorship Interests? 45
§ 3.2   Creating the Incident of Survivor-
        ship 45
§ 3.3   Severability 48
§ 3.4   United States Savings Bonds 50
§ 3.5   Avoiding Probate 51

		Page
§ 3.6	Taxation—In General	53
§ 3.7	Simultaneous Death	54
§ 3.8	"Totten Trusts" and "Pay on Death" or "Transfer on Death" Accounts	56
§ 3.9	Rights of the Surviving Spouse and the Divorced Spouse	57
§ 3.10	Conclusion	58
Chapter 4.	**Community Property**	**60**
§ 4.1	The Nature of Community Property	60
§ 4.2	Where the Community Property System Exists in the United States	61
§ 4.3	Community Property Differentiated from Separate Property	62
§ 4.4	Life Insurance	64
§ 4.5	Management and Disposition of Community Property	67
§ 4.6	Community Property and Federal Estate Taxation	68
§ 4.7	Community Property, Conflict of Laws, and Protection of the Surviving Spouse	69
§ 4.8	"Election" by a Surviving Spouse in a Community Property State	72
Chapter 5.	**"Simple" Wills**	**74**
§ 5.1	The Limited Function of the Will	74
§ 5.2	The Case Against Intestacy	75
§ 5.3	Interview with the Testator	79
§ 5.4	Drafting the "Simple" Will	79
§ 5.5	Dispositive Clause	82

		Page
§ 5.6	Caveats	85
§ 5.7	Guardianship	88
§ 5.8	Nominating the Executor	91
§ 5.9	Powers of the Executor	91
§ 5.10	The Closing Recitation	92
§ 5.11	The Attestation Clause	93
§ 5.12	Execution	95
§ 5.13	The "Self–Proved" Will	96
§ 5.14	Statutory Wills	99
§ 5.15	Safeguarding the Will	99
§ 5.16	Lists of Property and Benefits: Suggestions of the Decedent	100
§ 5.17	A "Simple Will" in Its Entirety	101
Chapter 6. Insurance		**105**
§ 6.1	Insurance and Estate Planning	105
§ 6.2	Why Life Insurance?	107
§ 6.3	Life Insurance Proceeds under State Law and under the Federal Estate Tax	110
§ 6.4	Why Property and Liability Insurance?	113
§ 6.5	Insurable Interest	114
§ 6.6	Kinds of Life Insurance	117
§ 6.7	Settlement Options	120
§ 6.8	Kinds of Settlement Options	122
§ 6.9	Change of Beneficiary of a Life Policy	124
§ 6.10	Assignment	126
§ 6.11	Assignment of Life Insurance	128
§ 6.12	Assignment of Fire Insurance	130

Page

§ 6.13   Assignment of Liability Insurance __ 131

Chapter 7. The Estate Arising From Status: Social Security; "Private" Pensions; Workers' Compensation; Veterans' Benefits _____ 132

§ 7.1   Providing for Dependents Through Status _____ 132
§ 7.2   Social Security_____ 133
§ 7.3   Becoming "Insured" under Social Security _____ 136
§ 7.4   Benefits under Social Security_____ 139
§ 7.5   Other Governmental and "Private" Pensions_____ 141
§ 7.6   "Vesting" and "Portability"_____ 144
§ 7.7   Forced Retirement _____ 146
§ 7.8   Workers' Compensation _____ 147
§ 7.9   Veterans' Benefits_____ 150
§ 7.10   Benefits from More than One Source 153

Chapter 8. Trusts—An Introduction _____ 155
§ 8.1   The Private Express Trust _____ 155
§ 8.2   The Statute of Frauds and the Statute of Wills_____ 158
§ 8.3   The Revocable Trust _____ 163
§ 8.4   Incorporation by Reference_____ 169
§ 8.5   The "Pour–Over" Will _____ 171
§ 8.6   Protecting the Beneficiary Against Himself _____ 176
§ 8.7   Trust Termination _____ 180

Page

§ 8.8   The Durable Power of Attorney 184
§ 8.9   The Living Will............................ 185

**Chapter 9. Future Interests—An Intro-
             duction**.............................. **186**
§ 9.1   Reversions, Remainders, and Execu-
         tory Interests............................ 186
§ 9.2   How Future Interests Change 190
§ 9.3   Using Future Interests................. 194
§ 9.4   The Language of Class Gifts 198
§ 9.5   How Class Gifts Work 200
§ 9.6   Drafting 204
§ 9.7   The Basic Language of Powers....... 210
§ 9.8   The Origin of Powers 213
§ 9.9   What Motivates the Creation of Pow-
         ers? 214
§ 9.10   How Powers Work..................... 216
§ 9.11   Drafting 218

**Chapter 10. Using   Private   Express
              Trusts; Charitable Trusts   223**
§ 10.1   Trusteeship versus Guardianship 223
§ 10.2   "Keogh" Trusts and Individual Re-
         tirement Accounts 228
§ 10.3   Marital Deduction Trusts 229
§ 10.4   Revocable Trusts Under Forced
         Share Statutes........................ 232
§ 10.5   Charitable Trusts..................... 234
§ 10.6   Mortmain Acts 239
§ 10.7   Community Foundations.............. 240

**Chapter 11. The Rule in Shelley's Case;
The Doctrine of Worthier
Title; The Rule Against
Perpetuities; The Rule
Against Accumulations** 242

§ 11.1 The Rule in Shelley's Case and the
Doctrine of Worthier Title 242

§ 11.2 The Rule Against Perpetuities 246

§ 11.3 The "Perpetuities Period" 251

§ 11.4 Class Gifts Under the Rule 252

§ 11.5 Powers and Appointments Under the
Rule 257

§ 11.6 Drafting Under the Rule 261

§ 11.7 Reforming the Rule 267

§ 11.8 The Rule Against Accumulations 269

**Chapter 12. Some Aspects of Fiduciary
Administration** 271

§ 12.1 Contract and Tort Liability of the
Fiduciary 271

§ 12.2 The Duty of Loyalty 277

§ 12.3 Trust Investments 280

§ 12.4 Administrative Powers 284

**Chapter 13. The Federal Estate and Gift
Taxes** 290

§ 13.1 Introduction 290

§ 13.2 Using Lifetime Transfers to Avoid or
Minimize Taxes 294

§ 13.3 What Is a Gift for Federal Tax Pur-
poses? 295

Page

§ 13.4 The Unified Credit and the Annual Exclusion _____ 299

§ 13.5 Present and Future Gifts for Purposes of the Exclusion _____ 300

§ 13.6 The Annual Exclusion and Gifts to Minors _____ 302

§ 13.7 Split Gifts; The Marital Deduction 303

§ 13.8 The Orphan's Deduction_____ 305

§ 13.9 Property Qualifying for the Marital Deduction _____ 306

§ 13.10 "Survivorship" Clause and the Marital Deduction_____ 307

§ 13.11 Property Qualifying for the Estate Tax Marital Deduction_____ 308

§ 13.12 The Gross Estate _____ 310

§ 13.13 Survivorship Interests _____ 311

§ 13.14 Transfers within Three Years of Death_____ 316

§ 13.15 Sections 2036, 2037, and 2038 _____ 317

§ 13.16 Annuities _____ 324

§ 13.17 Life Insurance _____ 325

§ 13.18 Powers of Appointment_____ 326

§ 13.19 The Charitable Deduction_____ 329

§ 13.20 Generation–Skipping Transfers _____ 331

§ 13.21 What is a "Generation"?_____ 334

INDEX_____ 335

TABLE OF CASES
References are to Pages

Bendall v. Home Indem. Co., 286 Ala. 146, 238 So.2d 177 (Ala. 1970), *131*

Cattlin v. Brown, 11 Hare 372, 68 Eng.Rep. 1319 (Ch.1853), *254, 255, 256*

Chandler, United States v., 410 U.S. 257, 93 S.Ct. 880, 35 L.Ed. 2d 247 (1973), *8, 9*

Claflin v. Claflin, 149 Mass. 19, 20 N.E. 454 (Mass.1889), *179, 198*

Claus, In re Estate of, 197 N.E.2d 898, 29 O.O.2d 262 (Ohio App. 1963), *7*

Estate of (see name of party)

Francis v. Francis, 89 Wash.2d 511, 573 P.2d 369 (Wash.1978), *67*

Harris v. Commissioner of Internal Revenue, 340 U.S. 106, 71 S.Ct. 181, 95 L.Ed. 111 (1950), *298*

Harvard College v. Amory, 26 Mass. (9 Pick.) 446 (1830), *281*

Higgins v. Higgins, 458 S.W.2d 498 (Tex.Civ.App.1970), *64*

In re (see name of party)

John Hancock Mut. Life Ins. Co. v. Jedynak, 250 Mich. 88, 229 N.W. 413 (Mich.1930), *124*

Jubinville v. Jubinville, 313 Mass. 103, 46 N.E.2d 533 (Mass. 1943), *278*

Kessler, In re Estate of, 177 Ohio St. 136, 203 N.E.2d 221, 29 O.O.2d 348 (Ohio 1964), *70*

Leake v. Robinson, 2 Mer. 363, 35 Eng.Rep. 979 (Ch.1817), *195*

Lewis v. Baldwin, 11 Ohio 352 (Ohio 1842), *47, 49*

Lippincott Estate, 17 Pa.D. & C.2d 80 (Orphan's Ct.1959), *240, 241*

XIII

Nelson, Estate of, 224 Cal.App.2d 138, 36 Cal.Rptr. 352 (Cal. App. 1 Dist.1964), *64*

Old Colony Trust Co. v. United States, 423 F.2d 601 (1st Cir. 1970), *319*

Pearce v. National Life & Acc. Ins Co., 12 La.App. 608, 125 So. 776 (La.App.1930), *67*
Phipps v. Ackers, 9 Cl. & F. 583, 8 Eng.Rep. 539 (H.L.1835), *191*

Shapira v. Union Nat. Bank, 39 Ohio Misc. 28, 315 N.E.2d 825, 68 O.O.2d 187 (Ohio Com.Pl.1974), *34*
Shelley's Case, *242, 243, 244, 245*
Steinhauser v. Repko, 30 Ohio St.2d 262, 285 N.E.2d 55, 59 O.O.2d 334 (Ohio 1972), *52*
Stone v. Stephens, 155 Ohio St. 595, 99 N.E.2d 766, 45 O.O. 11 (Ohio 1951), *125*
Storrs v. Benbow, 3 De Gex, M. & G. 309, 43 Eng.Rep. 153 (Ch. 1853), *254, 256*
Svab, In re Estate of, 11 Ohio St.2d 182, 228 N.E.2d 609, 40 O.O. 2d 166 (Ohio 1967), *51*

Toledo Trust Co. v. Toledo Hospital, 174 Ohio St. 124, 187 N.E.2d 36 (Ohio 1962), *282*
Trimble v. Gordon, 430 U.S. 762, 97 S.Ct. 1459, 52 L.Ed.2d 31, 4 O.O.3d 296 (1977), *43*
Trusteeship Under Agreement with Mayo, In re, 259 Minn. 91, 105 N.W.2d 900 (Minn.1960), *282*

United States v. ____ (see opposing party)

Weld v. Bradbury, 2 Vern. 705, 23 Eng.Rep. 1058 (Ch.1715), *202*

INTRODUCTION TO
ESTATE PLANNING
IN A NUTSHELL

*

CHAPTER 1

THE ESTATE AND ESTATE PLANNING

§ 1.1 Estate Planning and This Book. "Estate Planning" is applying the law of property, trusts, wills, future interests, insurance, and taxation to the ordering of one's affairs, while keeping in mind the possibility of retirement and the certainty of death. "Estate Planning" is often used as a synonym for "Tax Planning" or "Business Planning" or "Insurance Planning." Although taxation and the existence of business interests unquestionably affect estate planning, and adequate insurance coverage is often a part (and conceivably the most important part) of an estate plan, the emphasis in this book is on estate planning in the more traditional sense, with allusions to taxation, business interests, and insurance to the extent that they are necessary and helpful.

Estate planning in the more traditional sense is of principal interest to the middle class, the well-to-do, and the wealthy because it deals with the conservation and transmission of wealth from generation to generation. Nonetheless, it is error to think of this part of the law as "rich men's law" that emphasizes tax avoidance. Most of "estate planning" is a part of legal literacy. A properly educated lawyer is expected to be acquainted with

1

it. Although only a small fraction of the practising bar regularly engages in probate and trust work, many lawyers draft wills and trusts. Lawyers in general practice represent clients who are beneficiaries, or disappointed putative beneficiaries, or executors, administrators, or trustees. They encounter problems in fiduciary administration, including difficult matters of conflict of interest. Lawyers themselves are often fiduciaries.

To the extent that estate planning is a specialty, a somewhat disproportionate amount of a student's time is spent mastering legal doctrines that are encountered infrequently, and examining legal devices that are of questionable value. For example, in drafting trust instruments, lawyers do not "use" the Doctrine of Worthier Title or the Rule Against Perpetuities in the same sense that they use the law on powers of appointment, but some knowledge of Worthier Title and the Rule is nevertheless desirable. And the "pour-over" will having been made generally available by statute, it is probable that the device called "incorporation by reference" will fall into disuse. But incorporation by reference is still available to lawyers drafting wills, and its limitations should be understood. A lawyer does not knowingly supervise the "execution" of a will by a person lacking testamentary capacity, but if testamentary capacity of a testator might be questioned after the testator's death, the lawyer takes account of that fact in representing the client as effectively as possible. In short, the specialist must be an exceptionally well-informed lawyer.

The more informed the general practitioner is, the more effective the representation of clients with problems in wills, trusts, future interests, fiduciary administration, taxation, and related areas.

The materials in this book are prepared principally for a person who has had an introduction to property law, but who has not yet studied such subjects as trusts and future interests. It does not follow that this book purports to "cover" any subject fully. On the contrary, coverage with respect to a topic is selective, and is intended to acquaint the reader as quickly as possible with some of the information required for determining what a person's property arrangements are, whether they are vulnerable to unexpected loss, whether the arrangements are such that they might be changed, and how change might be brought about (if change is possible and desirable). For example, a person might be a "contributing" participant in a pension system that is compulsory as an incident to his employment. Although he cannot refrain from the forced saving that results from his required "contribution" to the pension "fund," he might nonetheless review such choices as are given to him under the pension system with respect to designating the beneficiary of (say) a "survivor annuity" should he die either before or after retirement. Here, the person's property arrangements are not altogether a matter of choice, but even so, to the extent that choice exists, it should be exercised with care.

Materials on estate planning, particularly those prepared for practising lawyers, often assume familiarity with the vocabulary, the subject matter, and the process of gratuitous transfers (gifts made during life or at death). This chapter 1, and chapter 2, cover such aspects of the vocabulary, subject matter, and process of gratuitous transfers as are essential to understanding some of the subsequent chapters.

§ 1.2 Lifetime Gifts. If a person makes a gratuitous transfer during lifetime, the gift is called an "inter vivos" gift (as differentiated from a testamentary gift—that is, a gift made by will). If an inter vivos gift is made by way of trust, the trust is called an inter vivos or "living" trust (as differentiated from a testamentary trust—that is, a trust created by will).

Making inter vivos gifts is sometimes recommended as an "estate planning" device. Whether it is wise in a particular case to make lifetime gifts is a matter of informed judgment. In arriving at that judgment, both the prospective donor and the donor's lawyer should remember that in the United States the average lifespan is increasing in length. The proportion of older persons in the population is increasing. In times of economic recession, early retirement of employees is "encouraged" or "suggested" in order to reduce costs. Some persons live a long time after their more customary sources of income have been displaced by some kind of "benefits." Property is a source of consideration and respect. Many an old person who would otherwise be shunted aside gets kind treatment because it is known or suspected (perhaps erroneously) that he or she is a person of some wealth. There are, of course, the usual exceptions, but generally speaking there is much to be said for keeping property until death. Refusal to make substantial lifetime gifts may frustrate or inconvenience those who would benefit from such transfers. But it might prove easier for a prospective donor to bear their ill-will while they wait then it would be to bear their open contempt after nearly all of the donor's property has been transferred to them.

§ 1.3 "Simple" (Non–Trust) Inter Vivos Gifts of Personal Property. Making an inter vivos gift of personal property of any kind requires subject matter of the intended gift, an intention to give by the transferor (the "donor"), an acceptance of the intended gift by the recipient (the "donee"), and "delivery" of the subject matter of the gift. Acceptance seldom causes much difficulty, and indeed there is a "presumption" of acceptance. (Unless it is demonstrated that the donee does not accept the gift, the donee is deemed to have accepted it.) Intention to give might alone occasionally cause legal problems, but frequently intention is in doubt because of difficulties with the abstraction called "delivery."

Suppose that A owns a ring that she is wearing, and she removes it, hands it to B, and says, "B, I give you this ring. It is yours." B takes the ring

and says, "Thank you." A has made a gift to B
because the subject matter of the intended gift,
intention to give, acceptance, and delivery are
clear. But suppose that A, instead of removing the
ring, merely twirls it on her finger, and the words
of both A and B are the same as those just described. In these circumstances there is no gift
because there is no delivery (relinquishment of
"dominion and control") by A, and furthermore,
the matter of intention to give is in doubt. A
intends to give, but arguably she does not intend to
give presently—rather, she intends to give in the
future. (Relinquishment of the subject matter of
the intended gift to demonstrate "delivery" of personal property can be dispensed with if a "deed of
gift" is executed by the donor and "delivered," but
making a gift of personal property by means of a
"deed of gift" is neither common nor well understood—even by lawyers.)

Occasionally the subject matter of an intended
inter vivos gift is not relinquished to the intended
donee; rather, the subject matter is put into the
hands of a third person. The practice at times is
both understandable and defensible—for example,
the intended donee might be a small child, and the
subject matter might be handed by the donor to
the parent of the child. This method of making a
gift is effective where circumstances are such that
the intention to give, acceptance, and delivery are
clear. (A hands one hundred dollars to C, parent
of B, age 4, and says, "I am giving this to B.") But
if the motive for failure to hand over directly to

the intended donee is obscure, litigation is encouraged. In the case In re Estate of Claus (1963),
Ruby A. Claus handed a metal box in a brown
paper bag to a neighbor, and written on the bag
was Ruby's name and the name of her niece, Alma
Koenig, a married woman. Ruby requested her
neighbor to hold the box and deliver it to Alma at
Ruby's death. When Ruby died, the neighbor
handed over the box to Alma. The administrator
of Ruby's estate claimed the contents of the box for
the estate, and Alma tendered the property to the
probate court, and contested the administrator's
claim.

The judgment of the Probate Court that Ruby
had made a completed gift to Alma during Ruby's
lifetime was affirmed on appeal, the Ohio Court of
Appeals saying:

> A gift inter vivos must be completed during the
> lifetime of the parties, but the delivery may be
> made to a third person for the donee and so long
> as this is done under such circumstances as to
> indicate that the donor has relinquished all con-
> trol and dominion over property, the gift is com-
> plete and irrevocable and is not affected by the
> death of the donor before the property comes
> into the hands of the donee.

What was in the metal box? The report of the case
does not say.

Where personal property that is the subject matter of an intended gift is in the hands of the donor
and consists of cash or tangible personal property

easily handed over ("delivered") to a donee (a ring, watch, or antique rocker), the matter of satisfying legal requirements is no bar to making inter vivos gifts. If the subject matter of an intended gift is a certificate of stock, corporate bond, United States Savings Bond, balance in a savings account, or life insurance policy (to name the more common "intangibles"), making a gift can be more complicated. For example, in United States v. Chandler (1973), Mary E. Baum purchased United States Savings Bonds in "coownership" form ("A or B"). Several years later she delivered the bonds to the respective coowners, her granddaughters, with the intention of making complete, irrevocable inter vivos gifts. On Mary's death, the value of the bonds was nonetheless held includible in her estate for Federal Estate Tax purposes by the Internal Revenue Service under § 2040 of the Internal Revenue Code, and taxed accordingly. In a suit for refund of the tax, the Supreme Court of the United States said:

> Mary E. Baum, the decedent here, whatever the reason may have been, chose not to have the bonds in question reissued in the names of her granddaughters, as she might have done pursuant to the applicable regulations. Instead, she merely delivered the bonds to the granddaughters with donative intent. Our issue is whether that delivery, accompanied by that donative intent, was sufficient to remove the bonds from the decedent's gross estate. We conclude that it was not.

The lesson of *Chandler* is clear: An owner of property who wishes to make a gift of the property that is complete for all purposes should take whatever steps the nature of the property dictates for changing both ownership and the indicia of ownership. If A owns a certificate of stock registered in his name, the overwhelming weight of authority is that a manual delivery of the certificate with the required donative intent results in a completed gift. But the evidence of the gift is buttressed if the certificate is re-registered in the name of the donee. So, if A has a savings account solely in his name, he makes an effective gift of the balance to B by surrendering his passbook to the issuing bank, having a new passbook issued solely in B's name, and delivering the new passbook to B. Something less than that might indeed suffice, but if A dies, B surviving, having the savings account already in B's name is less likely to give rise to controversy than having B in possession of a passbook issued solely in A's name.

A gift causa mortis (in contemplation of approaching death) is a revocable gift. Its effectiveness turns in part on the death of the donor. A, seriously ill, is about to enter a hospital for treatment. She owns a ring. She hands it to B, saying, "B, this is yours unless I return from the hospital." A enters the hospital and dies, B surviving. The gift not having been revoked by A prior to death, it becomes irrevocable at A's death. Being testamentary in character, gifts causa mortis are commonly subject to claims of creditors of the donor. Because words and other conduct of a donor in apprehension of death are at times ambiguous, gifts causa mortis provoke litigation.

To facilitate making gifts to minors, states have enacted Gifts to Minors statutes. Under such statutes, property that is the subject matter of a gift to a minor is held by a "custodian" for the benefit of the minor. Parents make gifts to children under such statutes in the expectation that as young adults the children will use the gifts wisely. In this connection it is well to remember that such gifts are completed gifts that are irrevocable.

§ 1.4 **"Estate" in the Largest Sense.** Persons acquire tangible personal property (an automobile, household furniture, and the like) and real property (the family home) that they use and give to their families or other successors in interest during their lives, or that they own at death, and then in some way pass to their families or other successors in interest. Tangible personal property and real property constitute the traditional "estate" of a decedent. But to an increasing extent, the estate in its largest sense is not confined to tangible personal property or real property. Instead the estate consists of an aggregate of tangible personal property, real property, and various kinds of "intangibles." Some of the intangibles are familiar: certificates of stock in corporations, corporate or government bonds, and bank accounts, for example. Other intangibles are familiar, but frequently overlooked as part of the estate because they are of relatively recent origin: such things as Social Security benefits, benefits in other governmental or "private" pension systems, benefits under state Workers' Compensation acts, and veterans' benefits. The proceeds of insurance on the life of the decedent (frequently the most sizable benefit that a decedent leaves to his family) are often viewed inconsistently: "He didn't leave much of anything, but I understand that he was heavily insured."

Viewed realistically, the estate that a contemporary decedent leaves to his family or other successors in interest consists in large part of various means of competing for the goods and services that are available from time to time. A widow solely dependent upon a "survivor annuity" originating in a pension system has a certain sum per month from which to sustain herself. An incompetent person or a totally disabled child who is the sole beneficiary of a trust fund of substantial corpus has the means to compete with those who are self-sustaining for the goods and services that he needs to survive. Put briefly, the contemporary decedent leaves to successors in interest various kinds of rights to a status. Where the decedent was unquestionably wealthy in his own right, and established a trust giving rights to his disabled child, the receipt of such rights is the acceptance of a gift made solely by the decedent. Where the beneficiary or beneficiaries of rights are without means of support other than the rights, and the decedent having little or no wealth died while still young, it is clear in some cases that the rights of the beneficiaries are not gifts at all. For example, if a young

married man who is "covered" by Social Security
dies at the age of thirty survived by his wife, and
by three children under the age of six years, the
aggregate of the benefits receivable by the family
over a period of years is considerable. Even
though the decedent paid Social Security taxes
during his lifetime, the aggregate of the benefits
receivable by his family is much greater than the
tax paid. Here, it is realistic to view "coverage" by
Social Security as an important element (and sometimes the only significant element) of the available
means of providing for one's dependents. But it is
not realistic to view the aggregate of Social Security benefits as a gratuitous transfer from the decedent to his family. In this connection, even that
bastion of skepticism, the Federal Estate Tax law,
takes a realistic view. Social Security and Workers' Compensation benefits payable to a decedent's
surviving spouse and children are not a part of the
decedent's "gross estate" for Federal Estate Tax
purposes.

Even an expanded and more realistic view of an
"estate" does not include an element that is unquestionably valuable to those benefiting from it,
namely, the existence of professional, political, union, or fraternal ties created or developed by the
decedent that enable "placement" of a favored
dependent or other successor in interest with (say)
a commercial, financial, or charitable institution.
This kind of "benefit" does not lend itself to either
count or valuation, and it is therefore ignored for
estate purposes.

§ 1.5 Administration of the Estate. Every
year persons die in the United States owning property that is not "administered" by the probate
court in the usual sense of that word. This is not
because decedents have skillfully arranged their
affairs to "avoid probate." Rather, non-adminis-
tration is attributable to lack of assets of appreciable value, or to lack of assets of the kind that
induce "probate," or to indifference to the desirability of administering the estate. If the decedent
owns very little property at death, a simplified
procedure for "settling the estate" may be available in the jurisdiction, and might be used. If the
decedent owns no land at death, no registered
automobile, no registered certificates of stock or
bonds, and no bank accounts, the family might
simply "take over" the decedent's assets at his
death, even though they are of considerable value,
and (perhaps) pay his debts. Even if the decedent
is the record owner of land at death, the family
might simply continue to occupy it, and to pay the
tax bills that continue to arrive in the name of the
decedent. United States Savings Bonds that are
registered solely in the name of the decedent might
lie undisturbed where the decedent put them. Dividend checks on certificates of stock registered in
the name of the decedent might arrive at his
address and accumulate, uncashed.

In sum, court-supervised administration of a decedent's estate, as it is usually visualized, is not a
process that occurs automatically on the death of a
decedent. It must be started by someone. And it
might not occur at all because the motives for

seeking court-supervised administration are not present in the particular case.

Just as there is no administration unless it is initiated by someone, so too, there is ordinarily no probate (that is, "proving") of the will unless some person brings the will forward. The executor designated in the will or some other interested person might petition the probate court to probate the will and grant "letters testamentary" to the executor. If the decedent died intestate, heirs or next of kin or a creditor might petition the probate court to grant "letters of administration" to an administrator. Letters testamentary or letters of administration are the badge of authority of the personal representative. Bankers, stock transfer agents, and the like, want to see them during administration of the estate. Notice of hearing on the petition is given to interested persons in conformity to statute. If there is a will, admitting it to probate as the last will of the decedent might not be a matter of controversy. But an heir who would benefit if the will were spurious might "contest" the will. If he does, the "will contest," a lawsuit in itself, must be disposed of.

Because the executor or administrator is appointed by, and is under the control of, the probate court, the executor is designated in the decree of probate or administration. Unless the will exempts the executor from furnishing bond, the executor, like the administrator, must furnish bond for the faithful performance of his duties. Either the executor or the administrator is commonly called the "personal representative" of the decedent.

The function of the personal representative is, in general, to collect and preserve assets, to pay debts of the decedent, expenses of administration, and taxes, and to distribute the property then remaining to devisees and legatees (to the extent that the will has dispositive effect) and to successors in interest under the statute of descent and distribution (to the extent that the decedent died intestate).

In connection with these matters, the personal representative prepares an "inventory" (list) of assets in the decedent's estate and gets an "appraisal" (estimate of their value). In conformity to statute, the representative gives notice to creditors of the decedent to present their claims. Commonly a general creditor who fails to present a claim for payment within the period set by statute for presentation of such claims will find the claim forever barred. If the personal representative rejects a claim, the effectiveness of the claim may be determined by a lawsuit.

After debts of the decedent, expenses of administration, and taxes have been paid, what is left is distributable to the devisees, legatees, or heirs of the decedent, as the case may be, and administration of the estate ends.

§ 1.6   **Responsibility of the Executor or Administrator.** An executor or an administrator of

an estate (like the trustee of a trust) is a fiduciary—a person managing property that partly or
entirely, as the case may be, belongs to others.
Even if the personal representative of the estate of
a decedent is the sole beneficiary of the estate,
there might nonetheless be duties to persons such
as creditors of the decedent, or tax collectors. For
example, § 2002 of the Internal Revenue Code (on
the Federal Estate Tax) provides that "[t]he tax
imposed by this chapter shall be paid by the executor"—that is, the personal representative is made
responsible for payment of the tax. Although the
liability for payment of the tax is liability in a
fiduciary capacity, the failure of the personal representative to fulfill properly this fiduciary responsibility might result in personal liability for payment of the tax. It is undeniably true that persons
have made an excellent living acting as fiduciaries,
and that state of affairs is likely to continue. Even
so, an inexperienced person should not accept fiduciary responsibility lightly. The matter of coping
with unfamiliar matters aside, the task might result in altogether unexpected personal liability if a
loss of estate or trust property occurs that is attributable to a failure of the fiduciary to meet the
standards on fiduciary conduct imposed by law. In
short, being named personal representative of an
estate or trustee under a trust instrument should
not invariably be viewed as leading to a windfall.
In a particular case, the result might be otherwise.

§ 1.7 Settling "Small" Estates. All states
have statutes of one kind or another facilitating
the settlement of estates of low value without
court-supervised administration in the usual sense.

For example, the New York Surrogate's Court Procedure Act section 1301 states:

In this article [Article 13 of the Act—Settlement of Small Estates Without Court Administration]

1. A small estate is the estate of a domiciliary or a non-domiciliary who dies leaving personal property having a gross value of $10,000 or less *exclusive of property required to be set off....*   (Emphasis added.)

2. A voluntary administrator is a person who qualifies and undertakes to settle the estate of the decedent without the formality of court administration....

In an appropriate case, the summary procedure for settling an estate that is available under Article 13 of the New York Surrogate's Court Procedure Act may be used whether the decedent dies testate or intestate. Because of required set offs, the gross amount of a small estate might amount to $36,150.

Under § 1303 of the Act, the right to act as "voluntary administrator" is given first to the "surviving adult spouse" of the intestate decedent, then, in order, to "a competent adult who is a child or grandchild, parent, brother or sister" of the decedent, or to "the guardian of the property of an infant, the committee of the property of any incompetent person or the conservator of the property of a conservatee who is a distributee," or "to the chief fiscal officer of the county except in those counties in which a public administrator has been appointed." If the decedent died testate, the right to act as voluntary administrator is given first to the named executor or alternate executor upon filing the last will and testament with the surrogate's court.

A statute facilitating settlement may deal with property of a particular kind. For example, § 257.236 of the Michigan Vehicle Code provides in part as follows:

> In event of the death of an owner of 1 or more vehicles whose total value does not exceed $60,-000.00, who does not leave other property necessitating procuring of letters of administration or letters of authority . . ., the surviving husband or wife . . . may apply for a title, after furnishing the secretary of state with proper proof of the death of the registered owner. . . .

Because there is no uniformity in statutes dealing with settlement of estates without full-fledged court supervision, one must simply check to see what the law on the matter is.

§ 1.8 Property "Outside" the Probate Estate. Persons who survive the decedent may benefit from arrangements that are not affected by the probate process.

For example, the decedent may have been the "life insured" under a policy of insurance designating the surviving spouse as beneficiary of the proceeds. The proceeds are not a part of the probate estate of the decedent.

Similarly, the decedent as an incident to employment may have been a member of a "pension" or "profit-sharing" or "retirement" plan that pays benefits to designated survivors of the "covered" employee. The value of benefits payable to designated survivors is not an asset of the employee's estate for probate purposes.

The decedent may be "covered" by Social Security or Workers' Compensation at death, and may leave a surviving spouse and minor children entitled to Social Security or Workers' Compensation benefits. These benefits are not assets of the decedent for probate purposes.

Some (but not all) "survivorship" arrangements of property do not fall within the probate process. Suppose that the decedent acquired title to the family home from A, the seller, in the form "B and C and the survivor of them." B, the decedent, is survived by C. At B's death, B's interest ceases, and C is the sole owner of the property. With respect to the home, B has "avoided probate."

A wealthy or well-to-do decedent may have created revocable or irrevocable trusts during lifetime under the terms of which the decedent was divested of all interests in the subject matter of the trusts. If so, no part of the subject matter ("trust property" or "corpus" or "principal") is a part of the decedent's estate for probate purposes.

§ 1.9 The Importance of State Law. Property and trust law is state law, and estate planning is

in large part an application of both. For purposes
of illustration, this book might summarize a reported case or set forth a statute from a particular
jurisdiction, or it might demonstrate the application of a property doctrine in a particular state. If
the reported case reaches an unexpected or unac-
ceptable result, that is stated; and if the statute is
unique, that is noted. If the application of a property doctrine is unusual, attention is directed to
the deviation from the norm. But even if a reported case is representative of cases from numerous
jurisdictions, or a statute is one enacted in some
form nearly everywhere, or the application of a
property doctrine is exemplary, one should not
assume uniformity throughout the United States.
There is diversity of doctrine and practice, and
particularly in the detail of law and practice.

A significant number of states seeking to improve the law and to reduce diversity have enacted
the Uniform Probate Code. In some states that
have not enacted the uniform act, some features of
the act have led to amendment of existing statutes
affecting the probate process.

§ 1.10 **The Importance of Federal Law.** Because "Estate Planning" is often used interchange-
ably with the expression "Tax Planning," it is
reasonable to think that the Federal Income, Estate, and Gift Tax provisions of the Internal Revenue Code are the parts of Federal law that have
most deeply affected arranging for one's possible
retirement and certain death. But the matter of
Federal influence on estate planning goes beyond
the obvious direct impact of tax statutes.

Tax statutes (including the Federal Income, Estate, and Gift Tax statutes) are used for purposes other than raising revenue. For example, Federal tax statutes through the "deduction" and "exemption" features of the law are used to encourage the creation (and to police the administration) of so-called "private" pension plans—pension plans for executives and employees sponsored by employers, or labor unions, or by both employers and unions acting together. Federal tax statutes are used both to encourage and police gifts to "charity." Under Federal law, the expressions "disqualified person," "party in interest," and "prohibited transactions" have become a part of the vocabulary of fiduciary administration. Statutes enacted by states during the last forty years are often no more than attempts by state legislatures to accommodate local property and trust law to the ever-changing vagaries of Federal tax law. It is not necessary to speculate about a "Federal law of property" in order to document the influence of Congress on property and trust law in the states.

Furthermore, through enforcement of laws by Federal departments (and in particular through the Social Security system), the Federal government every day extends its influence into areas of day-to-day living that formerly were largely a matter of private family arrangements (if, indeed, there were any arrangements at all).

Therefore one thinking through providing for retirement, or providing for dependents should death occur at an early age, should remember that (for example) whether a surviving spouse and minor children have an income might very well turn on whether there is "coverage" under Social Security, rather than on whether there is sufficient wealth to leave an adequate "net probate estate." Property and trust law is still "local" law, but it is not as local as it used to be.

§ 1.11 Community Property. Eight states— Louisiana, Texas, New Mexico, Arizona, California, Nevada, Washington, and Idaho—are the traditional "community property" states. Virtually all the rest—and the District of Columbia—are "common law" jurisdictions. The traditional community property states consist of a tier of states in the Southwest, plus Washington and Idaho in the Northwest, that have been influenced by the Civil Law. Wisconsin's community property act took effect in 1986.

The principal feature of a "community property" system of ownership is this: If A, married to B, acquires property through (say) his employment (as opposed to inheritance, devise, bequest, legacy, or gift), one-half of that acquired property belongs to B as "community property." Property that a spouse owned before marriage, and which he or she brings to the marriage, along with property that the spouse acquires by inheritance, devise, bequest, legacy, or gift during the marriage, is "separate property." If A dies, survived by B, generally speaking A has testamentary power of disposition over his half of the community property (B already owned the other half before A's death), and his separate property. There are variations in the property law of community property states, but again, generally speaking, A's testamentary power of disposition over his separate property is unrestricted. That a spouse in a community property state owns an undivided one-half of community property not only at the death of his or her spouse, but also during the marriage, is particularly important because a marriage might be dissolved before death by divorce.

§ 1.12 **"Foreign" Assets.** Many Americans move from one state to another during their working years, or they seek a "retirement home" in a better climate when customary work has ceased because of retirement or failing health. Persons move from "common law" states to "community property" states (and back again). Even persons who remain in the same state throughout their lives acquire property in states other than that where they are "domiciled." Therefore the estate of a decedent might include assets that for such purposes as administration of estates or death taxation are affected by the law of a state other than that where the decedent was domiciled at death. (An estate might even include assets in a foreign country.)

Language in some dispositive documents reflects the fact that property arrangements are frequently affected by the laws of more than one jurisdiction. For example, the prospective testator who owns land in more than one state might anticipate probate of the will in more than one state, and the will might explicitly nominate both a "primary" personal representative (a person resident in the state of domicile, to administer the estate in the state of domicile) and an "ancillary" personal representative (a person resident in another state, to administer the estate there to the extent required in that other state). A clause in a will explicitly giving the ancillary personal representative a power to sell land without court approval may originate in the knowledge of the lawyer drafting the will that absent such a power, court approval for sale of land must be sought in the state where the land lies and the ancillary personal representative is appointed.

The matter of "what law governs" with respect to various kinds of property arrangements can be a very complicated one. Persons who move (or have moved) from state to state, or who own property in more than one state, may find that putting their property affairs in order requires more thought and attention (and entails considerably more expense) than they had anticipated.

CHAPTER 2

THE TRANSFER OF PROPERTY AT DEATH BY WILL AND UNDER THE INTESTATE LAW

§ 2.1 **The Probate Estate.** Estate planning is associated with death. If a person dies owning property that is administered by the probate court, there is a "probate estate." Assets constituting the probate estate are listed in an "inventory" filed in the probate court. If the probate estate is not exhausted by payment of claims allowed against the estate, funeral expenses, expenses of administering the estate, and death taxes ("estate" or "inheritance" taxes), the person who dies—the decedent—leaves a "net probate estate."

§ 2.2 **Testacy and Intestacy.** If a person dies owning property that is administered by the probate court, he or she might die "testate" (leaving a will) or "intestate" (without a will). If the decedent dies testate, the decedent is called the "testator," if male, the "testatrix," if female. If the decedent dies intestate, he or she is called "the intestate." Because the will might not purport to dispose of all of the net probate estate of the testator, or because the will might not effectively dispose of all of the testator's net probate estate (although it purports to do so), a decedent might die testate with respect to part of the net probate estate, and intestate with respect to the balance.

To the extent that a decedent dies intestate, distribution of the net probate estate is governed by statute. Such a statute is called the "statute of descent and distribution." It governs the distribution of all kinds of property—real property and personal property, tangibles and intangibles, present interests and future interests. Statutes of descent and distribution in the United States are not uniform in their provisions. Nonetheless, one aspect of such statutes is noteworthy. Years ago the surviving spouse was not an heir of a decedent (a widow, for example, instead of succeeding to real property as an heir of the decedent, might assert "dower" in his land). Today, a surviving spouse is commonly made an heir under the statute of descent and distribution. (Dower—and its counterpart for husbands, "curtesy"—either has been abolished altogether or modified greatly by statute in many jurisdictions.)

§ 2.3 **Those Who Take the Net Probate Estate.** Persons who succeed to the property of a decedent under the statute of descent and distribution are called "heirs," "next of kin," "distributees," or "successors in interest" of the decedent. Persons who succeed to the property of a testator under his will (by "testamentary" gift) are called "beneficiaries." A beneficiary taking land (a "devise") under a will is a "devisee," a beneficiary taking money, a "legatee." A testamentary gift of personal property is a "bequest." Those taking

"all the rest, residue, and remainder" of the testator's property under his will are "residuary devisees and legatees." (All of the foregoing terms are
used at times in an imprecise way. For example, if
A leaves land to B by will, B is a "devisee" under
the will, not an "heir." Nonetheless, B might be
referred to as an "heir under A's will.")

§ 2.4 **Executor and Administrator.** The person who administers the estate of a decedent is
called the "personal representative" of the decedent. "Executor" and "administrator" are simply
more precise synonyms for personal representative.

If a person nominated by a testator to administer
the estate is appointed by the probate court, he is
an "executor" of the will ("executrix," if female).
A person not nominated by the testator to administer the estate, but nonetheless appointed by the
probate court to administer the estate is an "administrator" or "administratrix." (A testator
might fail in his will to nominate an executor, or
the nominee of the testator might refuse to accept
appointment, or the nominee might be unsuitable
for appointment, or the appointed executor might
undertake his duties and not complete them, or the
decedent might simply die intestate. In all such
cases, appointment of an administrator might be
appropriate.)

§ 2.5 **Intestacy: Estate Planning "By Operation of Law."** The provisions of statutes of descent and distribution, or "intestate laws," vary,
but in general such statutes direct the net probate

estate of the intestate decedent to persons related to him by "consanguinity" (blood) rather than "affinity" (marriage), and preference under the statutes is given to those blood relatives most closely related to the intestate, who take to the exclusion of more distant relatives. Blood relatives in a direct line of descent are preferred over "collaterals." For example, the intestate dies a widower, leaving no child or children, but survived by one grandchild. The intestate is also survived by his brother. The grandchild, a descendant of the intestate in the direct line of descent, takes to the exclusion of the brother of the intestate, who is a "collateral" relative. (Where the intestate leaves neither spouse nor descendant, but leaves parents who survive him, the parents as "ascendants" tend to be preferred over collateral relatives.)

A very important exception to the emphasis that the intestate laws put on blood relationship originates in the preference given the surviving spouse as an heir. For example, Ohio Revised Code § 2105.06(B) provides in part that "[i]f there is a [surviving] spouse and one child ..., the first sixty thousand dollars if the spouse is the natural or adoptive parent of the child, ... plus one-half of the balance of the intestate estate to the spouse and the remainder to the child...." (Under § 2105.06(D), if the intestate leaves a surviving spouse, but no children or lineal descendants of children, the surviving spouse takes all.)

It is sometimes said that a statute of descent and distribution creates an "estate plan by operation of law," that is, that to the extent the net estate is

not effectively disposed of by will, it passes according to statute. In this connection, one should note
the generality of the intestate laws. Suppose that
A at the age of sixty dies intestate, domiciled and
owning real and personal property in Ohio. A is
survived by his wife B, and his only child C. Under Ohio Revised Code § 2105.06(B), quoted above,
B takes either all or part (as the case may be) of
the net probate estate. B is A's surviving spouse
irrespective of whether she is twenty years of age
or sixty, and irrespective of whether she has been
married to A for one month or for forty years. C is
A's surviving child irrespective of whether he is
five or forty. C is A's child irrespective of whether
in his own right he is wealthy at A's death, and
irrespective of whether he is "deserving." In
short, "spouse" under Ohio Revised Code § 2105.-
06(B) means that person married to the intestate
who survives the intestate, and "child" means the
immediate offspring of the intestate who survives
the intestate.

Under some circumstances, a "laughing heir"
might succeed to the property of an intestate. Under Ohio Revised Code § 2105.06, if the intestate is
survived by no spouse, no children or their lineal
descendants, no parent, no brothers or sisters
("whether of the whole or the half blood") or their
lineal descendants, no grandparents or their lineal
descendants, then the property of the intestate
passes to his "next of kin." Next of kin might be
remote relatives of the intestate, who never expect-

ed to share in his estate—hence the expression "laughing heir."

§ **2.6 Lapse.** A testator cannot make a transfer of property by his will to his devisee or legatee until the testator dies (a will, it is said, "speaks at death"). An intended beneficiary under a will might predecease the testator. If so, the intended gift "lapses." (A testator can anticipate the death of his intended beneficiary during the interval between the time the will is executed and the time that the testator dies, and provide in the will for a gift to an alternate beneficiary. If such provision is made, the gift to the alternate beneficiary takes effect if he survives the testator.)

If lapse occurs, and the jurisdiction has an "anti-lapse" statute, a gift by substitution might exist under the statute. Suppose for example that A, domiciled and owning real and personal property in Ohio, executes a will under which he devises his farm to his son B. B predeceases A, survived by several children. A dies survived by B's children. Ohio Revised Code § 2107.52, the "anti-lapse" statute, provides in part as follows:

When a devise of real or personal estate is made to a relative of the testator and such relative was dead at the time the will was made, or dies thereafter, leaving issue surviving the testator, such issue shall take the estate devised as the devisee would have done if he had survived the testator....

Under the Ohio anti-lapse statute, B's children who survive A take by will what B would have taken had he survived A—the farm.

In the context of the devise or bequest attempted by will that fails because the devisee or legatee predeceases the testator, a substituted gift created by an anti-lapse statute serves the same purpose as the statute of descent and distribution serves when intestacy occurs—it directs the devolution of property in a way that the decedent might have preferred had he considered the circumstances that in fact arise. Like statutes of descent and distribution, anti-lapse statutes in the United States are not uniform in their provisions.

§ 2.7 **Ademption.** Because there is so frequently an interval of time between the execution of the will and the death of the testator, property that is the subject matter of a devise or bequest contained in the will might be disposed of by the testator (or used up, or accidentally destroyed, as the case may be) before the testator dies. For example, A executes his will containing the words "I give my gold pocket watch to my son B." Thereafter A gives the watch to another son, C. A dies, survived by B and C. The gift originally intended for B fails—it is said to be "adeemed."

Ademption, like lapse, can be anticipated by the testator. For example, A's will might provide as follows: "I give my gold pocket watch to my son B, but if I do not own a gold pocket watch at my death, I give my son B the sum of $200."

§ 2.8 Codicil. The matter of changes in a "will" brought about by lapse or ademption aside, a change in the terms of the document might be made by the testator himself by his execution of an instrument affecting his will called a "codicil." For example, A's will at execution has a provision leaving his farm to his son B. Thereafter, A executes a codicil to his will by which he revokes the devise intended for B, and instead leaves the farm to another son C. (When a testator dies leaving a "will" and one or more "codicils" thereto, all of the documents constitute the "last will" of the testator for purposes of regulating the administration and ultimate distribution of his estate.)

§ 2.9 "Provision" for the Surviving Spouse. Each person has his or her own picture of the surviving spouse—and all pictures mirror reality, even if all differ. The surviving spouse is conventionally an "old" widow with no children, or an "older" widow with grown children, or a "young" widow with minor children, but in any event a widow who was wholly dependent upon her husband, the deceased breadwinner. It is possible that all three of these views of the surviving spouse, when taken together, do indeed cover more cases than not (the life expectancy of American women is greater than that of men), but in a particular case they may miss the mark altogether. The surviving spouse may not be a widow at all. He may be a young man of twenty-five who is childless and will marry again before the year is out. Or if the surviving spouse is indeed a widow, she may be self-supporting in every respect (she may have supported the decedent), or she may be independently wealthy (the decedent may have made an "advantageous" marriage). In short, the surviving spouse is a person whose marriage (or most recent marriage, as the case may be) has been dissolved by death rather than annulment or divorce. "Provision" for the surviving spouse often means trying to maximize annual income over a period of years when the surviving spouse cannot be gainfully employed. But in some cases, "provision" for the surviving spouse means nothing other than taking account of the fact that at the death of the decedent, he or she might leave a surviving spouse. "Provision" in the usual sense might not be made for the surviving spouse because under the circumstances, provision is not appropriate.

§ 2.10   The Right of Election of the Surviving Spouse. If a surviving spouse of a testator is dissatisfied with the provision, if any, made for him or her under the will, statute may afford a "right to elect" to "take against the will"—that is, to take some part of the net probate estate regardless of the terms of the will. A statute affording such a right of election is called a "forced share" statute or an "election" statute (and what is procured by use of the statute is called a "forced share" or an "elective share" of the net probate estate). Forced share statutes are part of the movement to abolish (or greatly modify) dower and curtesy as means of providing for a surviving spouse, and instead to make the surviving spouse an heir under the statute of descent and distribution (in case of intestacy), or to give the surviving spouse a "right to elect" (where the decedent died leaving a will).

The prevalence of divorce and successive marriages has fostered the use of prenuptial (antenuptial) agreements. An enforceable prenuptial agreement can affect the distribution of an estate at
death and the right of election of the surviving
spouse in particular. When marriage occurs later
in life, either or both partners to the marriage
might be much more concerned about providing for
children and other descendants than providing for
a surviving spouse.

§ 2.11 **Freedom of Testation.** Persons making dispositions by will occasionally attach conditions to a gift, or they make a devise or bequest
that others think to be at best bizarre. Within
very broad limits, what is called "testamentary
freedom" exists in the United States, and therefore
a gift on condition or an unusual devise or bequest
may be lawful. For example, in Shapira v. Union
Nat. Bank (1974), the testator made bequests to his
sons on condition that they marry girls of the
Jewish faith. The condition was found to be only a
partial restraint upon marriage which was reasonable, not contrary to public policy, and therefore
valid.

The kind of testamentary disposition that is
much more likely to raise hackles is exemplified by
Eleanor Ritchey's 1969 bequest of her $4 million
Quaker Oil fortune in trust for the care of 150
mongrel dogs she had collected. Her will was
contested, and three of her relatives received $1.5
million in an out-of-court settlement. But the rest
of the fortune ($14 million in 1974) continued in

trust for care of the dogs and, ultimately, for animal research at Auburn University.

A statutory right in the surviving spouse to "take against the will" shows that there are limits imposed by law on testamentary freedom. Along with the body of law that has developed in connection with this right in the surviving spouse, there is law on such matters as "capricious devises and bequests," "illegal conditions," "restraints on alienation," "pretermitted heirs," "mortmain acts," "rules against perpetuities," and "rules against accumulations"—all of which affect freedom of disposition at death. Some of this law is no longer taught in law schools. A lawyer requested to draft a devise or bequest that is anything other than an outright, immediate devise or bequest to an identified (or readily identifiable) person or group of persons should be aware that limits on freedom of testation exist, and that the effectiveness of the conditional, postponed, or bizarre devise or bequest is often established only through a lawsuit.

§ 2.12 Revocation. Because a will cannot make a transfer of property until the testator dies, a will can be "revoked" by the testator (called back) in the interval between the execution of the will and the decedent's death. Revoking an existing will by executing a new will containing an express clause of revocation of prior wills and codicils is a common method of revocation. Others are tearing, cancelling, obliterating or destroying the will with the intention of revoking it.

Revocation can occur "by operation of law" (as differentiated from express revocation by the testator), but one must check to see what the law with respect to revocation by operation of law is in the jurisdiction. For example, a divorce with settlement of property rights between the parties to the divorce is often treated as a revocation of prior devises and bequests in favor of the divorced spouse. (Apart from devises and bequests to the divorced spouse, the will remains effective.)

§ 2.13 Survivorship: What Is Required? In order to take property of a decedent either as his successor in interest under the statute of descent and distribution, or as his beneficiary under his will (as the case may be), it is not necessary that the successor in interest or the beneficiary of the decedent survive to the time that the net probate estate is actually distributed. Administration of an estate takes some time and it might take several years. Generally speaking, the successors in interest of an intestate or the beneficiaries under a will are identified as of the time the decedent dies. But in this connection (as in so many others), one must check for relevant statutes. Ohio Revised Code § 2105.21 reads in part as follows:

> When the surviving spouse or other heir at law, legatee or devisee dies within thirty days after the death of the decedent, the estate of such first decedent shall pass and descend as though he had survived such surviving spouse, or other heir at law, legatee or devisee....

This "30 day statute" prevents property from passing at death to a person who cannot "enjoy" it in the ordinary sense of the word because the intended beneficiary dies shortly after the decedent dies. (In the absence of such a statute the same property passes through two estates, instead of just one, within altogether too short a period of time.) Suppose that A, domiciled and owning real and personal property in Ohio, dies testate. His will leaves his entire estate to B, who survives him. B dies ten days after A's death. Under Ohio Revised Code § 2105.21, A's net probate estate is distributed under the statute of descent and distribution as if B had predeceased A. No part of A's probate estate becomes a part of B's estate. (The Uniform Probate Code § 2–104 has a survival requirement of 120 hours.)

Further, it should be remembered that the interest a person acquires at the death of a decedent might be of a kind that does not entitle the taker to immediate possession even though the estate is fully administered and "closed," as it is said, within a relatively short time after the decedent's death. For example, A by his will devises his farm "to B for life, remainder to C and his heirs." Both B and C survive A. Under the will, C takes an indefeasibly vested remainder—a future interest in the land. C acquires his interest in the farm at A's death, but he is not entitled to possession of the farm until B dies. (Because B's interest is a transferable interest, C might acquire it during B's lifetime by gift or sale, and thus be entitled to possession of the farm before B dies.)

§ 2.14 Advancement. If a person who dies without a will—an intestate decedent—made a gratuitous transfer of property during his lifetime to a person who thereafter qualifies as an heir of the decedent, the property transferred is under some circumstances called an "advancement"—a transfer before death of part or all of an intestate share. If there is an advancement, the donee must bring the property "into hotchpot" if he wishes to share in the distribution of the net probate estate. That is, he must permit the value of the advancement to be included in the value of assets to be distributed as intestate property if he wishes to share in the distribution of intestate property.

§ 2.15 Satisfaction. Just as an advancement made to an heir affects distribution of the estate of an intestate decedent, so too "satisfaction" affects payment of legacies. Suppose that A's will says "I give $10,000 to my son B." Between the time of the execution of the will and A's death, A gives B $5,000. A dies, survived by B. If the lifetime transfer to B is in "satisfaction" of the legacy, B takes only $5,000 under A's will.

To avoid controversy over satisfaction, a testator might disclaim satisfaction: "No gift of any kind that I make under this will shall be considered either fully or partially satisfied by any inter vivos gift that I hereafter make."

§ 2.16 Abatement. Where the assets of the testator's estate are insufficient to satisfy all the

gifts that he intended to make by will, "abatement"—that is, reduction of gifts occurs. Assets
may prove to be insufficient because the decedent
depleted his assets before death, or because debts
of the estate or death taxes payable from the estate
are substantial, or because a surviving spouse
elects to take a share of the estate "against the
will," or a "pretermitted heir" takes a share of the
estate. Abatement occurs in the following order:
First, "residuary" devises and bequests are abated,
then, "general" devises and bequests, last, "specific" devises and bequests. (The specific gift is favored in abatement, but it is subject to "ademption.")

A residuary devise and bequest commonly is
introduced by "All the rest residue, and remainder
of my estate...." A general bequest is "I give
$10,000 to B." A specific bequest is "I give my
gold and diamond brooch to C."

Abatement can be anticipated by the testator,
and he can direct that his intended gifts be abated
in an order different from that otherwise required
under the substantive law on abatement. In short,
the testator can prefer one beneficiary over another where his assets prove insufficient to satisfy his
intention in all respects.

§ 2.17 **Per Capita and Per Stirpes.** "Per capita" means "by heads," "per stirpes" means "by
roots." Suppose that A had only two children, B
and C, both of whom predeceased A. B was survived by two children, D and E. C was survived by
four children, F, G, H, and I. All six grandchil-

dren of A survive him, and they succeed to his net probate estate under the statute of descent and distribution. (A leaves no widow.) Whether they take per capita or per stirpes is a matter of local law. If they take per capita, each grandchild takes a share in A's net probate estate equal to that of any other grandchild. If they take per stirpes, the children of B take what B would have taken had he survived A, and the children of C take what C would have taken had C survived A. Grandchild D, for example, takes one-half of one-half of A's net probate estate, or one-fourth. Grandchild F takes one-forth of one-half of A's net probate estate, or one-eighth. (Because the grandchildren of A are all related to him in the "same degree of consanguinity"—blood relationship—statutes often require a distribution per capita in this kind of case.)

The words "per capita" and "per stirpes" do not have the same connotation in all jurisdictions. In the example stated in the preceding paragraph, both B and C, the children of A (the decedent), predeceased A. Nonetheless, they might be treated as the "roots" or "stocks" so that the children of B take what B would have taken had B survived A, and the children of C take what C would have taken had C survived A, and the distribution is called "per stirpes" or "by representation." A jurisdiction might restrict a "per stirpes" distribution to those cases where there are effective claimants in more than one generation. For example, suppose that A had only two children, B and C, and that B predeceased A. B was survived by two children, D and E, who also survive A. C, the child of A who survives A, has four children, F, G, H, and I, who also survive A. (A leaves no widow.) There being effective claimants in more than one generation, a distribution "per stirpes" or "by representation" gives grandchild D one-half of one-half of A's net probate estate, or one-fourth, grandchild E (D's brother or sister) one-fourth, and C (A's surviving child), one-half of the net probate estate. F, G, H, and I take nothing because their parent C survived A.

§ 2.18 From Whom Property Is Acquired.

Precisely how property passes is worth emphasizing. Suppose that A had only two children, B and C, both of whom predeceased A. Because B and C predeceased A, they themselves cannot inherit from A if A dies intestate with respect to any of his net probate estate, and they cannot take as devisees or legatees under A's will if A dies testate. If both B and C were survived by children who survive A, and such grandchildren of A succeed to his net probate estate under the statute of descent and distribution, they take from A, not from their parents, and this is true irrespective of whether they take "per capita" or "per stirpes."

Similarly, one who takes a gift by substitution under an anti-lapse statute, takes directly from the testator. If A dies leaving a will reading "I leave my entire estate to B," and B predeceases A, the testamentary gift intended for B lapses. If an applicable anti-lapse statute creates a gift by substitution in B's children who survive A, the children of B who take under the anti-lapse statute take from A himself, not their parent B.

Suppose that A is the absolute owner of land and that he transfers it (by deed or will, as the case may be) under the following language "to B for life, and if C survives B, remainder to C and his heirs, but if C fails to survive B, then to C's daughter D and her heirs." B is married to C, and D is their child. B as "life tenant" enters into possession of the land. C dies survived by both B, the life tenant, and by D. Then B dies, survived by D. D is then the absolute owner of the land, but her ownership is traceable directly from A. B's life estate ceased when B died, and D in no respect takes from B. C's interest "failed by its own terms," as it is said, on C's dying during B's lifetime, so D in no respect takes from C.

How property interests pass is important not only to potential takers themselves, but also to interested observers, such as creditors and tax collectors. Tracing interests can be, and often is, a matter of considerable complexity.

§ 2.19 **Adoption.** Statutes regulating adoption are not uniform, but generally speaking an adoption statute takes the adopted person out of the family into which he was born and puts him into the family of his adopting parent or parents. But the general thrust of an adoption statute may be subject to qualifications either set out in the statute itself or read into the statute as a matter of construction in litigated cases. The consequence of

adoption for property purposes is still very much a
matter of state law, and that law must be consult-
ed in connection with a particular problem involving such matters as intestate succession, trusts,
and wills.

§ 2.20 **Illegitimacy.** Generally speaking, an
illegitimate child in the United States can inherit
from its mother, and the mother of an illegitimate
child can inherit from her illegitimate child. The
status of the illegitimate child with respect to its
father under both wills and intestate succession
laws is undergoing reexamination. In Trimble v.
Gordon (1977), the Supreme Court of the United
States held that an Illinois statute violated the
Equal Protection Clause of the Fourteenth Amendment where the statute permitted an illegitimate
child to inherit from its mother, but precluded an
illegitimate child from inheriting from its father
unless the parents intermarried and the father
acknowledged the child. Speaking for the majority
of the court, Mr. Justice Powell stated that "[f]or at
least some significant categories of illegitimate
children of intestate men, inheritance rights can be
recognized without jeopardizing the orderly settlement of estates or the dependability of titles to
property passing under intestacy laws." (In *Trimble,* the intestate decedent had been found to be the
father of the illegitimate child in a paternity suit,
and thereafter supported the child and acknowledged the child as his.)

§ 2.21 **Disclaimer.** Irrespective of whether a
donee is intended to take by means of an inter
vivos ("lifetime") gift or through the probate

process, the intended donee might refuse to take, that is, the donee might "disclaim." (One cannot be forced to accept a gift from the donor.) When the intended donee disclaims a gift under the intestate law or by will, the heir, devisee, or legatee is treated as having predeceased the decedent, and the property is distributed accordingly. An intended donee who disclaims is not thereby making a gift to that person or those persons, if any, who benefit from the disclaimer. The person or persons, if any, who benefit from a disclaimer take from the donor.

CHAPTER 3

SURVIVORSHIP INTERESTS

§ 3.1 What Motivates the Creation of Survivorship Interests? In trying to "avoid probate" or escape death taxes or disinherit a spouse, persons often resort to property arrangements that include an incident of survivorship. For example, B and C, husband and wife, take title to their residence from A in the form "B and his heirs and C and her heirs, and then in fee simple to the survivor of them." Thereafter B dies, C surviving. If the arrangement works as intended by B and C, C is then the sole owner of the property, and the property is not included in B's estate for purposes of administration by the probate court.

Putting property in survivorship form does not always achieve the objectives of those tempted to take advantage of its availability. Furthermore, the survivorship form of ownership has some disadvantages. We will consider both of these matters in some detail after first considering briefly how the incident of survivorship is created.

§ 3.2 Creating the Incident of Survivorship. Not all forms of coownership have the incident of survivorship. For example, if A, owning land in fee simple absolute, grants or devises "to B and his heirs and C and his heirs," B and C are tenants in

common. Each owns an undivided one-half interest in fee simple absolute in the land, and that
undivided one-half interest is alienable, devisable,
and descendible. If B dies, C surviving, B's undivided one-half interest passes under B's will to B's
devisee, or alternatively, it passes to B's successor
in interest under the statute of descent and distribution. Although C might be the devisee of B's
undivided one-half interest under B's will, or, alternatively, B's successor in interest under the statute
of descent and distribution, C in either case takes
by devise or descent, not by virtue of an incident of
survivorship. The incident of survivorship is not a
characteristic of the tenancy in common.

The incident of survivorship was a characteristic
of both the joint tenancy and the tenancy by the
entirety as those tenancies existed at Common
Law. The tenancy by the entirety existed only
between husband and wife. Both the joint tenancy
and the tenancy by the entirety as they existed at
Common Law have been affected by statutory and
judicial modification. Therefore, to determine
both the method of creating the incident of survivorship and the kinds of property to which the
incident attaches, one must consult applicable
state or Federal law. With respect to land, savings
accounts, checking accounts, certificates of deposit,
certificates of stock, mutual funds and safe-deposit
boxes, one looks to state law. With respect to
United States savings bonds, one looks to Federal
law. One should not assume that a method of
creating the incident that is effective in one state

will necessarily be effective in another, nor should one assume that a method effective with respect to one kind of property will necessarily be effective with respect to another.   There is considerable variation in these matters (with consequential misunderstanding and frustration).

For example, B with his separate funds purchases a United States savings bond and has it registered in the form "B or C."   Either B or C, in possession of the bond, may effectively seek payment.   On the other hand, were B to agree with A to purchase land from A, it would be unwise as a matter of state law for B to attempt to take title in the form "B or C" because questions might arise as to the effectiveness of the instrument of transfer. If B wishes to take title to land in a way which creates a present possessory interest in C, or a future interest in C, or an incident of survivorship ultimately advantageous to C, there are generally acceptable means of doing so.   For example, in Ohio the deed from A, owner in fee simple absolute, might run "to B and his heirs and C and his heirs, and then in fee simple to the survivor of them."   Under this language, both B and C have present possessory interests in the land, and on the death of either B or C, the survivor has a fee simple absolute in the entire parcel.   Lewis v. Baldwin (1842).   There is room for "innovation" in property matters, but generally speaking, one should not innovate unless conventional methods are inadequate to the task at hand.

§ **3.3 Severability.** If B and C are tenants in common of a fee simple absolute (each owning an undivided one-half interest), the interest of each is alienable, devisable, and descendible. Because a prospective purchaser of the entire parcel must negotiate with two persons rather than but one, the existence of the tenancy in common may affect marketability of the land. But such a prospective purchaser is no more likely to be discouraged by the necessity of dealing with several tenants in common than he would be if a tract of like size consisted of several parcels each of which was wholly owned by one of a number of different persons. (In either case, he must acquire the interests of all of the owners if he is to acquire all of the acreage he wants.) Where property is held by joint tenants or tenants by the entirety, transferability is more complex. For example, if B and C were joint tenants in fee simple of land at Common Law, either could sever the joint tenancy by conveying his interest to a third person. If B conveyed all of his interest in the land to D, C and D were thereupon tenants in common (the incident of survivorship having been destroyed).

If, rather than convey to D, B were to devise all of his interest in the land to D, D would take nothing if B died, C surviving, because at B's death, C would become sole owner by survivorship. (The incident of survivorship is not destroyed by a devise, as opposed to a conveyance.) Because joint tenancy has been deeply affected by both statutory and judicial development in the United States, one should not assume that the characteristics of joint tenancy as at Common Law are characteristics of what is frequently called "joint tenancy" today. If A in Ohio owns land in fee simple absolute and conveys it to B and C under survivorship language such as "to B and C for their joint lives, and then in fee simple to the survivor of them," and B thereafter conveys all of his interest in the land to D, the survivorship interest is not destroyed by the transfer, whereas it would have been were B and C joint tenants as at Common Law. If B dies, C surviving, C has a fee simple absolute by virtue of A's deed. As stated in Lewis v. Baldwin (1842), the survivor "holds title, not upon the principle of survivorship, as an incident to a joint tenancy, but as a grantee in fee, as survivor, by the operative words of the deed."

Tenancy by the entirety at Common Law existed only between husband and wife. Like the joint tenancy, the tenancy by the entirety has been deeply affected by statutory and judicial modification in those jurisdictions which have such a tenancy today. Unlike the joint tenancy at Common Law, the tenancy by the entirety could not be severed by an attempted conveyance by one of the spouses to a third person. That characteristic of the tenancy by the entirety is likely to be present where the tenancy by the entirety exists today.

When joint ownership exists between husband and wife, the inability under state law of either spouse, acting alone, to destroy the incident of survivorship may be of little moment. But if joint owners are brothers, or brother and sister, or father and son, the inability of one to destroy the incident of survivorship may effectively bar sale of his interest in the land.

§ 3.4 United States Savings Bonds. One purchasing or advising another on purchasing United States Savings Bonds should keep in mind that the issue, reissue, and payment of such bonds are matters of Federal law. It is true that the consequence of payment under Federal law may be affected by such state law devices as the constructive trust, but as a matter of the rational ordering of one's family affairs, one ought not to rely on a lawsuit to effect intention. If B with his separate funds opens a savings bank account in the names of C and himself in survivorship form, it is likely as a matter of state law and banking practice that B, in possession of the passbook, can close the survivorship account and open a new one solely in his own name. Suppose that B with his separate funds purchases a United States Savings Bond in "coownership" form "B or C." May B thereafter, in possession of the bond, have the bond reissued solely in his own name, irrespective of C's consent? This is a matter of Federal law, not state law, and one should not assume that the reissue of a United States Savings Bond will proceed in the same fashion as closing a savings bank account and opening a new one. The characteristics of United States Savings Bonds have been developed through regulation and court decision, and constitute a body of substantive law. Title 31, Code of Federal Regulations, § 315.51 states in part that "[a] request for reissue of bonds in coownership form during the

lifetime of the coowners *must be signed by both
coowners . . . .* " (Emphasis added.) By way of contrast, § 315.37 states in part that "[a] savings bond
registered in coownership form will be paid to
either coowner upon surrender with an appropriate request, and, upon payment . . ., the other
coowner will cease to have any interest in the
bond. . . . "

A United States Savings Bond may be registered
in beneficiary form rather than coownership form.
Suppose that B with his separate funds purchases
a bond in the form "B, payable on death to C."
Title 31, Code of Federal Regulations, § 315.38
states in part that "[a] savings bond registered in
beneficiary form will be paid to the registered
owner during his or her lifetime upon surrender
with an appropriate request. Upon payment . . .,
the beneficiary will cease to have any interest in
the bond."

A bond registered in beneficiary form serves
substantially the same purpose as one registered in
coownership form, because the survivor is entitled
to payment or reissue. But the two forms are not
identical. If B purchases a bond in the form "B,
payable on death to C," there is nothing in the
Regulations suggesting that C during B's lifetime is
entitled to payment or reissue.

§ 3.5 Avoiding Probate. Putting property in
survivorship form does not necessarily assure that
the property will escape administration by the
probate court. In the Ohio case of In re Estate of

Svab (1967), the decedent opened savings bank accounts in joint and survivorship form with her daughter, Mary Ann Beaver. Monies deposited in the accounts came solely from the decedent. At issue on the death of the decedent, Mary Ann surviving, was includibility of the accounts in the estate of the decedent. The Supreme Court of Ohio found that the accounts were opened in survivorship form as a matter of convenience to the decedent. The Supreme Court held that the burden was on Mary Ann to show by means other than the form of the accounts that the decedent intended to transfer an interest to her. Because Mary Ann failed to sustain that burden, the accounts were includible in the estate of the decedent, and were subject to administration by the probate court.

Use of the survivorship form of ownership is not confined to real property, bank accounts, and United States Savings Bonds. In Steinhauser v. Repko (1972), the decedent and his sister-in-law, Mildred L. Repko, rented a safe-deposit box in joint and survivorship form. At the decedent's death, Mildred surviving, the administratrix of the estate sought a declaratory judgment that currency in the box at the decedent's death was the sole property of the decedent and includible in his estate. The Supreme Court of Ohio held that the lease agreement for the safe-deposit box, like a joint and survivorship bank account agreement, is a contract under the terms of which the survivor of the co-lessees became the sole owner of the currency in the box at the decedent's death.

§ 3.6 Taxation—In General. Just as one must consult applicable state or Federal law with respect to the creation of ownership having the incident of survivorship, so too one must look to applicable state and Federal law to determine the tax consequences of joint ownership with the incident of survivorship. The Internal Revenue Code includes both gift and estate taxes. A few states tax gifts, and some states tax transfers at death by either an inheritance tax or an estate tax. (Inheritance and estate taxes are commonly called "death taxes.") In determining whether either a gift tax or a death tax applies to a transaction involving the incident of survivorship, one should pay particular attention to the kind of property to which the incident attaches. Interests in land may be treated differently from interests in savings bank accounts. The tax question must be stated with care. For example, one might sensibly ask this question: If B solely with his own funds opens a savings bank account in the names of B and C (B's brother) with the incident of survivorship, has B made a gift to C for purposes of the Federal Gift Tax on opening the account?

Putting property in survivorship form does not necessarily result in a tax advantage, and it may result in an unnecessary tax liability. For example, B and C are husband and wife, and B with funds inherited from his father acquires a residence and takes title from A, the grantor, in the form "B and his heirs and C and her heirs, and then in fee simple to the survivor of them." Thereafter C dies, B surviving. Under Ohio Revised Code § 5731.10(B) providing that "[w]hen the person holding property jointly are a husband and wife, the amount includible in the gross estate [of the decedent] shall be one-half the value of said property," one-half the value of the residence is includible in C's estate although C made no contribution toward the acquisition of the property. Of course, had B died, C surviving, only one-half the value of the residence would have been includible in *his* estate although he had been the sole contributor toward acquisition. But it is impossible to predict with certainty who will be the survivor of two or more persons, and therefore in a particular case, viewed solely from the standpoint of the tax law, it might be better for B to take title to the residence solely in his name. (C in her own right might be much wealthier than B. If title were taken in survivorship form, inclusion of one-half the value of the residence in C's estate were she the first to die would result in a tax on the estate of C that is greater than it would be on the estate of B were B to take title solely in his name, and B were the first to die.)

§ 3.7 Simultaneous Death. Section 3 of the Uniform Simultaneous Death Act states in part that "[w]here there is no sufficient evidence that two joint tenants or tenants by the entirety have died otherwise than simultaneously the property so held shall be distributed one-half as if one had survived and one-half as if the other had survived.... The term 'joint tenants' includes owners of property held under circumstances which entitled one . . . to the whole of the property on the death of the other . . . ."

The statute applies only where there is "no sufficient evidence" of survivorship. If one of the joint tenants has survived the other, even briefly, the statute has no application.

If the same person or persons are the successors in interest (under the statute of descent and distribution) or the devisees (under wills) of both joint tenants, the subject matter of the joint tenancy passes ultimately to the same persons irrespective of whether the simultaneous death statute applies. For example, suppose that B and C, husband and wife, own property as tenants by the entirety. B's will leaves his entire estate to C if she survives him, and if she does not, to their only child D. C's will leaves her entire estate to B if he survives her, and if he does not, to D. If B and C die under such circumstances that the simultaneous death statute applies, the property held as tenants by the entirety passes to D (one-half from B and one-half from C under their respective wills). If B and C die within a short time of each other, so that the simultaneous death statute does not apply, the survivor has the property by virtue of the tenancy by the entirety, and it passes to D thereafter under the will of the survivor.

By way of contrast, suppose that B and C, in no way related to each other, own property as joint tenants with the right of survivorship. B's will leaves his entire estate to D. C's will leaves his entire estate to E. B and C die simultaneously, and the simultaneous death statute applies. D takes one-half of the property under B's will, and E takes one-half of the property under C's will. But if B and C die under such circumstances that the statute does not apply, the survivor has the property by virtue of the right of survivorship, and it passes thereafter to the beneficiary of the survivor under the will of the survivor.

§ 3.8 "Totten Trusts" and "Pay on Death" or "Transfer on Death" Accounts. Just as a United States Savings Bond registered in beneficiary form serves much the same purpose as one registered in coowner form, so too the "Totten trust" and the "pay on death" bank account serve much the same purpose as joint ownership with the incident of survivorship. And the two property devices are like joint ownership with the incident of survivorship in that the characteristics of the devices are a matter of state law. If B with his separate funds opens a savings bank account in the form "B, in trust for C," and B dies, C surviving, C is ordinarily entitled to the balance of the account in a jurisdiction recognizing the Totten trust. But the characteristics of the Totten trust and the pay-on-death bank account, like joint ownership with the incident of survivorship, are a matter of state law. As a matter of state law, B may be empowered to bequeath the balance of a Totten trust account to someone other than the beneficiary designated in the account. If that is the case, the Totten trust differs in that important respect from joint ownership with the incident of survivorship.

(Under the Uniform Probate Code § 6–213(b), a will cannot affect the incident of survivorship of a joint bank account, a beneficiary designation in a Totten trust, or a pay-on-death payee designation in a bank account.)

§ 3.9 Rights of the Surviving Spouse and the Divorced Spouse.

A disaffected spouse may use joint ownership with the incident of survivorship or some other kind of will substitute in an effort to disinherit his spouse. Whether the effort is successful is a matter of state law. To make the law consistent with respect to a variety of will substitutes, New York enacted § 5–1.1(b) of the Estates, Powers and Trusts Law which states in part that the following inter vivos dispositions shall be treated as testamentary for the purpose of election by the surviving spouse: "(B) Money deposited ... in a savings account in the name of the decedent in trust for another person.... (C) Money deposited ... in the name of the decedent and another person and payable on death ... to the survivor.... (D) Any disposition of property ... whereby property is held ... by the decedent and another person as joint tenants with a right of survivorship or as tenants by the entirety.... Transactions described in subparagraphs (C) or (D) shall be treated as testamentary substitutes in the proportion that the funds on deposit were the property of the decedent immediately before the deposit or the consideration for the property held as joint tenants or as tenants by the entirety was furnished by the decedent. The surviving spouse shall have the burden of establishing the proportion of the decedent's contribution. Where the other party to a transaction described in subparagraph (C) or (D) is a surviving spouse, such spouse shall have the burden of establishing the proportion of his contribution, if any...."

Under § 5–1.1(b) the surviving spouse in New York seeking a forced share of the decedent's estate is put on a rough parity with the tax collector with respect to the subject matter of will substitutes. It bears emphasis that the position of the surviving spouse is not so advantageous in this respect in all states.

If a married person executes a will making provision for a spouse, and the couple thereafter divorce, statute commonly intervenes to revoke the provision in the will for the divorced spouse. There are numerous property arrangements, including survivorship interests, that serve as "will substitutes." A statute that on divorce revokes provision for a spouse made by will might be extended to cover will substitutes of which a divorced spouse is beneficiary. But there is no assurance that a statute will be so extended. Section 2–804 of the Uniform Probate Code, enacted in some states, revokes provision for a divorced spouse by various kinds of will substitutes, including life insurance. The lesson is clear: On divorce, all property arrangements should be re-examined to determine whether they still reflect the desires of the owner of the property.

§ 3.10 **Conclusion.** When one has little property, coownership with the incident of survivorship is justifiable both as a matter of convenience and as a means of avoiding probate. But as a couple accumulates considerable amounts of property, use of coownership with the incident of survivorship should be confined to kinds of property and amounts of property which do in fact further sensible arrangement of property matters. The tax advantage of coownership with the incident of survivorship is illusory, and unscrambling interests held in survivorship form is troublesome. Generally speaking, viewed from the tax standpoint, couples of some means should seek to equalize their respective individual holdings of property. Coownership with the incident of survivorship serves limited purposes. It does not defeat the tax collector. It might not defeat a surviving spouse seeking a forced share of the decedent's estate. And the savings achieved in avoiding probate may not be worth the trouble caused by putting property in survivorship form.

CHAPTER 4

COMMUNITY PROPERTY

§ **4.1 The Nature of Community Property.**
If A, married to B in a community property state, acquires property through (say) employment (as opposed to inheritance, devise, bequest, legacy, or gift), an undivided one-half of that acquired property belongs to B as "community property." Property that A owned before marriage, and brought to the marriage, along with property that A acquires during the marriage by inheritance, devise, bequest, legacy, or gift, is A's "separate property." If A dies survived by B, generally speaking A has testamentary power of disposition over both the separate property and an undivided one-half of the community property. By way of contrast, if A, married to B in a common law state, acquires $100,000 through (say) employment, A has power of disposition over the entire $100,000 during lifetime. If A dies survived by B, A has testamentary power of disposition over the $100,000 at death, subject only to any statutory right in B to elect to "take against the will"—that is, to take some part of the net probate estate regardless of the terms of the will. The principle underlying the system of community property is that whatever property is acquired during the marriage by the efforts of either husband or wife belongs to both of them—to the "community" of which each is a member. Be-

cause each member of the community during the marriage owns an undivided one-half of such acquired property, on the death of one survived by the other, the survivor already owns one-half of such acquired property, and he or she does not "take" that half from the decedent. Whether the survivor takes part or all of that undivided one-half of the community property owned by the decedent at death turns on the provisions of the decedent's will, or on the law of intestacy (to the extent that the decedent dies intestate).

§ 4.2 **Where the Community Property System Exists in the United States.** Eight states are the traditional community property states: Louisiana, Texas, New Mexico, Arizona, California, Nevada, Washington, and Idaho. Wisconsin's community property act took effect in 1986. All the rest of the states and the District of Columbia are common law jurisdictions. (A handful of common law states adopted the community property system in the 1940s to gain a Federal tax advantage. This system was abandoned in those states after Congress in 1948 made the split-income provision of the Income Tax, the split-gift provision of the Gift Tax, and the marital deduction of the Gift and Estate Taxes a part of the Federal tax law in an effort to put taxpayers in common law states and community property states on a rough parity.)

The eight traditional community property states are those that have been influenced by the Civil Law of Spain. Six of those states had the community property system of ownership on joining the Union. Washington and Idaho adopted the system because of the influence of California. A substantial share of the total population of the United States lives in community property states. Such states account for about one-third of the total land area of the United States, excluding Alaska and Hawaii.

Although it is conventional for purposes of considering marital property to refer to the eight states influenced by the Civil Law as "community property states," those states generally speaking recognize common law forms of ownership of property between spouses insofar as the common law forms are consistent with the community property system. For example, A, married to B in a community property state, might hold real estate as community property with B, and maintain a bank account in joint tenancy with B. In community property states, as in common law states, it is at times essential to know the detail of property law and practice in a particular jurisdiction in order to determine ownership and resolve disputes over property.

§ 4.3 Community Property Differentiated from Separate Property. Separate property is property that a spouse owned before marriage and brought to the marriage, and property that a spouse acquires during the marriage by inheritance, devise, bequest, legacy, or gift. Property acquired during the marriage by the efforts of either spouse—property acquired by "onerous" title—is community property. Rents, issues, profits, and fruits of community property are community property. Whether rents, issues, profits, and fruits of separate property are separate property or community property turns on the jurisdiction.

It bears emphasis that all property in possession of either spouse during or on dissolution of marriage in a community property state is presumed to be community property, and all property acquired by either spouse during marriage is presumed to be community property. The burden of proving that property is separate property is on the party asserting separate ownership. The quantum of proof required to overcome the presumption of community ownership has been described as "clear and convincing," and although in practice this might amount to no more than a preponderance of the evidence, it might be difficult to overcome the presumption of community ownership in a particular case. If A, married to B, dies in a community property state, survived by B, knowledge possessed by A regarding evidence of ownership might be irretrievably lost. Where there is no evidence of the time or means of acquisition of property, or where the evidence is scanty or nicely balanced, both presumptions and allocation of the burden of proof are important.

By "transmutation," separate property is changed to community property, or community property is changed to separate property. There are variations among the community property states with respect to both the permissibility of transmutation and the means of effecting change. In Texas, for example, property that a spouse acquires by inheritance, devise, bequest, legacy, or gift cannot be changed to community property because the statute that defines separate property is mandatory. Higgins v. Higgins (1970). By way of contrast, in California separate property can be changed to community property, and community property to separate property, comparatively easily. In re Estate of Nelson (1964), the decedent had owned an apartment house at the time of his marriage. During the marriage the decedent referred to the apartment house as the mutual property of himself and his wife, and conduct of the spouses during the marriage was found to be "additional evidence of an executed oral agreement" to change the separate property of the husband to community property.

§ 4.4 Life Insurance. Difficulties in classifying property as separate property or community property, and differences in classification among community property states, are illustrated by the treatment of life insurance policies, and the proceeds of life insurance policies.

A policy of life insurance is a form of property (a "chose in action" in the form of a "specialty"). Questions on life insurance are complicated by whether the insurance is on the life of the decedent or the life of another; whether the policy was procured before marriage or after marriage; the original beneficiary designation, attempts to change the beneficiary designation, and whether the decedent retained the right to change the beneficiary designation; the source of funds used to pay premiums; how one makes gifts to a spouse or to a third person in a community property state; and when rights with respect to an insurance policy or its proceeds "vest."

Suppose that A before marriage purchases a policy of ordinary or straight life insurance on his own life and designates his mother M as beneficiary. The policy is kept in force by the periodic payment of premiums, and the policy has customary "incidents of ownership," such as the right to change the beneficiary designation, the right to any cash surrender value of the policy, the right to use the policy as collateral for a loan, the right to assign the policy, and the right to select a method of payment under a settlement option.

While the policy is in force, A marries B. Thereafter A pays premiums on the policy with community funds. A dies survived by both his mother M and his wife B. A has never changed the beneficiary designation on the policy. What are B's rights, if any, in the proceeds of the policy?

Because A procured the policy before marriage and brought it to the marriage, the policy was separate property initially, and under the "inception of title" rule, the proceeds at A's death are separate property, and the community is entitled to reimbursement for community funds used to pay premiums. (The use of community funds to pay premiums on life insurance is treated like the use of community property to improve land that is the

separate property of a spouse—the improvements
follow the property.) Under the "apportionment"
rule, proceeds are allocated in accordance with the
amount of premiums paid with separate funds and
the amount paid with community funds. (This
allocation accords with the community property
principle that the increase in value of separate
property should be shared by the community
where community property increases value.) Another possible view is that B has no rights in the
proceeds because A had the power to make "reasonable" gifts from community property during his
lifetime (and did so when paying premiums from
community funds), or because the proceeds did not
"vest" until A died, when the community had
ended.

Suppose that A, married to B, purchases a policy
of ordinary life insurance on his own life and
designates his indigent mother M as beneficiary.
The policy has the customary incidents of ownership, including the right to change the beneficiary
designation. A keeps the policy in force by the
payment of premiums with community funds. A
dies survived by both his wife B and his mother M.
What are B's rights, if any, in the proceeds of the
policy?

In Washington, neither spouse can give community property without the express or implied consent of the other, but each spouse has the right to
devise and bequeath one-half of the community
property. West's Rev.Code Washington Ann. 26.-

16.030(1) and (2). B can effectively claim one-half of the proceeds of the policy. Francis v. Francis (1978). By way of contrast, in Louisiana it has been held that A had the right to purchase insurance on his own life in favor of any designated beneficiary, that under the circumstances outlined above A had made no gift either inter vivos or causa mortis, that M acquired no vested rights until after A's death (when the community had ended), and that B has no effective claim to the proceeds. Pearce v. National Life & Accident Ins. Co. (1930). A third view is that the transaction is voidable by B as to half of the proceeds of the policy (the policy having been procured by community funds).

§ 4.5 **Management and Disposition of Community Property.** Because of contemporary emphasis on the equality of husband and wife, community property states, generally speaking, give husband and wife equal powers of management and disposition of community property. Contemporary law should be differentiated from the traditional view which gave the husband a dominant role in management of community assets.

Joinder of spouses is commonly required to buy, sell, encumber, or dispose of community real property. Either spouse, acting alone, frequently has full power to manage, encumber, or dispose of community personal property. But in this connection, gratuitous transfers (gifts) should be differentiated from commercial transactions. For example, in a community property state a spouse who has full power, acting alone, to encumber community personal property might be disabled from making gifts (other than nominal) of such property unless the other spouse consents. Furthermore, the law of management and disposition of community property continues to be complicated by the origin of the community property in question, and the way in which title to the property is held.

§ 4.6 Community Property and Federal Estate Taxation.

In a common law state, if A, married to B, by his earnings amasses property valued at $400,000 and dies survived by B, all of the property is a part of A's gross estate for Federal Estate Tax purposes. In a community property state, if A, married to B, by his earnings amasses property valued at $400,000 and dies survived by B, only one-half of the property, being community property, is included in A's gross estate for Federal Estate Tax purposes. The other one-half of the community property was B's property during the marriage and at A's death, and B does not "take" it from A at A's death.

Because of this and other disparities in the Federal tax treatment of married persons in common law and community property states, Congress in 1948 made the marital deduction a part of the Federal Gift and Estate Taxes, the "split-gift" a part of the Federal Gift Tax, and "income-splitting" a part of the Federal Income Tax. These devices were intended to put taxpayers in common law states on a rough parity with taxpayers in community property states. Therefore, they are of principal interest to taxpayers in common law states.

Nonetheless, a married person in a community property state might be affected by law intended to put his counterpart in a common law state on a rough parity with him. For example, suppose that in a community property state A, married to B, by his earnings amasses property valued at $900,000. A has no separate property. A dies survived by B. A's gross estate of $450,000 consists solely of A's one-half of the community property. A wills his entire estate to B. Under the Economic Recovery Tax Act of 1981, the marital deduction is an unlimited deduction. Both community property and separate property included in the gross estate of a decedent that passes to the surviving spouse absolutely (or by another qualifying form of disposition) qualifies for the marital deduction.

§ 4.7 **Community Property, Conflict of Laws, and Protection of the Surviving Spouse.** Difficult questions on classification of property frequently arise because of the proclivity of Americans for moving from state to state, including moves from common law states to community property states and vice versa. In either a common law state or a community property state, tax collectors, purchasers, creditors, or the spouses themselves might be vitally interested in how property is treated for a particular purpose. For example, suppose that in a common law state, A, married to B, by his earnings amasses personal property valued at $400,000. If A were to die survived by B, a "forced share" statute in the common law state affords B protection against a testamentary attempt by A to disinherit B. A and B move to a community property state, A taking his personal property with him. A dies in the community property state, still owning that personal property, survived by B. A's will leaves his entire net probate estate to C, A's child by a prior marriage, who also survives A. The community property state has no "forced share" statute. Have A's change of domicile and change of situs of A's personal property permitted A to disinherit B?

Classification of property interests of married persons who move from state to state is determined in part by applying principles of conflict of laws. A generally recognized principle is that the character of property is determined at the time of acquisition, and it is not changed by moving the property to another state. This principle was recognized in In re Estate of Kessler (1964), where A, married to B and domiciled in California, acquired community property consisting of shares of stock issued in A's name. Thereafter the couple moved to Ohio and A died, survived by B. The Supreme Court of Ohio held that the shares of stock remained community property even after the change of domicile and change of situs of the shares. Therefore, one-half of the shares of stock were the property of B on the death of A. (Nonetheless, B's acquisition on A's death of "full and complete enjoyment" of one-half of the shares of stock "divested of the many restrictions and contingencies which had theretofore diluted her vested interest" was deemed a taxable succession for Ohio death tax purposes.)

If the principle that the character of property is determined at the time of acquisition is applied to the case where A, married to B, moves and takes his personal property from a common law state to a community property state, then A can effectively disinherit B with respect to that personal property. Even though A acquired the property during marriage by his earnings, it is "his" in a common law state and is, therefore, separate property on his removal to a community property state. Even so, California by statute precludes disinheritance in this kind of case. Had A acquired his property in California while married to B, it would have been characterized as community property. And as "quasi-community property" it is so treated in California for purposes of devolution at death. At A's death, one-half of the quasi-community property is B's. The other one-half is subject to unrestricted testamentary disposition by A. West's Ann.Cal. Prob.Code, § 6101.

Succession to real property on the death of the owner testate or intestate is governed by the law of the situs. In a common law state if A, married to B, by his earnings acquires real property in the common law state, and A and B thereafter move to a community property state, a testamentary attempt by A to disinherit B can be thwarted with respect to the real property by applying the law of the situs. For example, the law of the situs might give B a forced share of the real property through the right to elect to take against the will.

§ 4.8 "Election" by a Surviving Spouse in a Community Property State. In common law states, such protection as is afforded against disinheritance of a spouse is achieved through forced heirship ("elective share" statutes), dower, and curtesy. These devices are not a part of the community property system of ownership. In a community property state, a surviving spouse already owns an undivided one-half of community property at the death of the other spouse, and therefore, the survivor does not "take" that one-half of the community property from the deceased spouse, and the deceased spouse had no power of testamentary disposition over that one-half.

Nonetheless, the will of a deceased spouse in a community property state might affect the devolution of the one-half of the community property owned by the surviving spouse. For example, in a community property state A, married to B, dies testate survived by B and owning community property. A's will purports to put A's separate property and all of the community property (including B's undivided one-half) in a testamentary trust of which B is a primary beneficiary, but not the sole beneficiary. B must elect whether to take her undivided one-half of the community property (thus denying A's power to dispose of B's one-half of the community property, and rejecting A's provision for B) or to take under the will (thus assenting to A's disposition of B's undivided one-half of the community property).

CHAPTER 5

"SIMPLE" WILLS

§ 5.1 The Limited Function of the Will. It bears emphasis at the outset that the will, like the statute of descent and distribution, affects only the net probate estate of the decedent—property distributable at death under the supervision of the probate court. Inter vivos or lifetime dispositions of property are ordinarily beyond the purview of the probate court. The testator may have purchased United States Savings Bonds payable on his death to a person who in fact survives him. He may have taken title to his residence in the names of himself and his wife in survivorship form, and his wife in fact survives him. He may have designated his surviving spouse as beneficiary of insurance on his life, and as beneficiary of a retirement plan to which he made contributions. He may have created a revocable or an irrevocable inter vivos trust under the terms of which he divested himself of all interests in the property that was the subject matter of the trust. In all of these cases persons surviving the decedent enjoy interests in property originating with the decedent, but for probate purposes, the interests do not pass from the decedent to a beneficiary at death. For purposes of taxation, or election by a surviving spouse, a lifetime transaction may be viewed as essentially testamentary in nature, and treated accordingly,

but with that we are not here concerned. In any
event, a client unlikely to be aware of the limited
effect of the will should be informed that lifetime
arrangements for the disposition of property are
unlikely to be affected by the execution and subsequent probate of a will. That information in itself
may motivate him to consider his property arrangements in their entirety, and to make such
changes as are appropriate.

§ 5.2 The Case Against Intestacy. For many
persons the will is an important dispositive document. For one of modest or moderate means the
will is frequently the most important dispositive
document he executes. It certainly should not be
assumed that if one has little property, it is of little
consequence whether or not he executes a will.

If a wealthy person dies intestate survived by a
spouse and children, distribution of the estate
among the surviving spouse and the children under
the statute of descent and distribution may cause
no hardship to the spouse because the amount of
property the spouse receives is ample for his or her
needs. But suppose the intestate is a person of
moderate means. Requiring the surviving spouse
to share a small estate with children may effectively deprive the spouse of property sufficient for the
spouse's support. Furthermore, if one or more of
the children are minors, property passing to them
under the statute of descent and distribution may
require guardianship that is relatively expensive
and depletes a child's estate. When a couple has
little property, it is ordinarily preferable that the

entire estate of the decedent pass to the surviving spouse on the reasonable assumption that the survivor will provide for others to the extent that he or she can.

Even if one were indifferent to the devolution of his estate at death, he might be deeply concerned about the care of minor or incompetent children. Executing a will affords a parent an opportunity to state preferences regarding custody of his child or children when circumstances at death require guardianship. Just as devolution of an estate under statutes on intestate succession may work out satisfactorily, so too guardianship of minors or incompetents might proceed smoothly in the absence of direction by the decedent. But there is little to be said for leaving so important a matter to chance. Young parents with little property frequently overlook this important function of a properly prepared will, and for them, appointment of an appropriate guardian for the person of a minor child may be the most important function of the will.

In this connection, it is appropriate to emphasize that both the husband and the wife should execute wills. When either the husband or the wife dies, the surviving spouse is ordinarily the guardian of the person of a minor child of their marriage. The husband's designating a guardian of the person for a minor child in his will in the event his wife predeceases him avails nothing if she in fact is the surviving spouse. Both husband and wife in their

respective wills should anticipate possible guardianship of the person and of the estate of a minor
child. (If prospective estates are more than nominal, trusteeship of the estate of a minor as an
alternative to guardianship should be considered.)

If a husband and wife have no children or descendants, each may assume that on his or her
death intestate, the surviving spouse will take the
entire probate estate. That notion may be erroneous. The Uniform Probate Code § 2–102(2) provides that the intestate share of the surviving
spouse is "the first [$200,000], plus three-fourths of
any balance of the intestate estate, if no descendant of the decedent survives the decedent, but a
parent of the decedent survives the decedent...."
(The parent or parents take that one-fourth of the
balance of the intestate estate not passing to the
surviving spouse.) If a couple are in their mid-
fifties, each having an aged parent or parents, it is
possible that the husband or wife would prefer that
on death, his or her estate be shared by the surviving spouse and an aged parent or parents. If so,
that should be a matter of informed choice, not
chance. One must know the terms of the applicable statute. Although statutes regulating intestate
succession are similar from state to state, they
differ in important respects, and even if one is
familiar with the statute of his state of domicile, he
should not assume that the devolution of his estate
on his death intestate will follow the same course
should he move to another state.

Viewed solely from the standpoint of the devolution of the probate estate, the statute of descent and distribution may in a particular case direct distribution in accordance with the preferences of the decedent. But a statutory distribution that is satisfactory to the prospective decedent at a particular time may become unsatisfactory a moment later because of birth or death. A, married to B, has no parent or issue. A has no will. Were A to die survived by B, all of A's estate would pass to B under the applicable statute of descent and distribution. But were A to die predeceased by B, all of A's estate under the statute (including property received from B) would pass to cousins for whom A cares nothing. It is possible that A might execute a will after B's death for the purpose of leaving his estate to a person or persons other than his cousins. It is better for A to execute a will during B's lifetime setting out an alternative disposition of the estate should B predecease A.

The will affords an opportunity to nominate a suitable executor of the decedent's choice to administer his estate. The executor thought by the decedent to be appropriate to the task of administering an estate (including, perhaps, a business) may be someone other than the person entitled under state law to preference in appointment as administrator were the decedent to die intestate. The person entitled to preference in appointment as administrator might be unsuitable to administer an estate. A will may give the personal representative powers to administer the estate that are more efficient than those available under statute, and the will may exempt the executor from the requirement (and expense) of furnishing bond.

Execution of a will by no means solves all of the problems connected with the orderly disposition of property, but a will is an extraordinarily useful device for making gratuitous transfers at death. And it serves purposes beyond directing the devolution of the estate. Put briefly, there is usually little to be said for dying intestate.

§ 5.3 Interview with the Testator. Before drafting the will, it is necessary to interview the prospective testator to determine the nature and extent of his property and the identity of his intended beneficiaries. The client should be encouraged to bring relevant personal papers (deeds, insurance policies, savings bank passbooks, and the like) to the initial interview. The client's perception and memory of his property arrangements may be unreliable. Examination of documents reveals how the prospective testator holds title— under what name, and in what form. The client should be encouraged before the initial interview to consider alternative dispositions of his estate should there be births and deaths in the interval between execution of the will and death of the testator. Generally speaking, a lawyer should altogether avoid drafting a will for a person not personally interviewed.

§ 5.4 Drafting the "Simple" Will. It is customary for the testator to identify himself or herself in the introductory clause or the opening paragraph of the will. In this connection it may prove helpful in the administration of his estate for the testator to identify himself by names used by him or by which he is known to others. For example, the will might begin "I, William J. Smith, also known as William John Smith, William Smith, and Will Smith. . . ." The testator may have acquired title to real or personal property, tangible or intangible, in a variation of his name that is different from the one he commonly uses. To facilitate working with deeds, certificates of stock, certificates of title, bonds, bank accounts, mutual funds, and insurance policies after the testator's death, it is essential that the letters of appointment issued to the personal representative of the testator reveal the names under which he held property at death.

Next, the testator should state his place of permanent residence, for example, ". . . of the City of Columbus, County of Franklin, State of Ohio. . . ." The domicile of the testator affects such matters as jurisdiction of courts and choice of governing law. The testator may state his testamentary capacity: ". . . being of full age, sound mind and disposing memory, and knowing the nature and extent of my property and the objects of my bounty. . . ." On disputed issues of domicile or testamentary capacity, the declarations of the testator are of course not conclusive, but they are evidence. The declaration on testamentary capacity is frequently omitted altogether. The testator should state his purpose in executing the document: ". . . do make, publish, and declare this to be my last will. . . ."

A principal purpose of the introductory part of the will is the revocation of all prior wills and codicils: "... and I hereby revoke all wills and codicils heretofore made by me." In the absence of express revocation of prior wills and codicils, the new instrument revokes them only insofar as its provisions are inconsistent with those of prior wills and codicils. Unless circumstances are such that preparation of an entirely new will is difficult for the testator (he may be very old, or he may be easily exhausted, or he may be depressed), it is not usually desirable to draft a codicil to effect a change in the testamentary plan. Applying a single document at the testator's death is at times difficult. Creating the "last will" of the testator from several documents executed at different times under different circumstances tends to compound problems.

The introductory clause ("exordium") in its entirety is:

I, William J. Smith, also known as William John Smith, William Smith, and Will Smith, of the City of Columbus, County of Franklin, and State of Ohio, being of full age, sound mind and disposing memory, and knowing the nature and extent of my property and the objects of my bounty, do make, publish, and declare this to be my last will, and I hereby revoke all wills and codicils heretofore made by me.

Or, more simply (omitting the declaration of mental capacity):

I, William J. Smith, also known as William John Smith, William Smith, and Will Smith, of the City of Columbus, County of Franklin, and State of Ohio, do make, publish and declare this to be my last will, and I hereby revoke all wills and codicils heretofore made by me.

§ 5.5 Dispositive Clause. If the testator is a person of modest means with a spouse and several children, and he does not desire to make specific bequests or devises, the dispositive clause might be couched in alternatives:

I give, devise, and bequeath all of my property of whatever kind and wherever situate, as follows:

(1) to my wife Mary A. Smith;

(2) if my wife, Mary A. Smith predeceases me, to such of my children as survive me, in equal shares, provided, however, should a child of mine predecease me, survived by a child or children who survive me, such grandchild or grandchildren of mine shall take the share his or their parent would have taken had such parent survived me;

(3) if my wife Mary A. Smith and all of my children predecease me, to such of my grandchildren as survive me, in equal shares;

(4) if my wife Mary A. Smith, all of my children, and all of my grandchildren predecease me, one-half to my parents, William M. and Anne R. Smith, or to the survivor of

> them, should only one of my parents sur-
> vive me, and one-half to the parents of my
> wife, Thomas E. and Eleanor C. Rundell, or
> to the survivor of them, should only one of
> the parents of my wife survive me.

"Pretermitted heir" statutes are common. Under such a statute a child omitted from his parent's
will may nonetheless in some cases share in the
estate. A testator desiring to leave all of his estate
to his surviving spouse should anticipate the possible application of a pretermitted heir statute and
avoid it by appropriate language:

> Except as hereinbefore provided, I intentionally
> make no provision for children of mine now
> living, or for any child or children born to or
> adopted by me hereafter.

Section (4) of the above clause assumes that the
testator and his wife view their property as resulting from common effort, and that in the absence of
a surviving spouse or descendants, it should be
split between the families of husband and wife.
Property in an estate that is not disposed of by will
passes in accordance with the applicable statute of
descent and distribution. Generally speaking, laws
on intestacy direct the devolution of property to
blood relatives of the decedent, not to relatives of a
spouse who predeceased the decedent. If rather
than naming persons specifically, the testator prefers generality at this point, an alternative to the
language of Section (4) above is as follows:

(4) if my wife, my children, and all of my grand-
    children predecease me, one-half to those per-
    sons who would have been the heirs of my
    wife had she died immediately after my
    death, and

   one-half to my heirs, it being my intention
   that those persons, now unascertained, who
   prove to be my heirs, shall, by his will, take
   as purchasers.

If the testator desires to make a specific bequest
or devise, he might set out such a gift after the
introductory clause, and then set out gifts of the
residuary estate in the alternative:

[Introductory clause]

I, William J. Smith, also known as.....

[specific bequest]

I give the gold watch which was left to me by my
father to my son John. If my son John does not
survive me, I give the gold watch to my son
James.

[residuary clause]

All the rest, residue, and remainder of my estate,
of whatever kind and wherever situate, including
gifts that fail through lapse or otherwise, I give,
devise, and bequeath as follows:

(1) to my wife Mary A. Smith;

(2) if my wife Mary A. Smith predeceases me,
    to such of my children as survive me in
    equal shares, provided, however.....

§ **5.6   Caveats.** Do not direct that the debts or the "just" debts of the decedent, funeral expenses, taxes, and expenses of administration be paid. Payment of debts, taxes, and expenses is provided for by statute. Direction that "just" debts be paid may unnecessarily raise questions about payment of debts discharged in bankruptcy, or payment of debts the collection of which is barred by the running of the statute of limitation. Specific directions to the executor concerning the procurement and erection of an appropriate marker for the testator's grave, or disposition of the testator's body, or a part thereof, are appropriate parts of a will, although with respect to what are now called "anatomical gifts," sole reliance should not be put on the will.

Avoid expressions such as "per capita" or "per stirpes." These words are unfamiliar to laymen, and may be incomprehensible to the testator. Instead of "equally to my surviving children and the issue of any deceased child, per stirpes," write "to such of my children as survive me in equal shares, provided, however, should a child of mine predecease me, survived by a child or children who survive me, such grandchild or grandchildren of mine shall take the share his or their parent would have taken had such parent survived me."

Do not use precatory language in connection with a gift. "I give $1,000 to my brother John hoping he will use it for his family" at a minimum may cause ill feeling should John disregard the testator's hope. Worse, it may provoke litigation.

Do not accept without further inquiry the testator's description of his gift. A testator who says he wants his "new Cadillac" to go to his nephew John may mean "any automobile that I own at my death." The interval between execution of the will and the death of the testator (and changes in persons and property) should be considered in choosing language to describe the gift. Although it unquestionably is wise at times to be quite specific, specificity should give way when ascertained intention is a mix of generality and specificity.

Avoid expressions such as "if my wife Mary and I die as a result of a common disaster...." Persons may reasonably disagree on whether or not a particular event is a "common disaster." "If my wife Mary and I die at about the same time" is subject to the same kind of objection. If the testator desires that beneficiaries take only if beneficiaries survive the testator by some specified period of time, a clause of this kind might be used:

Any beneficiary under this will who dies within one hundred and twenty (120) days after the date of my death shall be treated for the purposes of this will as having predeceased me.

Remember that given names are frequently common within a family. To avoid difficulties in identification, it may be necessary to identify a beneficiary by describing in full a blood relationship or using a street address. As opposed to writing "to my nephew James W. Smith," it may be essential to write "to my nephew James W. Smith, son of my brother John" because the testator has two nephews named James W. Smith.

Do not forget that if the intended beneficiary of a gift predeceases the testator, a gift by substitution might arise under an anti-lapse statute. The beneficiary of the gift arising under the anti-lapse statute may be a person to whom the testator prefers to leave nothing. Application of the anti-lapse statute can be anticipated and avoided. The will might read:

> I leave my two-carat diamond ring to my niece Alice Kendall; if my niece Alice Kendall predeceases me, I leave my two-carat diamond ring to my niece Amy Kendall. If both Alice Kendall and Amy Kendall predecease me, my two-carat diamond ring shall be disposed of as a part of my residuary estate.

Be hesitant to create a legal life estate, or a legal life estate with a power to consume. Frequently the probate estate is so small that a legal life estate is altogether inadequate to the purpose it is intended to serve, its other disagreeable characteristics aside. A power to consume provokes litigation. A testator with wealth sufficient to justify the creation of a life estate might consider creating a trust. (If the testator insists on express provision in the will for successive enjoyment of an heirloom, the legal life estate with remainder is appropriate.)

Do not disinherit a child of the testator or any other person by leaving him one dollar. Simply write "I leave nothing to my sister Margaret."

The probate procedure ordinarily requires receipts
from distributees. A distributee of one dollar is a
distributee. Leaving a beneficiary one dollar may
amuse the testator, but it may cause unnecessary
trouble to the executor or administrator of his
estate.

Do not insert derogatory statements about beneficiaries or non-beneficiaries. The will is principally a dispositive document. It is not an appropriate
device for airing grievances. However, it may be
appropriate to indicate that the testator has
thought of a particular person:

> Having made occasional gifts to my brother John
> during my lifetime, I make no provision for him
> in this my last will.

§ 5.7 Guardianship. Because the testator
may die survived by a minor child or children
(irrespective of whether his spouse predeceases him
or survives him or they die simultaneously), he
should anticipate possible guardianship of the person and the estate of his minor child or children.
The law of guardianship, like the law of intestacy,
wills, and administration of decedents' estates, varies from state to state. But generally speaking,
one should anticipate judicial reluctance to designate a non-resident of the state as guardian of the
estate of a minor. On the other hand, a court may
be quite willing to appoint as guardian of the
person of a minor a non-resident nominated by the
testator, particularly when the nominee is a relative. The guardian of the person of a minor is
responsible for his care. The guardian of the es-

tate of a minor is responsible for the property of the minor. Although the same person may (and on occasion should) act as guardian in both capacities, guardianship of the person and guardianship of the estate draw on qualities that are only in part identical. A person who is acceptable as guardian of the person may not be suitable to manage property. In any event, nomination (or appointment) of guardians should be given careful thought by the testator prior to the drafting of the will, and the testator should assure himself that his nominees are willing to act in the capacities designated by him in his will. And here (as in the nomination of the executor), the testator should provide for an alternative or successor guardian. If we assume that the testator has left his entire estate to his spouse if she survives him, the clause on guardianship might read as follows:

> If my wife Mary A. Smith predeceases me, and I am survived by a minor child or children, I nominate my sister Helen E. Smith to be guardian of the person and estate of such minor child or children. If my sister Helen E. Smith predeceases me, or is unable or unwilling to accept such appointment, or, having undertaken her duties, is unable or unwilling to continue to serve, then I nominate my sister Georgia R. Kendall to be guardian of the person and estate of such minor child or children. I direct that any guardian nominated by me be exempted from the requirement of furnishing bond.

Exemption from the requirement of furnishing bond should be a matter of thought, not form. The usual justifications for the exemption are that the nominated guardian is honest, and exemption from furnishing bond saves the cost of the bond premium. But an honest person may err, and here (as elsewhere), the protection afforded by insurance may well be worth the price of the premium.

Where the prospective estates are more than nominal, trusteeship of the estate should be considered as an alternative to guardianship of the estate. The usual (but not the only) argument for preferring trusteeship over guardianship is that trusteeship permits greater flexibility.

If a minor child or minor children of the testator are at the execution of the will well beyond infancy, the testator might nominate as guardian of the person of the minor that person selected by the minor himself from a group listed by the testator:

If my wife Mary A. Smith predeceases me, and I am survived by my son Lawrence, still a minor at my death, then I nominate as guardian of the person of my son Lawrence that person selected by Lawrence from among the following: my sister Helen E. Smith, my sister Georgia R. Kendall, my brother Raymond S. Smith.

The matter of compatibility aside, consulting the minor himself with respect to guardianship may reveal facets of the matter (geographical location of the nominee) that may be important to the minor but overlooked by the testator, or unknown (and unknowable) to him at the execution of the will.

§ 5.8 Nominating the Executor. If we assume that the testator is an employee with only a moderate amount of property (a residence, an automobile, a few United States Savings Bonds, some bank accounts), and, in particular, that he is not operating a business that sensibly should be continued for an appreciable period of time after his death, it may be appropriate to nominate the surviving spouse as executor of the estate. As in nominating the guardian, so too in nominating the executor, the testator should anticipate an alternate or a successor. The clause might be drafted as follows:

I nominate my wife Mary A. Smith to be executrix of my last will. If my wife Mary A. Smith predeceases me, or is unable or unwilling to accept such appointment, or, having undertaken her duties, is unable or unwilling to continue to serve, then I nominate my sister Georgia R. Kendall to be executrix of my last will. I direct that any executrix nominated by me be exempted from the requirement of furnishing bond.

§ 5.9 Powers of the Executor. An executor, like a guardian or a trustee, is a fiduciary—he ordinarily is managing property that belongs to others. The statutory or judge-made law on fiduciary administration tends to be strict.

Generally speaking, a testator may free his fiduciary from restraints or rules which would otherwise apply to him. When the nominated fiduciary is a person of judgment in whom the testator sensibly has confidence, freedom of action may appropriately be provided for in the will by setting out express powers. Even if the executor has an enumerated power as a matter of local law irrespective of enumeration, those dealing with him may be more willing to act without explicit court approval if the power to act is set out in the will itself. When the testator is a person of modest means, the clause on powers might be correspondingly brief:

Without the necessity of obtaining leave of any court, my executrix shall have full power (1) to sell (at public or private sale), mortgage, transfer, and convey, in such manner and on such terms (including credit) as seem advisable, any and all property in my estate; (2) to settle, adjust, compromise, or pay claims asserted in favor of or against my estate, and to agree to any rescission or modification of any contract or agreement made by me; and (3) to make distribution in kind at a valuation set by her for such purpose, such valuation to be final and conclusive to the distributee or distributees.

§ 5.10 The Closing Recitation. The effort put into the proper drafting of a will is wasted if the will is not executed. The "testimonium" clause affords an opportunity to describe the format of the will ("... consisting of this page and the two preceding typewritten pages ..."), the means used to identify pages not signed by the testator ("... initialled by me at the left margin thereof ..."), and the circumstances, date, and place of execution:

In witness whereof I have hereunto set my hand
to this my last will, consisting of this page and
the two preceding typewritten pages initialled by
me at the left margin thereof, in the presence of
the three persons who have at my request and in
my presence and in the presence of each other
acted as witnesses this _____ day of _____
19__, at Columbus, Ohio.

Even if there is no statutory requirement that
the date and place of execution appear in the will,
the closing recitation should note both. The date
of execution assists in determining whether or not
the document offered for probate is the last will of
the decedent. The place of execution is an index to
compliance with the requirements for execution.
Most jurisdictions accept as valid a will executed
according to the law of the state of execution.

The usual place for the signature of the testator
is below the closing recitation and above the attestation clause. Typing the testator's signature below the line on which he signs assists in execution
of the will. The testator should sign his name in
the same form as it appears in the title to the will
and in the introductory clause. Wills should not
be executed in duplicate or triplicate. Wills should
not be executed in duplicate or triplicate because
failure to produce all executed copies at death may
raise a presumption that the testator destroyed an
executed copy with the intention to revoke his will.

§ 5.11 **The Attestation Clause.** The attestation clause affords an opportunity to state that the

execution of the will complies with all requirements prescribed by law. Even if state law requires only two attesting witnesses, it is preferable
to use three. Several states require three witnesses. And although a will valid where executed may
be admitted to probate in a three-witness state,
producing two out of three witnesses at probate in
a two-witness state may be easier than producing
two out of two. If the names and addresses of the
witnesses are certain in advance of execution, it is
sensible to type each name and address immediately below the line on which each signs as an attesting witness. Locating a witness is important for
purposes of probating (proving) the will. A will
could be proved if all of the witnesses were dead,
but one starts by trying to get the witnesses themselves. Furthermore, typing in the names mini-
mizes confusion at the time of signing. If names
and addresses are not known in advance of execution, they should be typed thereafter on a carbon
copy or photocopy of the will for record purposes.
The attestation clause might read as follows:

> The foregoing instrument of three typewritten
> pages, including this page, was signed at the end
> by William J. Smith and by him acknowledged to
> be his last will before us and in our presence,
> and by us subscribed as attesting witnesses in his
> presence, at his request, and in the presence of
> each other on the day and year last above writ-
> ten. And we and each of us declare that we
> believe William J. Smith to be of sound mind
> and memory.

§ 5.12 Execution. Witnesses to the will should be persons younger than the testator, in good health, and likely to be available at probate of the will. Although all witnesses should be acquainted with the testator, none should be a beneficiary under the will (or the spouse of a beneficiary) and none should be an heir (or the spouse of an heir). The lawyer drafting the will is a permissible (some say desirable) witness. In advance of execution he should explain to the testator that the witnesses need know nothing of the contents of the will, although they must be told that they are asked to attest to execution of the will of the testator (as opposed to some other kind of document).

The lawyer, the testator, and all witnesses being assembled, the testator should state to the witnesses that the document to be signed is his will and that he asks that they act as witnesses. With the witnesses observing him, the testator then initials the pages to the will preceding the last page, and signs his name to the will at the end. Each witness then reads the attestation clause (or one witness reads the clause aloud, the others listening) and signs his name and writes his address.

If the lawyer drafting the will believes that the testamentary capacity of the testator (ability to execute a will) might be questioned, the lawyer might sensibly have the entire ceremony of execution of the will videotaped. A thoughtfully prepared videotape might be much more compelling as evidence of testamentary capacity than the recollections of attesting witnesses given long after the time of execution.

§ 5.13 The "Self–Proved" Will. Statute may provide for the "proving" (establishing the authenticity) of a will by affidavit. For example, Utah Code Ann.1953, 75–2–504 provides in part as follows:

> Any will may be simultaneously executed, attested, and made self-proved, by acknowledgment of it by the testator and affidavits of the witnesses, each made before an officer authorized to administer oaths under the laws of the state where execution occurs, whether or not that officer is also a witness to the will, and evidenced by the officer's certificate, under official seal....

The affidavits are required to take "substantially" the following form:

> I, _____, the testator, sign my name to this instrument this _____ day of _____, 19__, and being first duly sworn, do hereby declare to the undersigned authority that I sign and execute this instrument as my last will and that I sign it willingly (or willingly direct another to sign for me), that I execute it as my free and voluntary act for the purposes expressed in it, and that I am 18 years of age or older, of sound mind, and under no constraint or undue influence.

_____

Testator

We, _____, _____, the witnesses, sign our names to this instrument, being first duly sworn, and do hereby declare to the undersigned authority that the testator signs and executes this instrument as his last will and that he signs it willingly (or willingly directs another to sign for him), and that each of us, in the presence and hearing of the testator and of each other, hereby signs this will as witness to the testator's signing, and that to the best of our knowledge the testator is 18 years of age or older, of sound mind, and under no constraint or undue influence.

_____

Witness

_____

Witness

STATE of _____

COUNTY of _____

Subscribed, sworn to, and acknowledged before me by _____, the testator and subscribed and sworn to before me by _____ and _____, witnesses, this _____ day of _____.

(Signed) _____

_____

(Official capacity of officer)

The statute permits combining affidavits in "substantially" the following form:

STATE of _____

COUNTY of _____

We, _____, _____, and _____, the testator and the witnesses, respectively, whose names are signed to the attached or foregoing instrument, being first duly sworn, do hereby declare to the undersigned authority that the testator signed and executed the instrument as his last will and that he had signed willingly (or willingly directed another to sign for him), and that he executed it as his free and voluntary act for the purposes expressed in it; and that each of the witnesses, in the presence and hearing of the testator and of each other, signed the will as witness and that to the best of his knowledge the testator was at that time 18 years of age or older, of sound mind and under no constraint or undue influence.

_____

Testator

_____

Witness

_____

Witness

Subscribed, sworn to and acknowledged before me by _____, the testator, and subscribed and sworn to before me by _____ and _____ witnesses, this _____ day of _____.

(Signed) _____

_____
(Official capacity of officer)

§ **5.14 Statutory Wills.** A Uniform Statutory Will Act exists, and some states have enacted statutory will statutes. The uniform act provides lawyers with a simple will that can be modified to meet the differing requirements of clients, and the act also permits the testator simply to direct that his or her estate be distributed in accordance with the terms of the act, thus incorporating the statutory plan of distribution by reference.

§ **5.15 Safeguarding the Will.** Two carbon copies or photocopies of the unexecuted will should be made. One should be kept by the lawyer who drafted the will and one should be kept by the testator. The will itself should be put by the testator in his safe-deposit box, or deposited with the Probate Court (if permitted by law).

A photocopy of any prior will or wills should be made and deposited with the lawyer who drafted the last will, and thereafter any prior will or wills should be destroyed by the testator, or by his direction and in his presence. (If two "wills" are found by the executor, he might offer both for probate, and that is contrary to the intention of the testator and creates unnecessary problems.)

§ 5.16 Lists of Property and Benefits: Suggestions of the Decedent. Because the testator may own a great variety of both real and personal property at his death, and because his beneficiaries may be entitled to insurance benefits, Social Security benefits, veterans' benefits, pension fund benefits, deferred compensation benefits, fraternal lodge benefits and the like (many of which are unaffected by his will), he should be encouraged to prepare lists of his property (and their locations), and lists of benefits available to his beneficiaries at his death. These lists should be reviewed periodically to determine that they are up to date. They should be as complete as possible, so that essential information known to the testator about his property interests (but neither known nor easily ascertained by others) is immediately available to the family and the personal representative of the testator at the testator's death. (A properly prepared list, for example, facilitates informing the insurer of the death of the insured.) These periodically reviewed lists might be accompanied by such written suggestions as the testator might think appropriate with respect to items making up the lists. A testator may have sensible suggestions to make that are not appropriate parts of a will, but that are nonetheless worth committing to paper. Because of the great variety of rights in property that can exist today, even in persons of moderate means, it is conceivable that properly prepared and frequently updated lists of property and benefits, with accompanying suggestions, are just as important to a decedent's family as the will itself.

§ 5.17 A "Simple Will" in Its Entirety.

Will of William J. Smith

I, William J. Smith, also known as William John Smith, William Smith, and Will Smith, of the City of Columbus, County of Franklin, and State of Ohio, do make, publish, and declare this to be my last will, and I hereby revoke all wills and codicils heretofore made by me.

I give, devise, and bequeath all of my property of whatever kind and wherever situate, as follows:

(1) to my wife Mary A. Smith;

(2) if my wife Mary A. Smith predeceases me, to such of my children as survive me, in equal shares, provided, however, should a child of mine predecease me, survived by a child or children who survive me, such grandchild or grandchildren of mine shall take the share his or their parent would have taken had such parent survived me;

(3) if my wife Mary A. Smith and all of my children predecease me, to such of my grandchildren as survive me, in equal shares;

(4) if my wife Mary A. Smith, all of my children, and all of my grandchildren predecease me, one-half to my parents, William M. and Anne R. Smith, or to the survivor of them, should only one of my parents survive me, and one-half to the parents of my wife, Thomas E. and Eleanor C. Rundell, or to the survivor of them, should only one of the parents of my wife survive me.

Except as hereinbefore provided, I intentionally make no provision for children of mine now living, or for any child or children born to or adopted by me hereafter.

If my wife Mary A. Smith predeceases me, and I am survived by a minor child or children, I nominate my sister Helen E. Smith to be guardian of the person and estate of such minor child or children. If my sister Helen E. Smith predeceases me, or is unable or unwilling to accept such appointment, or, having undertaken her duties, is unable or unwilling to continue to serve, then I nominate my sister Georgia R. Kendall to be the guardian of the person and estate of such minor child or children. I direct that any guardian nominated by me be exempted from the requirement of furnishing bond.

I nominate my wife Mary A. Smith to be executrix of my last will. If my wife Mary A. Smith predeceases me, or is unable or unwilling to accept such appointment, or, having undertaken her duties, is unable or unwilling to continue to serve, then I nominate my sister Georgia R. Kendall to be executrix of my last will. I direct that any executrix nominated by me be exempted from the requirement of furnishing bond.

Without the necessity of obtaining leave of any court, my executrix shall have full power (1) to sell (at public or private sale), mortgage, transfer, and convey, in such manner and on such terms (including credit) as seem advisable, any and all property in my estate; (2) to settle, adjust, compromise, or pay claims asserted in favor of or against my estate, and to agree to any rescission or modification of any contract or agreement made by me; and (3) to make distribution in kind at a valuation set by her for such purpose, such valuation to be final and conclusive to the distributee or distributees.

In witness whereof I have hereunto set my hand to this my last will, consisting of this page and the one preceding typewritten page initialled by me at the left margin thereof, in the presence of the three persons who have at my request and in my presence and in the presence of each other acted as witnesses this _____ day of _____, 19__, at Columbus, Ohio.

_____

William J. Smith

The foregoing instrument of two typewritten pages, including this page, was signed at the end by William J. Smith and by him acknowledged to be his last will before us and in our presence, and by us subscribed as attesting witnesses in his presence, at his request, and in the presence of each other on the day and year last above written. And

we and each of us declare that we believe William
J. Smith to be of sound mind and memory.

_____ residing at _____
_____ residing at _____
_____ residing at _____

CHAPTER 6

INSURANCE

§ 6.1 Insurance and Estate Planning. Insurance on his own life (the "life insured" or "the insured") is important to a prospective decedent because it augments or creates his estate, using the word "estate" in the largest sense. Because the proceeds of a life insurance contract (the "policy") are commonly payable under the policy to the surviving spouse of the insured decedent, or to some other person (as differentiated from the estate of the insured), the proceeds ordinarily are not a part of the assets of the decedent that are administered by the probate court.

Kinds of insurance commonly lumped together and called "property and liability" insurance by lawyers (including, for example, "fire" insurance, "marine" insurance, "inland marine" insurance, and "casualty" insurance) are also important to the ordering of one's affairs because they protect against losses that decrease or deplete altogether the assets that the prospective decedent is accumulating to leave to his family. The person protected against loss under a property or liability insurance policy is also commonly called "the insured." (Because the expression "the insured" is used both to identify the life insured under a life insurance policy, and to identify the person protected against

105

loss under an insurance policy of any kind, the
meaning of "the insured" must be determined from
context.)

A fire insurance policy commonly covers loss or
damage to real and personal property of the insured caused by hostile fire or lightning. It might
also cover loss or damage caused by such events as
windstorm, flood, earthquake, or landslide. A
"personal property floater policy" covering loss or
damage to personal property of the insured is an
example of inland marine insurance. Casualty
insurance includes the "liability" insurance that is
a characteristic feature of "automobile" insurance
and of some "homeowners" insurance policies.

Traditionally, an insurance policy has been a
contract of indemnity—the insurer agrees to pay
because of a loss suffered. (A "bond" issued by a
surety company is not usually considered to be a
contract of insurance. The law on insurance and
the law on suretyship overlap to some extent, but
each has its own history.) Because a contract of
insurance even today is basically a contract to
indemnify for a loss, it is desirable that a person
buying insurance "protection" inform himself as
best he can with respect to "coverage"—that is,
what losses are insured against. In this connection, the most reliable source of information is the
insurance policy itself. It is undeniably true that
(say) a "homeowners" policy is replete with words
like "exclusions," "conditions," and "endorse-
ments," and that often only a person experienced

in insurance matters can determine in a particular case whether "coverage" exists. Nonetheless, any policy of insurance should be examined when received. For example, a buyer might be able to determine on examination of his policy that the dollar limit on coverage is lower than he thought he had specified.

Because a person's circumstances change as time passes, it is desirable to "review" (that is, to think systematically about) one's insurance periodically. For example, as the insured under a "homeowners" policy acquires additional possessions (or as inflation continues), he might consider increasing the dollar amount of "coverage" he has against fortuitous loss of his property. If an unmarried person with no dependents marries, he or she might consider acquiring (or augmenting) life insurance. Because ours is to an increasing extent an age of litigation, the kind of person who only thirty years ago might sensibly have thought "liability" insurance to be principally of interest to physicians, might today give serious thought to trying to protect assets from diminution or outright depletion as the consequence of a lawsuit.

§ 6.2 **Why Life Insurance?** There are various kinds of life insurance, and innumerable life insurance "plans." Regardless of the kind of insurance on a person's life, if he dies while insured under the policy (and there is no effective "defense" available to the insurer), the proceeds are payable to the beneficiary. This result follows even though the proceeds payable are $50,000 (the "face amount" of the policy), and the premiums paid total (say) only $2,500 when death occurs. The ability to create what is sometimes called an "instant estate" through buying life insurance is of particular interest to the prospective decedent who has little or no accumulated property. He might be young, never having had an opportunity to accumulate. He might be middle-aged, and unable to accumulate much property. In either case, he has never acquired substantial property by gift, devise, or descent that he might pass on to his dependents and successors.

Even if one is not motivated to buy life insurance to create an instant estate, he might procure insurance to provide ready cash to meet payments incident to his death: funeral costs, debts, family living expenses, and death taxes. Having cash available from insurance proceeds to meet such payments avoids a sale of estate assets that might otherwise be required, and that might occur under unfavorable market conditions.

Because of the way payments for insurance ("premiums") are calculated and paid, life insurance other than "term" insurance includes a forced savings feature. During the early years of the contract, the premium paid is greater than the sum required to buy "pure" insurance, and the savings accumulate in the hands of the insurer. Consequently, the insurance policy has a "cash surrender" value. The owner of the policy (the "policyholder") who has decided to terminate the

insurance can surrender the policy to the issuing
company (the "insurer") and receive its then cash
surrender value. More importantly, because the
insurance includes a savings feature, the policy can
be pledged to a commercial lender, or to an individual as security for a loan. The policy by its terms
might enable the policyholder to pledge it to the
issuing company as security for a loan from the
insurance company (sometimes at a favorable rate).
Although on (say) an "ordinary life" policy, premiums are payable during the lifetime of the life
insured, if the policyholder "drops" the insurance,
that is, simply fails or refuses to pay premiums,
the forced savings feature entitles him to "paid up"
life insurance at a reduced face amount. If the
policyholder lives to retirement age, the policy by
its terms might enable the policyholder to draw
retirement benefits payable over a period of years
from the accumulated savings. (While accumulating, the savings are not includible in the policyholder's gross income for Federal Income Tax purposes.)

A prospective decedent might be a partner in a
business. The partners might have an enforceable
agreement under which on the death of a partner,
the surviving partners have the right to buy the
interest of the deceased partner. Insurance on the
life of each partner, with the other partners being
designated beneficiaries under the policy, can provide the cash required to pay for the deceased
partner's interest on his death.

Regardless of whether the prospective decedent is a person of some means, he might procure insurance on his life to serve as the principal or even the sole basis of a trust for the benefit of the decedent's family. (The decedent might prefer that the proceeds of the insurance be paid out from time to time by a trustee having discretion to allocate among beneficiaries according to circumstances, as opposed to having the proceeds paid outright to a beneficiary in their entirety as a "lump sum," or even paid out over time under a "settlement option.")

Last, a person who is an employee might procure life insurance on his own life because he has no choice: Life insurance "protection" is a requirement of his employment relation. Commonly, this protection is afforded through "group" life insurance—usually one-year renewable term insurance.

§ 6.3 Life Insurance Proceeds under State Law and under the Federal Estate Tax. Because the insurance industry is well established and influential, statutes may give to the insurance contract or to insurance proceeds recognition not accorded other "property" of a decedent. If a decedent leaves assets at death that are subject to administration by the probate court, and he dies owing debts that are "allowed" as claims against the estate, such debts (as well as debts incurred during administration of the estate) are payable from estate assets (and as a consequence, probate assets might be exhausted, leaving none for distribution to the dependents of the decedent). By way of contrast, suppose that at the decedent's death, he owns policies of insurance on his own life, payable to his wife, who survives him. That the proceeds of the policies are not subject to administration by the probate court is implicitly recognized by the following language from Ohio Revised Code § 3911.10:

All contracts of life or endowment insurance ... upon the life of any person ... which may hereafter mature and which have been taken out for the benefit of, or made payable ... to, the spouse or children, or any relative dependent upon such person ..., or to a trustee for the benefit of such spouse, children, [or] dependent relative ..., shall be held, together with the proceeds or avails of such contracts ... *free from all claims of the creditors of such insured person....* (Emphasis added.)

Ohio Revised Code § 3911.14 makes explicit the validity of a "spendthrift" clause applicable to the interests of beneficiaries of the proceeds of a life policy:

Any life insurance company ... may hold the proceeds of any life or endowment insurance ... contract ... with such exemptions from legal process and the claims of creditors of beneficiaries other than the insured ... as have been agreed to in writing by such company and the insured or beneficiary.... Any life or endowment insurance ... contract ... may provide that the proceeds thereof or payments thereunder *shall not be subject to transfer, anticipation,*

*commutation, or encumbrances by any benefi-
ciary, and shall not be subject to the claims of
creditors of any beneficiary other than the insured....* (Emphasis added.)

Section 2042 of the Internal Revenue Code permits a decedent to pass proceeds of insurance on
his life to his beneficiaries at his death free from
the Federal Estate Tax even though the decedent
procured the policy himself, and paid the premiums on the policy from the time of procurement
until his death. Since 1954 the "incidents of ownership" test has been used to determine whether
the proceeds of insurance on the life of the decedent that are payable to a beneficiary other than
his estate are includible in the decedent's "gross
estate," that is, his estate for Federal Estate Tax
purposes. (The gross estate might include, and
commonly does include, property in addition to
that included in the probate estate of the decedent.) Incidents of ownership include the right to
change the beneficiary of the policy, the right to
surrender the policy for cash, the right to pledge
the policy as security for a loan, and the right to
designate the method of payment under a settlement option. If a decedent retains any incident of
ownership at his death, the proceeds of the policy
on his life are includible in his gross estate for
Federal Estate Tax purposes. If the decedent assigns all of his rights in his policy to another more
than three years before the decedent dies, no part
of the proceeds is includible in his gross estate at
his death.

§ 6.4 Why Property and Liability Insurance? Fire insurance and "allied lines," and marine and inland marine insurance are commonly called "property" insurance because the insured is protected against loss or damage to real or personal property originating in various kinds of perils or hazards. Liability insurance protects the insured against loss arising from legal liability.

If a person owns property outright, such as a house or an automobile, ordinary experience leads him to conclude, and properly so, that he can insure against loss or damage to the property, and accordingly he procures property insurance. Experience might also lead him to conclude, and properly so, that his ownership might expose him to legal liability. For example, his house guest might be injured on the premises and bring suit against him alleging negligence in failing to maintain the premises. To avoid diminution or depletion of assets that results from being held legally liable for loss or injury to another attributable to the fault of the homeowner and his family he carries liability insurance.

A trustee of a private express trust or a charitable trust (irrespective of whether the trustee is an individual or a corporation) is not the "beneficial" owner of the property that he holds in trust—the beneficial ownership is in an individual beneficiary or beneficiaries (of whom the trustee might be one) in the case of the private trust, and in the public in the case of the charitable trust. Nonetheless, the trustee, like the executor or administrator of an

estate, is under a fiduciary obligation to preserve
and protect the property he holds in trust. Fulfilling that duty might require, and ordinarily does
require, procuring property and liability insurance
to protect the trust property against loss or damage.

§ **6.5 Insurable Interest.** An insurance contract is aimed at indemnity, that is, reimbursement for loss or damage. The indemnity principle
underlies a doctrine called "insurable interest"—
one seeking to procure an enforceable contract of
insurance must have an "insurable interest" in the
subject matter of the contract, irrespective of
whether it is life or property. Insurable interest is
that relation between the insured and the fortuitous event that causes loss to the insured.

As to life insurance, insurable interest must exist at the time the contract is made. It need not
exist at the death of the life insured. As to property insurance, insurable interest must exist at the
time of loss. It often exists both at the time a
property insurance contract is made and when loss
occurs. For example, A, owning and occupying a
single-family residence, procures fire insurance
covering the house. Thereafter, while A is in
possession and the policy is in force, a fortuitous
fire damages the house. A had an insurable interest both at the time he procured the fire policy and
at the time loss occurred.

It is said that everyone has an insurable interest
in his or her own life. All this means is that a

person who is legally competent may effectively contract for insurance on his or her own life, designating anyone as beneficiary. A more useful statement is that generally a person may procure insurance on his or her own life without regard to insurable interest. Because persons so frequently procure insurance on their own lives, the "life insured" and the policyholder (or "owner") are frequently one and the same person. If one seeks to procure an enforceable contract of insurance on the life of another, one must have an insurable interest in the other's life.

Some kinds of family relationships give rise to generally recognized insurable interests. A husband has an insurable interest in the life of his wife, and she in his. A parent has an insurable interest in the life of his minor child, and the minor child has an insurable interest in the life of his parent. Beyond these standard kinds of family relationships supporting insurable interest, generalization on family relationship as a basis for insurable interest is difficult.

Outside the family relationships that give rise to an insurable interest, some kinds of business relationships suffice. A creditor has an insurable interest in the life of his debtor, a partner in the life of his co-partner, and a business entity in the life of a key employee.

There are three bases of insurable interest in property that deserve mention: property right, contract right, and legal liability.

A person who owns a valuable commercial building outright has a property right that can be
destroyed altogether or diminished if the building
is destroyed or damaged by fire. He therefore has
an insurable interest in the building. Even if the
building were "mortgaged"—that is, if the building
were security for a debt—the "owner" has a property right, and therefore an insurable interest, and
the creditor has a property right, and therefore an
insurable interest. Either can lawfully procure
insurance against loss by fire or similar hazard.
(Commonly, only the owner procures insurance,
with proceeds in the event of loss being payable to
both mortgagor and mortgagee as their interests
appear.)

Although a person does not have a property
right with respect to property, he may nonetheless
have such a relation to it, based on a legal right or
duty, so that he will derive a benefit from its
continuing existence or suffer a loss or liability
because of its destruction or damage. A merchant
who contracts to buy goods at a distance on condition that the goods arrive safely at the merchant's
place of business has an insurable interest in the
goods because he will suffer a loss of profit if the
goods do not arrive safely. Here, a contract right
is the basis for insurable interest in goods. Similarly, a building contractor who contracts to build
a structure on the land of another has an insurable
interest in the building as construction proceeds
because the contractor is under a contract duty to
rebuild even though the structure is fortuitously

damaged or destroyed before accepted by the owner. Here, a contract duty is the basis for insurable interest in the building.

A person may have a property right with respect to property, and also a duty with respect to the property, so that he has an insurable interest in the property based on more than one ground. A trustee of a private express trust or a charitable trust ordinarily has legal title to the subject matter of the trust (the "trust property" or the "trust corpus"). The trustee is under a fiduciary duty to preserve and protect the trust property. For breach of that duty, he is liable in damages to the beneficiary or beneficiaries of the trust. Both his property right as "title holder" of the trust property and his exposure to legal liability for failure to fulfill his duty to preserve and protect the trust property give the trustee an insurable interest in the trust property.

In virtually every instance in which a person seeks insurance for a sensible purpose, he has an "insurable interest," and therefore the doctrine is not a bar to advantageous arrangement of one's personal and business affairs. But lack of insurable interest is a defense occasionally raised with success by insurers defending actions on policies. A lawyer or an insurance advisor should be aware of it.

§ 6.6 Kinds of Life Insurance. There are many variations in the terms and conditions that make up a life insurance "plan." Below are some terms commonly employed to differentiate plans of life insurance.

"Whole-life insurance" provides coverage during the entire lifetime of the life insured and is payable only at his death. "Whole-life insurance" can be differentiated further: In the case of "ordinary" or "straight" life insurance, premiums are payable either throughout the lifetime of the life insured or until he has reached a specified advanced age (say) 100; in the case of "limited-payment" life insurance, premiums are payable for a specified number of years (say) twenty, or until the occurrence of a specified event, such as attaining age 60. (Under a limited-payment plan, the premiums are higher, and at the end of the payment period the policy is "paid up"—on the death thereafter of the life insured, the face amount of the policy is payable.) "Single-premium" insurance is what the words imply: Rather than pay premiums over time, the purchaser pays but one premium on procuring the policy. "Joint life" insurance covers more than one life (commonly, husband and wife or business partners). The face amount is payable on the death of the first of the lives insured to die.

"Endowment life insurance" provides for payment of a specified sum if death of the life insured occurs within the endowment period, or for payment at the end of the endowment period if the life insured survives the endowment period.

Both whole-life and endowment policies include a forced savings feature. That is, premiums are

the same amount ("level") throughout the time
that they are payable. Consequently, the policyholder pays more than is required for "pure" insurance during the early years of payment of premiums, and less than is required for "pure" insurance
during the later years.

Both "universal" life and "variable" life policies
include the savings feature, but a "variable" policy
allows the policyholder to invest the cash value in
investment instruments of choice.

"Term" life insurance is sometimes referred to
as "pure" insurance—it has no savings feature. If
the life insured dies while the contract is in force,
that is, during the term of the policy—commonly
one year or five years—a stated sum is payable to
the designated beneficiary. Because term insurance has no savings feature, it has no cash surrender value. And once the term has ended, there is
no insurance in force. Nonetheless, term is an
important form of life insurance. It is often sold
as "mortgage" insurance—decreasing term insurance assuring that on the death of the life insured,
the mortgage on the family home will be paid.
The term insurance contract might by its terms
permit optional "conversion" of the term insurance
to a more "permanent" plan of insurance without
regard to the state of health of the life insured at
the time conversion is sought. The term insurance
contract might also provide for optional renewal of
the term insurance for an additional term without

regard to the state of health of the life insured at the time renewal is sought.

If a policyholder (whether of whole-life or term insurance) is entitled to "dividends," the policy is a "participating" policy. (If a policy does not pay dividends, it is a "non-participating" policy.) Insurance dividends should not be confused with dividends on certificates of stock. A dividend is an annual payment made to the policyholder by the insurance company at its discretion, and represents an overpayment that is refunded. A policyholder determines his actual premium cost per year by subtracting his dividend (if any) from the total premiums paid during the year.

§ 6.7 Settlement Options. "Settlement options" are provisions of a life policy that permit flexibility in the payment of the proceeds of the insurance on the death of the life insured. Rather than pay the proceeds as a lump sum to the designated beneficiary, the insurer paying under a settlement option retains the proceeds and pays them out thereafter in accordance with the terms of the chosen option. Where the policyholder and the life insured are the same person (as is so often the case) the policyholder himself might select an optional method of payment before he dies. (The right to select the method of payment under a settlement option is an "incident of ownership.") Alternatively, he might leave selection of the method of payment to the beneficiary.

The insurer who pays in accordance with the terms of a settlement option does not hold the proceeds of the policy in trust. Insurance is a contractual device. Payment of the proceeds of a life policy is fulfillment of a contractual duty whether payment is by lump sum or under a settlement option. In a particular case, payment under a settlement option to the beneficiary over a period of time might well be preferable to payment of the proceeds in a lump sum, but the flexibility in payment achieved through using the settlement option might nonetheless be not as great as that achievable by designating a trustee as beneficiary of the entire proceeds of the policy, and using a separate instrument of trust to set out the manner of payment by the trustee to the person or persons intended by the owner of the policy to benefit ultimately from the proceeds. If the proceeds are payable to the designated beneficiary of the policy as a trustee in the way just outlined, a private express trust does exist, with the proceeds of the policy making up the trust property or "corpus." Both life insurers and trustees are ordinarily investors of funds, but a trustee holding the proceeds of life insurance in trust can be given investment powers by the trust instrument that are tailored to the situation of the beneficiaries of the trust, and he can be given powers to make payments to the beneficiaries from time to time in accordance with their respective needs. In sum, settlement options further flexibility in paying out the proceeds of a policy, but they do not in all respects achieve the flexibility available through the private express trust.

§ 6.8 Kinds of Settlement Options. Under an "interest option" or "deposit option," the proceeds of a life policy are left with the insurer, and only periodic payments of interest are made to the beneficiary. At a predetermined time, the proceeds themselves are payable to the beneficiary. Usually interest is payable at a "guaranteed" minimum rate, but the minimum rate is low. (By way of contrast, an ordinary income interest payable from a trust is not guaranteed, and because of investment experience, no income might be forthcoming in a particular case.)

An "installment" option is either for a fixed amount or for a fixed period of time. Under a "fixed amount" or "installment amount" option, periodic payments of both policy proceeds and income are made to the beneficiary until policy proceeds and income are exhausted. Under a "fixed period" or "installment time" option, periodic payments of both policy proceeds and income are made to the beneficiary for a predetermined period of time, the amount of each payment being dependent upon both the total amount available for distribution and the length of time over which periodic payments are to be made. Under a fixed amount option, if the first or "primary" beneficiary dies before the funds are exhausted, the balance is payable to the "secondary" beneficiary (or beneficiaries). Under a fixed time option, if the primary beneficiary dies before the predetermined period of time has elapsed, the periodic payment is payable to the secondary beneficiary for the rest of the predetermined period.

Because neither the amount payable nor the number of payments is contingent upon the survival of the primary beneficiary, the options described above do not involve "life contingencies." Other options commonly available do involve life contingencies. The "straight" life annuity, the "joint and survivor" annuity, and some combination of the installment and life annuity all involve a life.

Under a straight life annuity option, the proceeds of the policy are in substance used to pay for an annuity that provides periodic payments to the primary beneficiary for life. Nothing is payable to the secondary beneficiary, even though the primary beneficiary lives only a short time. Unless the proceeds of the policy are unusually large, or the primary beneficiary is sixty or seventy years of age, the periodic payments from a straight life annuity tend to be low in amount.

A "joint and survivor" annuity provides for periodic payments during the lives of two beneficiaries and during the life of the survivor of them.

A combination of the installment and the life annuity option might take this form: The primary beneficiary receives a fixed amount per month for ten years or life, whichever is the longer. If the primary beneficiary dies before the "ten years certain" have elapsed, the fixed amount per month is payable to the secondary beneficiary for the rest of the ten year period, when the annuity expires without value.

§ 6.9 Change of Beneficiary of a Life Policy.
When a person procures a policy of life insurance
on his own life, or on the life of another person
where he has an insurable interest in the other's
life, he ordinarily reserves to himself by the terms
of the policy the right to change the designation of
the beneficiary of the proceeds of the policy without the consent of the beneficiary. Under such
circumstances, the beneficiary has no vested rights
under the policy, but has a mere "expectancy."
(His situation is comparable to that of a person
who has been designated the devisee or legatee
under the will of a person not yet dead.) If the
policyholder makes a change in the designation of
the beneficiary in accordance with the formalities
prescribed in the policy for making such a change,
the change is effective even though the earlier
beneficiary did not consent, or even though the
earlier beneficiary had no knowledge of the
change. Indeed, if the policyholder clearly ex-
presses an intention to designate a new beneficiary, and the then designated beneficiary prevents
insurance company "endorsement" of the intended
change by withholding possession of the policy,
there is "substantial compliance" with the policy
provision for change of beneficiary, and if the life
insured dies, the substituted beneficiary is entitled
to the proceeds of the policy rather than the earlier
beneficiary. For example, in John Hancock Mutual Life Ins. Co. v. Jedynak (1930), the life insured
procured a policy of insurance that designated her
mother as beneficiary. Under the terms of the
policy, the insured could change the beneficiary in
writing upon presenting the policy to the issuing
company for endorsement. The insured executed a

proper writing to change the beneficiary, but the designated beneficiary would not relinquish possession of the policy for endorsement by the insurer. On the death of the insured, the insurer filed a bill of interpleader, paid the proceeds of the policy into court, and submitted the matter of who was entitled to payment to the court for decision. The intended substituted beneficiary was found to be entitled to the policy proceeds.

Despite the existence of litigated cases demonstrating that a change of beneficiary can be made by "substantial compliance" with the policy provisions governing change, the policy provisions should be complied with in every respect whenever that is possible. Determining by a lawsuit that an attempted change of beneficiary has been successful is an expensive way to make a determination. In particular, the policyholder should not attempt to change the beneficiary designation by his will. It is usually held that an attempt to change the beneficiary designation by will is not "substantial compliance" with the procedure for change fixed by the policy. In Stone v. Stephens (1951), for example, the life insured had designated his wife Jeannette as beneficiary of his insurance. Jeannette thereafter divorced the insured, and although the insured was aware of the divorce, he made no attempt to change the beneficiary of his insurance in accordance with policy provisions. But in a subsequently executed will, the insured provided that if he died unmarried, all of his property, including his insurance, should go to his grand-

mother. Both Jeannette and the grandmother of
the insured survived him. The insurers paid the
proceeds of the policies into court and submitted
the matter of who was entitled to payment to the
court for decision. It was held that the right of the
insured to change the beneficiary was a personal
right, exercisable only during the lifetime of the
insured. Jeannette was entitled to the proceeds as
the designated beneficiary of the insurance at the
death of the insured.

Designation of the beneficiary can be irrevocable, and an irrevocable designation frequently
occurs as an incident to the separation or divorce
of a married couple. Irrevocable designation is
ordinarily to be avoided. If the policyholder has
made an irrevocable designation of the beneficiary
with the knowledge of the insurance company issuing the policy, he no longer can act effectively as
sole owner of the policy. For example, if he wishes
to "cash in" the policy, he must procure the consent of the designated beneficiary.

§ 6.10 **Assignment.** "Assignment of insurance" is an expression that has more than one
meaning. The meaning of "assignment" is determined, if determinable at all, from context. "Assignment of insurance" might mean transfer of a
right to money under an insurance policy after loss
has occurred; it might mean transfer of all rights
or some rights under a policy before loss has occurred; and it might mean transfer of "coverage"
under a policy to a substituted "insured."

Some kinds of rights existing or arising under insurance policies are unquestionably transferable or "assignable" as it is usually said. For example, if proceeds are payable under a life policy on the death of the life insured, the beneficiary's right to the proceeds is a right to money that is assignable. Similarly, if loss has occurred under a fire policy, the insured's right to payment is a right to money that is assignable. Rights assigned under the circumstances just suggested are subject to the infirmity one expects: The assignor can transfer no greater right than he himself has. Therefore defenses to a claim to payment available to the insurer before assignment are available to the insurer after assignment.

It is not assignment of insurance proceeds after loss that is of principal interest to one arranging his personal and business affairs in the expectation of retirement or death. Rather, with respect to insurance of various kinds, he is interested in what is transferable before loss has occurred. In this connection it is desirable to differentiate among life insurance, property insurance, and liability insurance. It is also desirable to know whether the transfer is with the consent of the insurer. And for property and liability insurance purposes, it is essential to differentiate between assignment of rights and transfer of "coverage"—that is, substitution of another person as the "insured" under the policy. (The owner of a life policy can transfer his rights, but substitution of another person as the "life insured" under a life policy is not possible.)

§ **6.11 Assignment of Life Insurance.** An owner of a policy of (say) straight life insurance commonly has the right to change the designation of the beneficiary, the right to surrender the policy for cash, and the right to pledge the policy for a loan. He might also have a right to dividends paid by the issuing insurer, and a right to designate the method of payment under a settlement option.

The owner of such a life policy might transfer all of his rights irrevocably to another by way of gift or sale (thus making an "absolute" assignment), or he might assign some of his rights for the purpose (say) of providing security or collateral for a loan (thus making a "collateral" assignment). The life policy itself usually contains provisions covering assignment, and the procedures for assignment outlined in the provisions should be followed to minimize controversy and litigation. Under modern life policies, the designated beneficiary has no "vested right" in the policy or the proceeds of the policy where the claim of such right is based solely on the beneficiary designation. The owner under modern life policies reserves to himself the right to change the beneficiary designation, and the designated beneficiary usually has a mere "expectancy" in the proceeds. Therefore, if an assignment of rights in a policy is made in conformity with the provisions in the policy for assignment, the assignee has rights in the policy superior to those of the designated beneficiary. Although an assignment of rights is not a change of beneficiary, the assignee under an "absolute" assignment is entitled to the proceeds of the policy on the death of the life insured to the complete exclusion of the designated beneficiary. If the assignment is a "collateral" assignment (to secure a debt), the assignee is entitled to priority in the proceeds only to the extent of the unpaid debt.

If assignment of rights in a life policy is not made in conformity with the provisions in the policy for assignment, and the position of the insurer is not prejudiced by the failure to conform to policy provisions for assignment, the assignee should have (and usually does have) rights in the policy superior to those of the designated beneficiary. But to determine priority at the cost of a lawsuit is to pay a high price for the failure of the assignor to follow policy procedures for assignment.

Although an absolute assignment can result from a sale of all rights in a life policy to another, it is likely to arise as a result of a gift. Here it is well to remember that a "completed" gift is not subject to revocation. Suppose that A, a well-to-do widower with several children, namely C, D, and E, owns a policy of insurance on his own life. Wishing to exclude the proceeds of the policy from his estate for death tax purposes, he gratuitously assigns all of his rights in the policy to his daughter C who is married to F. C and F are childless. C dies survived by her husband F, and by A (the life insured), and by D and E. C's will leaves her entire estate to her husband F. C's estate includes the policy of life insurance on A's life, and it is irrelevant that A when assigning all rights in the policy to C intended that C benefit from the assignment, not F.

§ 6.12 **Assignment of Fire Insurance.** A contract of fire insurance is said to be a "personal" contract—the insurer is entitled to choose the person with whom he contracts in order to decrease the moral hazard. The fire insurer assumes the risk of the insured's carelessness, but he does not assume the risk of intentional destruction of the property by the insured in order to collect on the insurance.

Because a contract of fire insurance is a personal contract, coverage under an existing fire policy is not extended automatically on transfer of the "insured" property to a new owner. For example, if A has fire insurance on his residence, and he sells the residence to B during the term of the policy, and moves out, B is not "covered" by A's policy. By way of contrast, if unspecified personal property in A's residence (household furnishings, and the like) is covered by fire insurance, and A acquires additional furniture, the acquisitions are covered by the existing insurance. But in this connection it bears emphasis that fire insurance, like other kinds of insurance has a dollar limitation on coverage. A dollar limitation on coverage that is adequate at one time may prove inadequate as time passes.

Of course, if on sale of A's residence to B, A, A's insurer, and B all agree that on B's assuming ownership of the residence, B is to be substituted for A as the insured under the existing fire policy, B is then "covered." This arrangement is called a "novation" as a matter of contract law.

§ **6.13 Assignment of Liability Insurance.** Although automobile insurance is written with relation to a vehicle, a sale of the vehicle during the term of the policy does not carry insurance coverage with it. Tying the validity of a liability policy to vehicle ownership is demonstrated in Bendall v. Home Indemnity Co. (1970), where the named insured of an automobile liability policy had, together with her husband, signed a promissory note and a chattel mortgage to enable the sister of the named insured to purchase, and to become the registered owner of, an automobile. A person who was involved in an accident while the automobile was being driven by the registered owner was joined as a defendant with the registered owner, the named insured, and her husband, in a declaratory judgment suit brought by the insurer to determine its obligations. The Supreme Court of Alabama found no error in the finding of the trial court that the named insured had no insurable interest to support liability coverage of the policy, that the policy was therefore void, and that the insurer was not obligated to defend the named insured, or her husband, or the registered owner, and that the insurer was not obligated to pay any judgment against them in an action arising out of the accident.

CHAPTER 7

THE ESTATE ARISING FROM STATUS: SOCIAL SECURITY; "PRIVATE" PENSIONS; WORKERS' COMPENSATION; VETERANS' BENEFITS

§ 7.1 Providing for Dependents Through Status. Persons die each year in the United States without leaving an appreciable net probate estate, yet their dependents are nonetheless to some extent provided for by the decedent. Such provision for dependents does not originate in property arrangements with a survivorship feature intended to "avoid probate," or in life insurance, or in something as sophisticated as the "revocable trust." Rather, it originates in various kinds of arrangements based on the status of the decedent as (to list some categories) an employee "covered" by Social Security, or a participant in some other governmental or "private" pension plan, or a "veteran" of military service in the armed forces of the United States, or a member of a fraternal organization. To state the matter in another way, governments and other institutions and organizations over the years have created some means of providing to older persons "retirement" benefits, and of affording to families of deceased persons "survivors" benefits, "dependents" benefits, and "lump-sum" death benefits that range considerably in amount, and are payable under a great variety of conditions.

It is not feasible to consider (or even to list) all of the sources of benefits of the kind mentioned in the paragraph above. Rather, what follows is minimal information principally about (1) a system of providing benefits that is to some extent widely known (even if not well understood), namely, Social Security, (2) devices that have been a continuing source of profit, pillage, and controversy for at least thirty years—"private" pension plans, and (3) governmental arrangements for providing benefits to one of the many "special interest" groups that are a vital part of American life—"veterans" (as differentiated from retired career service personnel). A brief examination of these three distinct sources of retirement and dependents benefits gives some notion of both the nature of non-traditional estate "assets," and of the complexities accompanying their realization by the decedent himself during his lifetime, and by his dependents after his death.

§ 7.2 **Social Security.** Of the governmental arrangements, by far the most important is the Social Security system. Both the importance and the effect of Social Security are demonstrated by the following example: Suppose that A, married to B, and having four small children, dies at the age of thirty, survived by his wife and children. A at his death is "covered" and "fully insured" under Social Security. Benefits payable to his family over a period of years under Social Security might easily exceed $150,000.

For many millions of Americans, Social Security, like retirement or death, is a part of the future. Apart from payment of the Social Security tax (which from their standpoint might be simply a matter of another unavoidable payroll deduction), Social Security for these millions is of little immediate interest. But for some other millions some kind of Social Security benefit is a present reality.

The Social Security Act has been amended from time to time since its enactment in 1935, and further amendment is likely. That being so, it is more important to learn the basic structure of the benefits available, and to whom and under what conditions benefits are payable, than it is to learn the detail of the Social Security system, for the detail will certainly change. In its first years, Social Security covered only the "insured" himself, and provided retirement benefits. In 1939, survivors and dependents benefits were provided by amendment to the law. Disability benefits were added in 1954. "Medicare" was added in 1965, and expanded in the 1970s. Exactly what is available under Social Security, and to whom, is very much a matter of current law, and that should be kept in mind when considering the material that follows.

As Social Security now exists, it includes numerous programs of which only three are administered solely by the Federal government. Two of those programs are the old-age, survivors, and disability insurance program (commonly called "social security") and the program of health insurance (commonly called "medicare"). It is the old-age, survivors, and disability insurance program ("social security") that is of principal interest to those arranging their property matters. The programs not administered exclusively by the Federal government are operated by the states with Federal assistance.

At the inception of Social Security, "coverage" was confined principally to employees of business and industry. Over the years coverage has been extended to all sorts of persons, including the self-employed. (In the 1950s, coverage was extended to include self-employed persons, some state and local employees, farm and household employees, members of the armed forces, and clergymen.) Some persons are covered by Social Security whether they wish to be or not. Others are covered because they have elected to be covered. Those persons who are working and who are under Social Security pay a Social Security tax based on their earnings. (And as one might expect, both the maximum amount of earnings per individual subject to Social Security tax and the tax rate have increased from time to time.) This tax, along with a similar tax on employers, finances social security and health insurance benefits.

One of the most important features of Social Security is the "portability" (transferability) of status. If a person works for wages or salary as an

employee covered under the Social Security law,
and he changes employers, earned quarters of coverage are a part of his Social Security record and
are not "lost" merely because he changes employers. One of the drawbacks of many "private"
pension plans is that status as a "covered" employee is not transferable on a change of employment.
(There are exceptions. For example, a single pension system may prevail throughout an industry.
If so, change of employment within the industry
does not result in loss of status as a "covered"
employee for pension purposes.)

For purposes of arranging one's affairs for possible retirement and certain death, it should be
emphasized that under specified circumstances, Social Security benefits are available to the covered
taxpayer himself, as well as to members of his
family. In this respect, the Social Security system
parallels some "private" (corporate or industrial)
pension plans that assume possible retirement of
the employee himself (as well as payment of benefits to his family if he dies before retirement, or
even if he dies after retirement—there is great
variation in private pension plans with respect to
matters of this kind). It should also be emphasized
that to whom Social Security benefits are payable
is a matter of law, not a matter of choice on the
part of a covered taxpayer. In this connection,
"planning" has been done by Congress.

**§ 7.3 Becoming "Insured" under Social Se-
curity.** Just as a traditional language has devel-

oped with respect to traditional property devices such as the trust, a traditional language is developing with respect to the Social Security system. For purposes of considering Social Security benefits, some of that language should be noted. (Although not important for estate planning purposes, it is interesting that Social Security taxes paid to the Treasury as internal revenue collections wind up in the "Federal Old–Age and Survivors Insurance Trust Fund," the "Federal Disability Insurance Trust Fund," and the "Federal Hospital Insurance Trust Fund." The portions of each of these funds not needed for current withdrawals are invested in interest bearing obligations of the United States or in obligations guaranteed as to both principal and interest by the United States. The word "trust" is a long-time favorite, and shows up in all sorts of contexts, including that where the "trustee" is empowered to borrow the corpus.)

Before Social Security benefits are payable to a person or his family, he must be "insured" under the system. Being insured turns on the "quarters of coverage" that one has. One acquires a quarter of coverage by performing work for wages or salary as an employee covered under the Social Security law, or by earning income as a self-employed person covered under the Social Security law. Quarters of coverage are calendar quarters.

As a condition of eligibility for most of the benefits available under Social Security, one must be "fully insured." When one has 40 quarters of coverage, he is "fully insured" for life. (For example, if a man were "fully insured" at age 55, and ceased to work simply because he refused to work any longer, he would be entitled to old-age insurance benefits on attaining retirement age.) Under circumstances specified by law, a person can be "fully insured" even though he has not acquired 40 quarters of coverage (and is therefore fully insured for life).

One who has not attained "fully insured" status, might nonetheless be "currently insured." To be currently insured, one must have at least six quarters of coverage during the thirteen-quarter period that ends with the quarter one dies, or becomes entitled to old-age insurance benefits, or most recently becomes entitled to disability benefits. Benefits available when one is only "currently insured" are less than those available when one is "fully insured." (One might also be "transitionally insured." This status allows payment of limited benefits to aged workers and their spouses or surviving spouses where the worker has too few quarters of coverage to qualify as "fully insured.")

Disability benefits are also available under Social Security. A particular insured status is required to qualify for disability benefits. That particular insured status exists if one is "fully insured" and had not less than 20 quarters of coverage during the forty-quarter period ending with the quarter that disability begins. But the matter of insured status for disability purposes is more complicated than the preceding sentence suggests, and some idea of the complexity of the Social

Security system can be gained by examining representative sections of the United States Code (for example, Title 42, § 423(c)(1)).

To summarize, one must be "insured" under Social Security before retirement or disability or survivor benefits can be paid to him or his family. Being insured turns on the number of calendar "quarters of coverage" that one has. One acquires quarters of coverage by self-employment or by being employed under circumstances covered by the Social Security law. Under conditions outlined in detail in the law, an insured person is entitled to benefits on becoming disabled or on retirement, and benefits are payable to his family.

§ **7.4 Benefits under Social Security.** Benefits payable under Social Security are of four general kinds: (1) retirement or disability benefits paid to the "insured" himself, (2) benefits paid to dependents of the insured, (3) benefits paid to surviving family members of the deceased insured, and (4) lump-sum death benefits. These old-age, disability, and survivors benefits are commonly referred to as "OASDI" (old-age, survivors, disability insurance) benefits.

"Early retirement" is available to an insured under Social Security, but the benefits are not as large as they would have been had the insured retired at the normal retirement age. Retirement benefits are based on average earnings of the insured in "covered" employment that are subject to Social Security. Whatever the Social Security system ultimately develops into in the United States, it was originally intended to afford a base for retirement, and it was originally hoped that persons covered by the system would in some way have available to them in their retirement years means of support in addition to Social Security payments. Minimum monthly retirement payments made today reflect those earlier notions: They are modest.

A spouse or dependent child of a retired or disabled insured is entitled to Social Security benefits under circumstances specified by law. For example, a spouse of an insured retiree who herself (or himself) has reached normal retirement age is generally entitled to a monthly benefit equal to one-half that payable to the insured retiree. If an insured retires having a child unmarried and under age 18, or a child of any age if such child became disabled before age 22, such child is eligible for benefits equal to fifty per cent of the insured's retirement benefits. (No matter how many dependents a retiree has, however, there is a ceiling set on the total benefits payable to his family.)

Because of the death, disability, or retirement of a parent (or perhaps a grandparent) many thousands of persons receive monthly Social Security benefits because they have severe disabilities that began in childhood and continue into their adult years. Ordinarily, a child's benefits cease at age 18, but a child's benefits can continue indefinitely if he has a severe disability that began before age

22 and that prevents substantial gainful work. To qualify for such benefits, it is not necessary for a person disabled since childhood to have himself worked under covered employment. His benefits are payable on the basis of his parent's (or perhaps grandparent's) coverage. And a parent who might not in any other way qualify for Social Security benefits can do so by caring for the disabled child.

Although benefits receivable under Social Security are not affected by such other sources of income as interest on savings, income from investments, and the proceeds of life insurance, benefits might be affected by earnings from work of any kind. In this connection it is essential to differentiate among disabled beneficiaries, retired beneficiaries under age 70, and retired beneficiaries over age 70. (The rules on the effect of earnings on Social Security benefits reflect the persisting notion that Social Security benefits are a replacement of earned income, not a payment of insurance proceeds.)

§ 7.5 Other Governmental and "Private" Pensions. The Social Security Act became law in 1935. Prior to that time both governments (Federal, state, and local) and businesses had to some extent set up pension systems for their employees. During World War II, creation of new "private" pension plans (plans sponsored by private corporations, or labor unions, or corporations and labor unions together) was stimulated by the permissibility of extending to employees "fringe" benefits in the form of pension benefits at a time when wages were fixed or "frozen" by law.

A substantial share of all full-time nongovernmental employees in the United States are covered by private pension plans. Many persons employed by Federal and state governments are covered by government pension plans (often referred to as "civil service pension plans"). Accumulated funds of pension plans are enormous. They are so great that at times one gets the impression from periodicals that the impact of pension funds on the stock market, and the existence of pension funds as a direct source of "investment" money, are of greater interest to the public than the extent to which pension plans are properly fulfilling their ostensible purpose—namely, according to the retired employee a competence after regular employment ceases.

Some of the language that has become a part of a working vocabulary with respect to pensions should be noted. Under a "contributory" pension plan, both employees and the employer regularly contribute to creation of a source of benefits. (Where the plan takes the form of a trust, contributions result in a "trust fund.") Older pension plans were often of the "contributory" kind. Plans adopted since World War II tend to be "non-contributory"—the employer ostensibly bears the entire cost of the plan. If favorable tax treatment under the Internal Revenue Code is available under a pension plan, it is referred to as a "qualified" plan. (As an example of favorable tax treatment, a covered employee "defers" payment of income tax on employer contributions made on behalf of the employee until the contribution is actually received by the employee.)

If there is no accumulation of assets from which pension benefits are payable, the plan is an "unfunded" plan (as opposed to "funded"). Where "funding" exists, it should not be assumed that accumulations always result in a trust fund. Although many pension plans are "trusteed" plans (so that there is a trust fund), some are so-called "insured" plans—contributions are paid over to an insurance company that administers the pension plan. Although both trustees and insurers invest contributions, laws governing investments by trustees and insurers have their own histories. The insurer's obligation to pay under a pension plan is a contractual obligation, not an obligation that arises under the traditional law on trusts.

"Health" and "welfare" benefits are a part of the Federal Social Security system. There is great variation in the pension plans sponsored by state and local governments, by employers, by unions, and by employers and unions working in concert, but even so, health and welfare benefits are a characteristic feature of many such plans. And so one frequently encounters the expression "pension and welfare" plans. In this connection, it should be noted that "welfare" does not carry its common connotation of "dependent on public funds." Rather, the expression "health and welfare" benefits under a private pension plan usually refers to

benefits available other than retirement income
benefits.

§ 7.6 **"Vesting" and "Portability".** During
the past thirty years, criticism has been leveled at
both governmental and private pension plans that
lack "vesting" and "portability" of benefits. The
two notions are related, but they are not the same.
For example, suppose that A is a state employee.
The state has created its own pension plan for
state employees (as opposed to "covering" them
under Social Security). The plan is a "funded"
plan that requires continuing contributions by A
during the period of his employment. (Accumulated contributions are invested in a "trust fund.")
Under the terms of the pension plan, if A terminates his employment before retirement (but after
having been employed for five years), he does not
lose his right to a pension because he has acquired
"vested" rights. (Here, a typical plan might give
the employee a choice: (1) a right to withdraw his
accumulated contributions on terminating employment, or (2) a right to let the contributions remain
a part of the "trust fund" to afford the former
employee minimum pension benefits when he
reaches retirement age.) Nonetheless, A's "vested" rights might not be transferable at all to (say)
a retirement system in another state in which A
has relocated. In short, "vesting" does not assure
"portability." By way of contrast, one who is "insured" under Social Security carries his "quarters
of coverage" from one covered employment to another.

There are continuing efforts to improve pension plans. But the variations in both the structure and the quality of pension plans are great. The possible causes of loss of pension benefits are many. Therefore one either considering his own status under such a plan, or advising another who falls under such a plan, should be cautious in his assumptions about the availability of benefits on retirement or at death. The pension systems that work best tend to be those sponsored by the Federal government or by economically successful and financially sound corporations. Some "private" pension systems have been established by employers or unions (or the two working together) under economic conditions that make it rather improbable that the pension held out by the employer as an inducement to entering employment, or to continuing employment, will in fact be paid.

The Employee Retirement Income Security Act of 1974 (commonly referred to as "ERISA" or the "Pension Reform Act") was enacted to try to assure retirement incomes to those participating in "private" pension plans. Among the devices used to assure retirement incomes are provisions on early "vesting" of pension rights, and the creation of a fund (administered by the Pension Benefit Guaranty Corporation) from which benefits can be paid when a pension plan fails. Enforcement of ERISA is shared by the Department of Labor (which can impose civil penalties) and the Internal Revenue Service (which can impose excise taxes). It bears emphasis that ERISA does not extend to all pension plans, and that ERISA does not create pension plans for those persons who fall under no plan at all.

§ **7.7 Forced Retirement.** Propaganda accompanying the creation of private pension plans stresses affording to an employee an income on his attaining retirement age (reaching the "golden years") and leaving the work force. No thoughtful person can seriously quarrel with the desirability of working out an orderly system for providing those no longer employed because of age or disability (or no longer employed full-time for those reasons) with an income. But a matter that should not be overlooked by an employee (or his advisor) who is "thinking ahead" is that a pension plan can be used in more than one way. Conventionally a pension plan is viewed as an inducement to employees to remain "loyal" to the sponsoring employer in order to "build up" the highest possible benefit on retirement (both length of employment under a plan and rate of pay as a "covered" employee affect benefits). This conventional view ignores economic realities. A "loyal" employee might find his employment terminated merely because there is no longer a job for him to fill. And even if he remains loyal for years, he might find his employer "encouraging" him to retire "early" (that is, before the customary age 65 or 70) at a retirement income much less than his wage or salary (were he to continue employment), and significantly less than what he might reasonably expect by way of retirement income were he to continue to work until attaining (say) 65.

The point is this: All other contingencies that might occur aside, an employee "covered" by a private pension plan who is attempting to estimate what his financial position will be as of the time of "normal" retirement (for example, at age 65) should take account of the fact that he might be forced to retire at age 55. If forced retirement occurs, he might have to forego altogether the high income he anticipated receiving at that time as an employee, and he might find himself relying on retirement income that does not include Social Security retirement benefits. Just at a time in life when he thinks he might be building up his savings, he might be reduced to depleting them.

§ 7.8 Workers' Compensation. Workers' Compensation laws were enacted by all states during the period between 1911 and 1948, with coverage for Federal employees and the District of Columbia being established by the Federal government. Although the type of law, extent of coverage, and amount of benefits available vary from state to state, all such laws were designed to eliminate the Common Law procedure under which an injured workman, in order to recover damages, had to file suit and prove that the employer's negligence was the proximate cause of his injury. Depending upon the jurisdiction, recovery could not be had at Common Law against an employer who successfully defended on the grounds of assumption of risk, the fellow-servant rule, or contributory negligence.

Under Workers' Compensation, eligibility for benefits is determined on a "no-fault" basis, with the general standard requiring "personal injury by accident arising out of and in the course of employment." Occupational diseases are included in coverage everywhere. Most states provide for payment of unlimited medical benefits on behalf of injured workers. The quid pro quo of the availability to the employee of no-fault benefits is that Workers' Compensation is then the exclusive remedy of the employee against the employer, and the employee is precluded from seeking a higher tort liability award.

Workers' Compensation laws may be classified as compulsory or elective. Under compulsory laws every employer and employee subject to the law must comply with its provisions. Nearly all Workers' Compensation laws are compulsory.

Under elective laws the employer has the option of either accepting or rejecting the act, but rejection results in the loss of such Common Law defenses as assumption of risk, the fellow-servant rule, and contributory negligence.

In most states voluntary coverage is available for employments that are exempted from compulsory or elective coverage. Unlike the employer who rejects elective coverage, the employer who does not accept voluntary coverage preserves his Common Law defenses.

Whether compulsory or elective, many state Workers' Compensation laws provide for specific exclusion of coverage for employments such as agricultural, domestic service, and "casual." Further exclusion may result from numerical exceptions for employers having fewer than a prescribed number of employees in otherwise covered employment. However, exclusions will become fewer as states broaden coverage under Federal "encouragement."

Benefits payable to injured workers under Workers' Compensation are intended as income replacement while the worker is unable to return to employment. Consequently such benefits do not usually reflect the marital status of the worker or the number of children or other dependents he may have. The actual amount of benefits payable is determined by the rate set by the law (often 66⅔ per cent of the weekly wage), the term or period of payment, the weekly maximum, and the aggregate maximum.

In instances of permanent total disability the trend throughout the states is toward payment for the entire period of disability.

All states provide for sometimes contingent burial allowances and for the payment of death benefits to the spouse of a worker whose death results from a covered accident. Although some states provide for continued payments to the spouse for life or until remarriage, some limit the time over which payments are to be made, or the aggregate amount of payments. Further allowance for children or other dependents of deceased workers is common.

Although Workers' Compensation benefits can mitigate the financial effects of a disabling injury upon a worker's eventual estate at death, or in the case of death from a covered accident, perhaps result in an increase in the value of the estate, Workers' Compensation laws are of little use in arranging the affairs of one not yet injured. Unlike Social Security, which provides somewhat predictable disability and death benefits to and on behalf of those fully insured, the amount of benefits, if any, receivable under Workers' Compensation depends primarily on the jurisdiction in which the accident occurs, and may be determined by the nature of the accident, the type and extent of injury, the type of employment, the number of employees employed, and numerous other statutory restrictions on the size of benefits and the period of time over which they are payable. In short, for estate planning purposes receipt of any Workers' Compensation benefits could only be classed as a fortuitous event.

§ 7.9 Veterans' Benefits. Suppose that a decedent at death has so little property that he leaves no "net probate estate." He has never had occasion to create "survivorship" arrangements intended to "avoid probate." He has no "coverage" under Social Security, and he has never been under a "private" pension plan. He carries no conventional life insurance.

Because the United States has been at war inter-
mittently during the twentieth century, such a
decedent might nonetheless "leave" modest monthly benefits to (say) his surviving spouse solely because he was a "veteran" who served in the active
military, naval, or air service of the United States
during the Mexican border period, World War I,
World War II, the Korean "conflict," the Viet Nam
"era," or the Gulf War. Further, if he was at
death insured under service-related life insurance,
his widow, if the beneficiary of the insurance, is
entitled to insurance proceeds. A small sum might
also be available from the government toward payment of funeral expenses.

Benefits available to a veteran—as veteran—
during lifetime will not enable living a life of ease,
and benefits available to the veteran's family at
death are modest. Nonetheless, the availability of
such benefits should be noted as an example of the
broad range of "benefits" available today arising
out of status—employment covered by Social Security, employment requiring participation in a
private pension plan, "career" service as a member
of the armed forces of the United States, and so on.
A person who might otherwise accumulate nothing
for dependents and successors might nonetheless
leave "benefits" at death that in cumulative effect
are fairly substantial. (A veteran's surviving
spouse receiving only a small sum per month
might receive that monthly benefit for half a century.)

"Disability" pensions that are now a familiar feature of Social Security have their counterpart under veterans benefits. For example, a veteran who is permanently and totally disabled from a non-service connected cause is entitled to monthly disability benefits provided annual income is not excessive. (Monthly benefits are larger than they otherwise would be if the veteran is married or has a child, or if there is need of regular aid and attendance from another person because of disability.) Severely disabled veterans qualify for grants to assist them in acquiring suitable dwellings.

Under eligibility requirements that vary considerably to allow for such factors as when the veteran served, the duration of service, and the origin of mental or physical condition ("service-connected" or not), a veteran may receive either out-patient or in-hospital medical and dental care. In some circumstances, eligibility requirements include inability of the veteran to defray expenses from the veteran's own resources. Where hospital care is required, the capacity of Veterans' Administration facilities is a statutory limitation on the availability of benefits.

If a veteran dies, monthly benefits might be payable to the veteran's family (surviving spouse and children, if any). But as with payment of pension benefits to the veteran, the availability to the family of other income affects the amount of survivor benefits.

"Government" life insurance procured by a veteran during military service is frequently retained after the period of service ends. Government life insurance is similar to insurance procured from commercial life insurers in that, for example, the life insured who is the owner of the policy has the right to designate the beneficiary, a policy of term insurance is convertible into an ordinary life policy, and proceeds of the policy are payable in a lump sum or in installments. For payment of an additional premium, the insured is entitled to monthly benefits should the insured become totally disabled. Government life insurance is commonly regarded as a "good buy" because costs of administering the insurance system are borne by the taxpaying public.

§ 7.10 Benefits from More than One Source. Because rights based on status have developed on a piecemeal basis, it is not unusual for a beneficiary to qualify for disability benefits or retirement benefits or survivors benefits under more than one source of payments. For example, A, married to B, dies survived by B. As A's surviving spouse, B might prima facie be entitled to Social Security benefits, Workers' Compensation benefits, veterans benefits, and survivors benefits under a "private" pension plan created by A's employer.

The extent to which a beneficiary can lawfully draw benefits from more than one source turns principally on the existence of somewhat crude controls on payment of benefits that are features of the sources of payment, and the matter of "fairness" in making payments to the same beneficiary from multiple sources is still being worked out. Adjustments in benefits ("offsets") originating in multiple sources of payments are a continuing source of irritation to recipients, and ill-will between recipients and administrators of benefits.

CHAPTER 8

TRUSTS—AN INTRODUCTION

§ 8.1 **The Private Express Trust.** The private express trust (as differentiated from the charitable or public trust) is used to conserve wealth, and to transfer wealth from generation to generation within families. The private express trust need not include both present and future interests, but it frequently does. Where tax avoidance motivates or affects the creation of trusts, lawyers draw heavily on the law of future interests. Most of the future interests created today are created through trusts, and are equitable interests rather than "legal" interests. If A is the sole owner of securities and transfers them to a trust company in trust to manage and to pay the net income to B for life, and at B's death to pay the principal to C, C's remainder is an "equitable" remainder, not a legal one.

The private express trust may be created "inter vivos" (during the lifetime of the creator) or by will at death. (An inter vivos trust is sometimes called a "living" trust. A trust created by will is commonly called a testamentary trust.) An inter vivos trust is most commonly created by the transfer of property to a trustee (a natural person, or a corporation empowered by statute to act as a fiduciary) for the benefit of donees called beneficiaries. The creator of the trust (called the settlor, trustor, grantor, or donor) may himself be a beneficiary.

A trust created by will is a matter of public record because a will is probated ("proved") in a court. An inter vivos trust is not necessarily a matter of public record, but it may be so either at its creation or thereafter. If A owns real property and transfers it by deed to a trustee and designates beneficial interests in the deed itself, recording the deed makes the details of the trust public. If A creates an inter vivos trust of real property without revealing the fact of trust on the face of the deed, the trust may nevertheless become public as a result of litigation. (Because instruments of title revealing the fact of trust inhibit the transfer of trust property, many instruments of title to property held in trust do not reveal that fact.) The comparative confidentiality of the terms of the inter vivos trust (along with such factors as avoiding probate and general acceptance of the "pour-over" will) have made inter vivos trusts increasingly popular in the United States.

Property held in trust is referred to as the trust property, the trust corpus, the trust res, or the trust principal. An instrument creating a trust, particularly an inter vivos trust, may provide for additions to the trust property by the creator of the trust or by others. When the corpus of an existing trust is augmented by a transfer of property made by will, the will is frequently called a "pour-over" will. Either real or personal property may be the subject matter of a trust, but commonly today the subject matter consists of personal property, particularly stocks, bonds, or other intangibles. Ordinarily the trustee has "legal" title to property that is the subject matter of the trust, but the corpus of a trust may consist of a purely equitable interest.

Traditionally the trustee has been a person other than the creator of the trust: A, owning property, transfers it to T in trust for one or more beneficiaries. This transaction may have all of the elements of a contract, but for historical reasons it is seldom so analyzed. An owner of property may effectively declare himself to be a trustee for one or more beneficiaries, because no consideration is required for the creation of a trust. But there is little evidence that the self-declaration of trust is well understood. Just as the trust as a device for making gifts is less well-known than the will, so too the self-declaration of trust is less well known than the trust created by transfer of property to another in trust. Because there are doctrinal requirements with respect to both the transfer of property to another (whether in trust or not) and the creation of beneficial interests in property (whether by transfer in trust or by self-declaration of trust), questions on the existence of the trustee, the identity of the trustee, the identity of beneficiaries, and the fact of trust itself do arise.

The creation of trusts falls within that part of the law called "gratuitous transfers." Within rather broad limits, one may give away property under such restrictions as the donor sees fit to impose. It follows that the settlor or testator may condition the creation of a trust on the willingness of the named trustee to assume his duties; provision may be made for resignation of the trustee; successor trustees may be anticipated and provided for. Legal doctrines with respect to these matters are flexible and are of considerable interest to lawyers because effectively representing clients includes anticipating events, providing for alternatives, and avoiding controversy and litigation that deplete the trust assets.

§ 8.2　The Statute of Frauds and the Statute of Wills. The private express trust is a means of making gifts, and just as intention by the donor to make a gift of the more familiar kind is insufficient to create an interest in the intended donee, intention alone does not result in the creation of a private express trust. Similarly, the existence of property that is the intended subject matter of a trust, the designation of a trustee, and the designation of an intended beneficiary or beneficiaries are not in themselves sufficient to constitute the creation of a valid private express trust. There must also be an intention to create a trust.

Even if all the elements listed in the paragraph above exist, a trust may fail because the trustee refuses to perform his duties, and relief is unavailable to the beneficiaries because the trustee successfully interposes the Statute of Frauds or the Statute of Wills as a defense to a suit for enforcement. (In some instances where evidence is not receivable to establish an express trust because one or the other of these defenses is raised, courts have afforded relief against unjust enrichment by way of "constructive" trust.)

When a decedent attempts to create a trust by will, he or she must comply with the requirements of the jurisdiction's Statute of Wills. When an owner of property attempts to create an inter vivos trust, he or she must comply with the requirements of the jurisdiction's Statute of Frauds, if any. A majority of American jurisdictions have statutes requiring a writing for the creation of an inter vivos express trust of land.

Because most trusts are created through the assistance of lawyers and professional trustees, compliance with the requirements of the Statute of Frauds and the Statute of Wills ordinarily follows automatically. Where professionals prepare trust instruments, a written document or group of documents is used to identify the creator of the trust, the trustee, the beneficiaries, the subject matter of the trust, and the nature of the beneficial interests. Where problems arise in connection with such trusts, it is not because of failure to put such important matters in writing. By way of contrast, reported litigation involving noncompliance with the Statute of Frauds or the Statute of Wills often originates in informal family transactions that have nothing to do with making gifts. An owner of land may be trying to insulate it from claims of his creditors, and he "deeds it over" to a friend or relative. An aged person owning property may orally promise to devise or bequeath it as the price for the promise of another to provide continuing care to the prospective testator. These cases arise with regularity.

The requirements of the Statute of Frauds should be differentiated from the formalities of conveyancing. From the fact that a jurisdiction requires that an express trust of land must be created (or "manifested and proved") by a writing, it does not follow that the fact of trust and the identity of the beneficiaries must be revealed on the face of the deed when the trust is created by a "transfer out" (as opposed to a self-declaration of trust). If A owns land in fee simple absolute and he wishes to make T trustee of the land, he might execute and deliver a deed in which the operative words are "to T and his heirs, in trust, to hold, administer, and manage, and to pay the net income to B for life, and at her death to convey to my children C and D." But if A prefers, he may transfer title to T by "absolute deed," that is, by a deed that does not reveal that the grantee holds as a fiduciary. To comply with the requirements of the Statute of Frauds, A contemporaneously prepares a writing signed by T by which T agrees to hold the land as trustee for designated beneficiaries. (Because transfer of land and securities is facilitated if the owner designated in the deed or instrument of title appears to own "absolutely," institutional pressures and practices encourage the use of a separate writing to show that T holds as a fiduciary, and that he holds for the benefit of a beneficiary or beneficiaries.)

Formerly, a transfer of property by will, to be held in trust, was made by a will that revealed on its face all of the elements of a trust: "I leave my entire estate to T and his heirs, in trust, to hold, administer, and manage, and to pay the net income to B for life, and at her death to transfer and convey to my children C and D." The testator's use of "incorporation by reference" to create his testamentary trust did not amount to a departure from this common practice, because the matter incorporated by reference became known at probate (and indeed might be filed as a part of the probate procedure). Revealing all of the elements of the trust in the will itself was consistent with the requirements of the wills acts that gratuitous transfers at death be by a writing signed by the testator and attested to by a stated number of witnesses. (A mere transfer of legal title by will to the intended trustee, with the identities of the beneficiaries and the nature of the beneficial interests set out in a letter prepared by the testator does not satisfy requirements of the wills acts even though the letter is a writing.) During the past thirty years the "pour-over" will has become more popular. As a consequence, the terms of the testamentary transfer in trust, like the terms of the inter vivos transfer in trust based on the "absolute deed," remain private, and they become a matter of public record, generally speaking, only when the trust is the basis for litigation. The privacy achieved through using the pour-over will results from the fact that the trust to which an addition is made by will is often an inter vivos trust created by the testator himself, and the terms of that trust are not matters of public information.

If an intended private express trust is unenforceable because of failure to comply with the requirements of the Statute of Frauds or the Statute of Wills, and relief is sought by way of constructive trust, there is considerable variation in result. Where the instrument of transfer (a deed of land or a will) reveals on its face that the transferee takes as a fiduciary ("to T, in trust" or "to T, as trustee") there is reason for finding that the beneficial interest is in the transferor (or his successor in interest) by way of resulting trust. (The instrument of transfer reveals on its face that the transferee takes as a fiduciary, and no beneficiary being designated in the instrument, the fiduciary does not hold for himself; he holds for the transferor or the transferor's successor in the interest.) Nonetheless, there is support for the notion that where such a "secret" trust is attempted by will (as opposed to by deed) a constructive trust for the intended beneficiaries of the express trust (rather than a resulting trust for the successors in interest of the testator) should be imposed even though the will reveals on its face that the transferee (the devisee or legatee) takes as a fiduciary. If one keeps in mind the judicial generosity frequently demonstrated with respect to imperfect testamentary transfers, this result is not surprising. Because lawyers must contend with attempted dispositions of property that have gone awry, this part of trust law is relevant; but, again, the lawyer does not "use" it in the ordinary sense. Rather, being aware of it, he or she takes account of it in counseling and representing donors, and in sorting out property interests when an imperfect trust plan has led to controversy.

§ 8.3 **The Revocable Trust.** An inter vivos trust may be either revocable or irrevocable. If revocable, it is commonly revocable by the settlor acting alone. If the instrument of trust is silent with respect to revocability, the law in the United States is not uniform as to the consequence. In most jurisdictions, the trust is irrevocable. In a few, it is revocable. The lesson for the lawyer is clear: Be explicit regarding revocability or irrevocability. (And if the trust is revocable, be explicit regarding the method of revocation.)

The revocable trust is frequently used as a will substitute, not because it affords any tax advantage (for Federal Estate Tax purposes, it is treated as testamentary), but because using it reduces some expenses incident to administration of probate assets, and permits distributions to beneficiaries during the period that probate assets are being administered (as opposed to distributed). (Assets in the revocable trust are not part of the probate estate.) Perhaps more importantly, the revocable trust affords the settlor an opportunity while alive to observe the results of making property arrangements that frequently are still in effect at his death, that continue in effect during administration of his probate estate, and that endure after administration of his estate is completed. For example, A, the sole owner of securities, transfers them by a written instrument of trust to his son C to manage, and to pay the net income first to A for life, then to B (A's wife) for life, then to D (daughter of A and B) for life, and to pay principal to such of the children of D, to one or more to the exclusion of others, in such shares and proportions, and at such times and in such manner as D in her absolute and uncontrolled discretion appoints, and in default of appointment, to pay principal to E (the third child of A and B). A reserves the power to revoke, alter, amend, or modify the trust. Apart from the reserved income interest in A, the settlor, the terms of this revocable inter vivos trust are similar to those that A might create by will: There is an income interest in A's wife for her life, then a successive income interest in A's daughter D for her life, with a special power created in D to appoint the principal, or not, as she sees fit among her children, followed by a gift of principal "in default of appointment" (that is, in absence of an effective appointment) to E. In sum, if the creator of a trust elects to do so during his lifetime, he can create administrative and dispositive powers in a trustee, and beneficial interests in various beneficiaries, that approximate (and in some instances are identical to) those that will exist under the trust at his death. He can observe the administration of the trust by the trustee, and the effect of the existence of the trust on both the trustee (if a member of his family, or a family friend) and the beneficiaries. If existence of the trust proves to be altogether unsatisfactory, or unsatisfactory in some particular, destruction or modification of the trust can be effected by exercising the reserved power to revoke, alter, modify, or amend. Knowledge acquired by watching one's own trust in operation is, of course, available to the creator of an irrevocable inter vivos trust, but there is little evidence that most persons of means are willing to divest themselves completely of substantial amounts of property, by trust or otherwise, before death. The revocable trust, like the executed will before the death of the testator, may be destroyed or modified by the settlor as long as the power to revoke exists. (A trust is modified by "amendment"; a will is modified by "codicil.") But unlike execution of a will, creation of a revocable trust (unless corpus is nominal) results in the immediate creation of beneficial interests that persist until they end by their own terms, or are destroyed or modified by act of the settlor.

To execute a will, a testator must possess "testamentary capacity." To create an inter vivos trust (revocable or irrevocable), the settlor must be "competent." Nonetheless, there is reason to believe that disappointed putative beneficiaries of a donor's bounty have more difficulty in attacking trusts on the grounds of incompetency than they have in attacking wills on the grounds of lack of testamentary capacity. Therefore, one who thinks that a will he or she executes (particularly one executed later in life) might not withstand a vigorous assault by will contest, might create a revocable trust of substantial assets. Similarly, one fearful that a testamentary gift for the benefit of charity might be attacked might make an inter vivos transfer by revocable trust for the ultimate benefit of a charity or charities. Although possible application of a "pretermitted heir" statute to a will can be anticipated (and avoided) by the draftsman of a will, it is worth noting that pretermitted heir statutes do not apply to inter vivos trusts.

Since the general acceptance of the "pour-over" will, the revocable trust created by the testator during his lifetime is frequently used as the receptacle for probate assets at the settlor's death. Because the terms of the revocable inter vivos trust can to a considerable extent be kept confidential, using the revocable trust-"pour-over" will combination permits passing substantial amounts of property by will without making the identity of the beneficiaries and the nature of the beneficial interests a matter of public record.

Many persons who have neither inherited wealth nor accumulated wealth depend heavily upon insurance on their lives and employment-related death benefits to "create" an estate should death occur at a comparatively early age. Just as the revocable trust created by a testator during his lifetime can be used through his pour-over will to receive probate assets at his death, so too it can be

used to receive the proceeds of insurance on his life
and death-benefits attributable to his employment.
This is accomplished by designating the trustee of
the revocable trust the beneficiary of the insurance
or death-benefit. It is true that by taking advantage of "settlement options" often available under
an insurance policy, the insured decedent might
direct the payment of the proceeds of the policy
over time (as differentiated from a lump-sum payment) in much the same way that proceeds might
be payable when put into a trust. But settlement
options are a matter of contract, not trust, and the
insurer making payments under a settlement option does so in the performance of a contractual
duty, not in the performance of a fiduciary duty as
trustee. Generally speaking, administration of the
proceeds of life insurance through a trust affords
more flexibility than payment under a settlement
option. (For example, a trustee can be empowered
to withhold payments.) In any event, the revocable trust-insurance policy combination gives the
person of little property many of the advantages
commonly associated with the revocable trust-pour-
over will combination that is used by the more
affluent.

Although the revocable inter vivos trust is now
permissible in all American jurisdictions, and
serves many useful purposes, it is not always beyond successful attack. Although valid for many
other purposes, it is "testamentary" for death tax
purposes. In some jurisdictions a surviving spouse
of the settlor may successfully treat the revocable

trust as "testamentary" for purposes of electing to take against the settlor's will (and as a consequence, the corpus of the trust is treated for election purposes as part of the probate estate). If the settlor retained powers that rendered the trustee a mere title-holder, successors in interest to the probate estate (under the statute of descent and distribution, or under the will of the settlor) may successfully attack the revocable trust on the traditional ground that it was a mere agency that terminated at the settlor's death. If the revocable trust was created by self-declaration, and the settlor himself retained substantial interests in the subject matter, it may be successfully attacked on the traditional ground that it is a sham intended to circumvent the operation of the Statute of Wills. Put briefly, a revocable inter vivos trust, because it is revocable, will under some circumstances be treated as testamentary. It does not inevitably follow that the trust itself will be adversely affected by the decision to so treat it. For example, although the revocable trust created by the decedent is testamentary for death tax purposes, the decedent may direct in his will that all death taxes payable in connection with his death, including those originating in the revocability of trusts he created, be paid from his probate estate (and it happens that the estate is sufficient to satisfy the direction). On the other hand, the successful attempt by the surviving spouse to treat the revocable trust as "testamentary" for purposes of taking an elective share results in a reduction of assets in

the inter vivos trust. And if revocability combined
with other facts induces a court to label an inter
vivos trust arrangement an "agency" or a "sham,"
it ceases at the settlor's death.

Whether revocability alone is sufficient to enable
creditors of a settlor to reach the assets of the trust
(as differentiated from reaching (say) a reserved
income interest in the settlor) is a matter of state
law. Judge-made law denies the creditor's claim,
but statute may favor the creditor.

§ 8.4 Incorporation by Reference. The law
in many jurisdictions permits writings in existence
at the execution of a will to be "incorporated" into
the will by "reference." For example, Ohio Revised Code § 2107.05 provides in part as follows:

> An existing document ... may be incorporated
> in a will by reference, if referred to [in the will]
> as being in existence at the time the will is
> executed....

Compliance with the statute might take this
form:

> All the rest, residue, and remainder of my estate,
> including gifts that fail through lapse or other-
> wise, I give, devise, and bequeath to T, in trust,
> to hold, invest, administer, and distribute in ac-
> cordance with the terms of an existing trust
> instrument executed by me and agreed to by T,
> as trustee, on July 1, 19—, the terms of which
> trust I hereby incorporate into and make a part
> of this my will as if fully set forth herein.

Although it is conventional to say that a will is "ambulatory" or that it "speaks at death" (of the testator), it is a part of the accepted doctrine on "incorporation by reference" that material incorporated into a will by reference takes the form that it had at execution of the "incorporating" will. This aspect of incorporation by reference is of particular importance where the writing incorporated is itself a revocable instrument (such as revocable, modifiable, and amendable inter vivos trust created, perhaps, by the testator himself), or is a will executed by another that has not yet taken effect through death. Such an instrument may in fact be changed in important respects before the death of the testator who has executed the incorporating will. To incorporate by reference a revocable instrument that has been changed with respect to its dispositive provisions after execution of the incorporating will may be, and often is, intent-defeating: The testator may well have believed that his will would incorporate the terms of the writing as that writing stood at his death, but that belief finds little support in accepted incorporation by reference doctrine. For example, A creates a revocable, amendable inter vivos trust, of which B is the income beneficiary. Thereafter A executes a will, disposing of his residuary estate in accordance with the terms of the inter vivos trust, which he incorporates by reference into his will. Finding the attitude or conduct of B unsatisfactory to him, A amends his trust, removing B as income beneficiary, and putting C in his place. A, the settlor-testator, then dies, survived by both B, who was removed as income beneficiary of the inter vivos trust, and by C, the person who was substituted in his place. If accepted doctrine on incorporation by reference is followed, B, the original beneficiary of the inter vivos trust, is the beneficiary of the testamentary trust of the residuary estate arising at the testator's death through incorporation by reference.

Because incorporation by reference may frustrate intention, that in itself should discourage relying on it as a drafting technique. But there are other aspects of the matter. If a writing is worth incorporating, it is worth reproducing in the will. Reproduction in the will obviates preliminary inquiry into state requirements regarding incorporation by reference: Must the matter incorporated itself be attested? Must the matter incorporated be referred to in the will as being in existence at the time of execution of the will? Must the matter incorporated be offered for probate with the "will" itself? And these considerations aside, reproduction in the will resolves questions that otherwise might arise regarding just what is incorporated. Put briefly, arguments for incorporation by reference should be highly persuasive before it is used as a drafting technique.

§ 8.5 **The "Pour–Over" Will.** A drafting technique much more important than incorporation by reference is the revocable trust-"pour-over" will combination. General acceptance of the technique turned on treating the revocable, amendable inter vivos trust as a "fact of independent significance" for purposes of the Statute of Wills.

A "fact" is one of "independent" significance in this connection if it has a purpose other than attempting to dispose of property at death without complying with the requirements of the local Statute of Wills. Most frequently, complying with those requirements includes the preparation of a writing designating what property is disposed of at death, and to whom the property goes. The writing is signed by the testator in the presence of a number of persons who themselves sign the writing as attesting witnesses. If a decedent keeps cash in a safe-deposit box to which he has sole access, and in his will he states that "all the cash in my safe-deposit box at my death I give to my daughter Mary," cash in the box passes to Mary at the testator's death if Mary survives the testator. It is true that in the interval between the execution of the decedent's will and the time of his death, the decedent may add cash to that already in the safe-deposit box, or he may withdraw cash from the box, and either act affects the amount of cash that passes to Mary at the decedent's death under his will. But in upholding the testamentary bequest, courts justifiably assert that the maintenance of the safe-deposit box is for the purpose of safeguarding valuables, and that that purpose has a significance that is independent of attempts to make changes in a will without complying with the requirements of the Statute of Wills.

If A is a person of means, he might create a revocable, amendable trust. Thereafter he might execute a will under the terms of which he transfers some or all of his probate estate to the trustee of the inter vivos trust, to become a part of the corpus of the inter vivos trust and to be treated as an integral part of the inter vivos trust. Having executed his will, he might amend his trust, changing beneficiaries and the nature and duration of beneficial interests. Although the amendment is made in conformity to the requirements of the trust instrument, and is immediately effective, the method of amendment might not conform to the requirements of the Statute of Wills for modifying a will. When the testator dies, assets in the probate estate that pass to the trustee of the inter vivos trust, and are added to the corpus of the inter vivos trust, are administered under the terms of the trust as amended because the revocable, amendable inter vivos trust (like the safe-deposit box) has a "significance" that is "independent" of attempts to transfer property at death without complying with the requirements of the Statute of Wills. For example, A creates a revocable, amendable, inter vivos trust, of which B is the income beneficiary. Thereafter A executes a pour-over will under the terms of which A's residuary estate passes at A's death to the trustees of the inter vivos trust, to be added to the corpus of that trust, and to be administered as an integral part of that trust as amended from time to time. Finding the attitude or conduct of B unsatisfactory to him, A

amends his trust, removing B as income beneficiary, and putting C in his place. The amendment
conforms to the requirements in the trust instrument for amendment, but does not conform to the
requirements of the Statute of Wills. A, the settlor-testator, then dies, survived by both B, who
was removed as income beneficiary of the inter
vivos trust, and by C, the person who was substituted in his place. When A's residuary estate is
distributed by A's personal representative to the
trustee of the inter vivos trust, that part of the
probate estate becomes an integral part of the
inter vivos trust of which C is the income beneficiary. Of course the residuary estate originates in
A's gross probate estate, and the gross probate
estate is subject to the claims of A's creditors and
it is subject to death taxes. In common law states
the net probate estate might be reduced by an
election by the surviving spouse to take against the
will. In short, until estate assets are distributed,
the pour-over will is incapable of removing property from the probate estate. In the example just
stated, it directs devolution of probate assets in
accordance with the terms of an inter vivos instrument as that instrument stands at the decedent's
death.

Although acceptance of the revocable, amendable trust as a fact of independent significance for
purposes of the pour-over will is common, a lawyer
nonetheless should comply with local conservative
requirements for the revocable trust-pour-over will
combination. Because a revocable trust has a life

of its own, it should make no difference as a matter of logic whether at the time of execution of the pour-over will, the trust exists to which a "pour-over" is made by the will. The will does not "speak" until the testator dies. That being so, it should be sufficient for purposes of the effectiveness of the pour-over provision in the will that the trust exists at the testator's death. But the statute authorizing the pour-over technique may require that the trust (whether revocable or irrevocable, whether inter vivos or testamentary, whether created by the testator himself or by some other person) be in existence when the pour-over will is executed. If that is the requirement, the requirement should be complied with.

Compliance with a "pour-over" statute might take the following form:

All the rest, residue, and remainder of my estate, including gifts that fail through lapse or otherwise, I give, devise, and bequeath to the T Trust Company, as trustee, to hold, invest, administer, and distribute as provided in a trust instrument executed by me and agreed to by the T Trust Company, as trustee, on July 1, 19__, as amended by me thereafter and hereafter (as provided by the terms of the trust instrument), to be added to the corpus of the trust, and to be held, invested, administered, and distributed as an integral part thereof.

If the terms of an existing trust are incorporated into a will by reference, the incorporating language at the testator's death creates a testamentary trust of that part of the decedent's estate affected by the incorporating language. If the existing trust was, for example, one created by the decedent himself, and by its terms it continues after his death, two trusts exist—an inter vivos trust, existing when the will was executed, and still existing at and after the settlor-testator's death, and the testamentary trust created at the testator's death by the incorporating language of his will. By way of contrast, if an addition is made to an existing inter vivos trust by a pour-over will, there is but one trust, the corpus of which has been increased by an addition originating in the probate estate of the decedent. The trustee of the inter vivos trust is not required to account to the probate court, and unless the terms of the inter vivos trust are litigated, the terms of that trust remain (generally speaking) confidential.

§ 8.6 **Protecting the Beneficiary Against Himself.** Of the protective devices available to the creator of the trust, the spendthrift clause is the best known. Where fully accepted, the spendthrift clause protects a beneficiary's interest against involuntary alienation (forced sale to satisfy the claims of his creditors) and against voluntary alienation (transfer of the interest by the beneficiary before he has received it). A spendthrift clause does not affect a beneficiary's interest after it has become possessory. A donor can attach an effective spendthrift clause even to the interest of a beneficiary who is competent to manage his own affairs in every respect.

Judges say that no particular words are required to create a spendthrift restraint, but the formula has become standardized and ordinarily the lawyer intending to create interests subject to a spendthrift clause should use generally accepted language:

Before its actual receipt by a beneficiary of this trust, no income or principal payable or to become payable under this trust instrument shall be subject to anticipation, alienation, or assignment by such beneficiary, or to control or interference by any creditor of such beneficiary, or to attachment, execution, garnishment, or other legal or equitable process available to a creditor to satisfy any debt or liability of such beneficiary.

Although the spendthrift trust has achieved general acceptance, one should not assume that it is acceptable everywhere. Where accepted, it may be effective with respect to equitable gifts of income, but not equitable gifts of principal. A spendthrift provision is ineffective with respect to equitable interests retained by the settlor himself, such as an income interest for life. It may be ineffective with respect to claims of a kind particularly appealing, such as those of minor children of the beneficiary for support. More importantly, the spendthrift restraint does not protect the beneficiary after his interest has become possessory, and it is at that time that he may particularly require protection.

It is in this connection that the discretionary trust has come into its own.

The following language is typical of that used to create discretionary trusts:

> ... to T, in trust, and as long as any child or children of mine are alive, to pay to or apply for the benefit of such child or children as much of the net income and corpus of the trust as T in his absolute and uncontrolled discretion sees fit for their comfortable support, after taking into consideration any other income or resources of such child or children known to T....

The discretionary trust is a special power of appointment—an ability in T to allocate income and corpus among a class. Although the beneficiary of a discretionary trust has enforceable rights with respect to the trust property, it is clear that his rights are not so readily identified and described as are (say) those of B and C, trust beneficiaries of income and principal, respectively, subject to a spendthrift restraint. It is the nebulous nature of the interest of the beneficiary of the discretionary trust that affords him protection against his own improvidence where the trustee performs his function conscientiously.

A third well-known protective device is the "Claflin" restraint. A Claflin-type restraint is a restraint on possession of an equitable interest. A creates a trust for the sole benefit of B (or creates a beneficial interest for the sole benefit of B) and explicitly withholds possession: "... to T in trust

to pay $30,000 to B [18 years of age] in the follow-
ing manner, namely, $10,000 and accumulated in-
terest when he is of the age of 21 years, $10,000
and accumulated interest when he is the age of 25
years, and $10,000 and accumulated interest when
he is of the age of 30 years." B at his majority
cannot compel immediate payment to him because
A has created a gift that is less absolute than it
might have been. Claflin v. Claflin (1889). Claflin-type restraints are permissible in many states.

Because private express trusts are means of
making gifts, and donors within rather broad limits are permitted to fashion their gifts as they wish,
there is considerable variety in the protective devices available to the settlor or testator wishing to
insulate his beneficiary from the distasteful consequences of his own lack of foresight. In addition to
the spendthrift trust, the discretionary trust, and
the Claflin-type restraint, there are "protective"
trusts, "blended" trusts, and "support" trusts. Under the terms of a protective trust, B might be
given an income interest for life that ceases automatically should a creditor seek to subject B's
interest to his claim. On the happening of such an
event, the trust becomes discretionary—the trustee
is empowered to apply income for B's benefit. The
effectiveness of blended trusts and support trusts,
like that of the discretionary trust, is based on the
nebulous nature of the beneficiary's interest. In
this connection it is worth noting that in order that
there be a private express trust, there must be
intent, trust property, a trustee, and a beneficiary.

In his enthusiasm to protect a beneficiary, a lawyer should be careful not to attenuate the beneficiary's interest to such an extent that it ceases to
exist. If there is no outstanding beneficial interest, the intended express trust fails.

§ 8.7 Trust Termination. Private express
trusts commonly end "by their own terms." An
instrument of trust directs that income be paid to a
beneficiary or beneficiaries for a term of years or
for lives, and that at the end of the term, or at the
death of the last of the income beneficiaries, as the
case may be, principal be distributed. (A charitable trust may be so created that it can endure
indefinitely, but it, too, can be created to end by its
own terms.)

If A transfers property to a trustee to manage
and to pay the net income to B for life, and then to
pay the principal to C, A might logically assume
that the fact of trust alone is sufficient to assure
that B's income interest will be enjoyed by B over a
lifetime, and that payment to B over time will
assure to B protection against improvidence not
assured by (say) a gift of $10,000 to B in cash.

A's assumption may prove to be erroneous. If C
and B, having agreed to a division of the trust
assets, request the trustee to terminate the trust,
and to pay over the assets to them, he might do so
voluntarily. If the trustee does not do so on request, C and B are entitled to a court order of
termination, because it is the generally accepted
view that if all beneficiaries of a trust are in being,

all are sui juris, and all consent to termination, and no material purpose is served by continuation of the trust, termination can be compelled. In this connection, the law might well have developed otherwise, but the rule being well established, the creator of a trust and his lawyer should take account of it.

The settlor or testator can give his trust a "material purpose" by making the trust a spendthrift trust, or attaching a Claflin-type restraint to an interest, or by expressly using some other generally recognized drafting device intended to afford protection to the beneficiaries of a trust. For example, creating in the trustee a discretionary power to allocate income or corpus, or both, should demonstrate a "material purpose" of the settlor sufficient to defeat a suit by beneficiaries to compel termination.

In this connection however, it must be emphasized that the substantive law on duration of private express trusts is still developing in the United States, and the effectiveness of a protective device as a deterrent to forced termination of trusts is affected by the law on trust duration. If A creates a trust to pay the net income to B for life, then to B's children, for their lives, and at the death of the survivor of B's children, to pay the principal to C, the trust might last beyond the perpetuities period if "B's children" is given its usual construction of "B's children whenever born." The survivor of B's children might be a child unborn at the creation of the trust, and he might be alive more than twenty-one years after B, C, and B's children alive at the creation of the trust have died. Nonetheless, the trust is terminable within the perpetuities period because any child of B, even a child born to B after the creation of the trust, will attain twenty-one no later than twenty-one years after B's death (and an actual period of gestation).

Suppose that a "spendthrift" restraint is attached to all gifts of income in the trust just described. If B has died, and all children of B (including after-born children of B) have attained twenty-one, and they and C sue for termination, continuation of the trust serves a "material purpose" of the creator—protecting income beneficiaries against the consequences of their own improvidence. Should termination therefore be refused? It is said that a Claflin-type restraint created to last beyond the perpetuities period (lives in being plus twenty-one years) is void ab initio, and that therefore the beneficiaries may terminate the trust at any time. There is no persuasive reason for differentiating between a spendthrift clause and a Claflin-type restraint for purposes of trust termination. That being so, a lawyer should not create a protective device that might last beyond the perpetuities period. To do so is to jeopardize the device in its entirety. It is true that a statute may state a rule on trust duration. West's Ann.Cal.Civil Code § 716.5 provides in part that "[i]f a trust is not limited in duration to the time within which future interests in property must vest ..., a provision, express or implied, in the instrument creating the trust that the trust may not be terminated is ineffective *insofar as it purports to be applicable beyond that time.*" [Emphasis added.] But statutes on duration of private express trusts are not common, and the more prudent thing to do is to abstain from the indiscriminate use of protective devices. The discretionary trust is a protective device that has attained considerable use. (There is a body of literature on "sprinkling" and "spraying" trusts.) A discretionary trust may be nothing more than a special power to appoint. A special power to appoint that is so created that it is exercisable beyond the perpetuities period is void ab initio under the Rule Against Perpetuities in orthodox form.

Careful drafting to avoid violations of the Rule Against Perpetuities and developing rules on the duration of "indestructible" trusts can be supplemented by expressly providing in the trust instrument for termination of trusts at the end of the perpetuities period. Below is language typically used for that purpose:

Unless sooner terminated by its own terms, this trust shall terminate twenty-one years after the death of the survivor of me, my wife Mary, and our children John Jr., Alice, and Jane, and at that time the trustee shall pay over corpus of this trust to my grandchildren George and James Thomas, share and share alike, any provision in this trust to the contrary notwithstanding.

If some of the beneficiaries of a trust are unborn or incompetent, that inhibits termination, but it does not preclude it, because guardians can be appointed for purposes of a termination suit, and a court might order termination if appropriate under the facts of the particular case. If a court refuses termination at a particular time because of possible unborn beneficiaries, it might at a later time order termination because of changed circumstances. In trust termination cases, the conclusive presumption of fertility that for so long was a part of perpetuities law has been given short shrift. A settlor or testator intent on preserving his trust against forced termination should not rely on the fact of possible unborn beneficiaries to accomplish his purpose.

§ 8.8 The Durable Power of Attorney. By means of a power of attorney one person (the principal) makes another (the attorney-in-fact) an agent for a specified purpose or purposes. A power of attorney that is not by its terms a durable power ends when the principal dies or becomes incapacitated. Everywhere in the United States statute permits the creation of a durable power of attorney—a power of attorney that persists despite the incapacity of the principal. (A power of attorney that becomes effective only upon the disability or incapacity of the principal is sometimes called a "springing" durable power of attorney.)

Under a durable power of attorney the attorney-in-fact can be empowered to manage the assets of the principal in much the same way that a trustee of a private express trust manages trust assets. Therefore the durable power of attorney is sometimes used as an alternative to trusteeship or guardianship. If the principal creates an inter vivos trust, the durable power of attorney can be used to complement trusteeship. (For example, the attorney-in-fact can be specifically empowered to fund the inter vivos trust.) The durable power of attorney can specifically empower the attorney-in-fact to make health care decisions on behalf of the principal. (Some states have statutes specifically authorizing the durable power of attorney for health care decisions.) In this connection, a durable power can be used to complement a living will executed by the principal.

§ 8.9 The Living Will. Most states recognize the "living" will—a document in which the declarant states in advance directives for health care should the declarant become terminally ill or permanently unconscious. Statutes authorizing the living will are not uniform. Because the effectiveness of a living will turns on the cooperation of the family, friends, and health care providers of the declarant, executed copies of the living will should be made available to family, friends, and health care providers upon execution of the document.

CHAPTER 9

FUTURE INTERESTS—AN INTRODUCTION

§ 9.1 Reversions, Remainders, and Executory Interests. Before the English Chancellors laid the groundwork for the modern trust, the Courts of Common Law created a scheme of present and future interests in land. That scheme did not include what are now called executory interests. Both executory interests and powers of appointment became a part of the modern array of property devices as a consequence of the enactment of the Statute of Uses (1536).

Today if A owns land in fee simple absolute and he conveys "to B for life," he retains a reversion in fee simple in the land. One might also say that A has a "fee simple subject to a life estate in B," but that is not the conventional way of characterizing the matter. B's life estate is a present, possessory interest. A's reversion is a future interest.

If A owns land in fee simple absolute and he conveys "to B for life, remainder to C and his heirs," A retains no interest in the land. C's future interest is an indefeasibly vested remainder in fee simple. C's remainder serves the same purpose as A's reversion in the preceding example, and both A's reversion and C's remainder are

186

alienable (transferable inter vivos), descendible (transferable under the statute of descent and distribution), and devisable (transferable by will). If A by his deed were to create an indefeasibly vested future interest in C but retain the life estate himself rather than create it in B, he would be creating in C by his inter vivos transfer the equivalent of a fee simple devised to C by A at A's death. The purpose served by this (and similar) future interests is recognized by the tax law. Section 2036 of the Internal Revenue Code reads in part as follows:

> The value of the [decedent's] gross estate shall include the value of all property to the extent of any interest therein of which the decedent has at any time made a transfer ... under which he has retained for his life ... the possession ... or enjoyment of ... the property....

If A owns land in fee simple absolute and he conveys "to B for life, remainder to C and his heirs if C marries D," A retains a reversion because the remainder in C is a contingent remainder, and if C were to die without having married D, B (the life tenant) surviving, the remainder would "fail by its own terms." In that event, A (or A's successor in interest) would be entitled to possession of the land on the termination of B's life estate. Although the contingent remainder was created by English judges, they fashioned a rule called the destructibility rule which resulted in the destruction of legal contingent remainders in land in some circumstances. In the example just put, if B were to die, C and D surviving but not having married, the contingent remainder in C would fall under the destructibility rule. (And A, or his successor in interest, would be entitled to possession.) The destructibility rule has been abolished in many jurisdictions.

Executory interests are the modern counterparts of "springing" and "shifting" uses that existed in Chancery prior to the enactment of the Statute of Uses. Executory interests commonly displace or divest a prior interest. For example, if A owns land in fee simple absolute and he conveys "to B and his heirs, but if C marries D, then over immediately to C and his heirs," B's fee simple terminates immediately if C marries D. C's executory interest is capable of divesting B's interest.

A retained power in a grantor which somewhat resembles the executory interest is the right of entry for condition broken (or power of termination) which follows the fee simple on condition subsequent. If A owns land in fee simple absolute and he conveys "to B and his heirs, but if the use of the land for park purposes ceases, A and his heirs may enter and terminate the estate granted." A's power to end B's estate precludes B's interest in fee from being absolute just as C's executory interest does in the example set out immediately above. If the grantor varies his language somewhat he creates a fee simple determinable and a possibility of reverter. For example, if A conveys "to B and his heirs so long as the land is used for park pur-

poses," A retains a possibility of reverter by implication. It is commonly said that the possibility of
reverter (unlike the right of entry for condition
broken) takes effect "automatically" upon the happening of the event that terminates the determinable fee simple. In that respect the possibility of
reverter appears to resemble C's executory interest
more closely than the right of entry does.

An executory interest may be created to displace
the interest of its creator. If A owns land in fee
simple absolute and he conveys it "to B and his
heirs 10 years hence," B acquires an executory
interest which takes effect by displacing A's fee
simple at the expiration of ten years from the
effective date of the deed. There is no evidence
that owners of property commonly create such
interests.

It should not be assumed on the basis of the
examples ("limitations") set out above that a remainder or a reversion must be in fee simple, or
that a future interest cannot be classified as an
executory interest unless it may displace or does
displace a prior possessory fee simple. A remainder may be for life ("to B for life, then to C for
life"), and the executory interest is commonly so
created that it may displace a remainder ("to B for
life, remainder to C and his heirs, but if C fails to
survive B, then to D and his heirs"). There are
many variations with respect to limitations. Further, it should not be assumed that classification of
future interests is always easy and proceeds

smoothly. Those drafting dispositive instruments do not always use stylized language that lends itself to ready classification.

One more matter at this point. If A grants "to B for life, remainder to C and his heirs," the words "and his heirs" are traditional words of inheritance indicating that the remainder is in fee simple (rather than for life). They are also words of limitation indicating the duration of C's interest, as opposed to words of purchase indicating who takes. Words of inheritance were never required to pass a fee simple by will, and they are not required in most jurisdictions today to pass a fee simple by deed. If A grants "to B for life, remainder to C," the remainder is in fee simple nearly everywhere. Generally speaking, therefore, words of inheritance are dispensed with hereinafter in this chapter (and in this book).

§ 9.2 How Future Interests Change. The nature of a future interest can and often does change as time passes, and that characteristic of a future estate is of interest to both the lawyer preparing a document and the lawyer working with a dispositive instrument prepared by another. A, who owns land in fee simple absolute, grants it "to B for life, remainder to C provided he attains 35" (C not being thirty-five at the time of the grant). If C attains thirty-five during B's life estate, C's contingent remainder "vests" indefeasibly in C, and on B's death, C is entitled to possession of the land. If C has not attained thirty-five when B's life estate ends, A's reversion, being a "vested" interest, en-

titles A to possession and (assuming that the destructibility rule has been abolished) A then has a
fee simple, subject, however, to the future interest
in C. (C's future interest, strictly speaking, is no
longer a "contingent remainder" because it takes
effect, if at all, by way of "divesting" a fee simple.
Therefore, on B's death, it becomes an executory
interest.) Logically, there is no more reason for
putting A in possession at B's death than for putting C in possession—A's reversion is subject to an
implied condition (C's not attaining thirty-five) just
as C's remainder is subject to an express condition.
Possession is awarded to A on the basis of characterizing his interest as "vested." To further demonstrate the importance of the label attached to an
interest, consider this case: A, owning securities,
bequeaths them in trust "to pay the net income to
B for life, and at B's death, to pay principal to C
provided he attains 35, and if he does not attain 35,
then to pay principal to D" (C not having attained
thirty-five at A's death). C does not attain thirty-
five during B's life estate, and B dies. If the
limitations at A's death are construed to be a life
estate in B, and a vested remainder in C, subject to
possible divestment by an executory interest in D,
then on B's death, C and D surviving, C is entitled
to income from the trust, not A's successor in
interest, if Phipps v. Ackers (1835), is followed. C
is entitled to income because he has an interest
that is classified as "vested." (At B's death, C's
interest becomes an equitable estate, subject to D's
executory interest.)

In the case just stated, classification of interests
is used to solve a difficulty created by circum-

stances that the lawyer could have anticipated: disposition of income at B's death, C and D surviving, but C not then having attained thirty-five. (From the fact that D survived B, one should not infer that there is any requirement that D survive the income beneficiary. D must survive the testator, but having done that, there is no requirement that he survive any other person in order to qualify for the gift to him. If D survived the testator, but predeceased the income beneficiary, D's successor in interest—whoever that is—stands in his place.)

The difficulties created by imprecise drafting can be further demonstrated by elaborating somewhat on the case set out above. A, owning securities, bequeaths them in trust "to pay the net income to B for life, and at B's death, to pay principal to C provided he attains 35, and if C dies under 35 without leaving issue surviving him, then to D." B, C, and D survive A, but C has not attained thirty-five at A's death. C dies at thirty, survived by issue and devising his estate in its entirety to his surviving spouse E. B dies. Who is entitled to corpus of the trust? Clearly D is not, because his taking was conditioned both on C's dying under thirty-five, and on his dying without being survived by issue. Did A by implication make a gift to C's issue who survive C? Or on C's death, survived by issue, did his "vested remainder subject to possible divestment" become an indefeasibly vested remainder in C's estate? (There is support for the notion that C's interest under such circumstances does vest indefeasibly in C's estate. If so, that interest passed to E under C's will.) The drafting point is clear: If A intends to make a gift to C's issue who survive C, he should make the gift explicit: "... and if C dies under 35 survived by issue, to pay principal to such issue, but if C dies under 35 without leaving issue surviving him...."

The ability of future interests to change in character is of particular importance to lawyers engaged in trusts and estates work because future interests can and do exist for years before becoming possessory, and during that time, much may have happened to the interests. To resolve disputes between claimants (or merely to locate those persons entitled to property or a fund to which no claim at all has been asserted) it is often essential to determine the classification of an interest at its creation, and its subsequent change in classification (if any), as well as its ownership through time. Suppose that A, owning land in fee simple absolute, grants "to B for life, remainder to C provided C survives B." C's future interest is a contingent remainder and A has a reversion in fee simple by implication. If C executes a will purporting to devise his future interest to D, and dies thereafter, survived by both B and D, the attempted devise is ineffective because C's contingent remainder ceased to exist (it "failed by its own terms") at C's death. Had C granted (as opposed to devised) his contingent remainder to D, the grant in itself would be effective. (The contingent remainder is alienable.) Were D to then die, survived by B and

C, and by his sole heir E, D's contingent remainder would pass to E under the statute of descent and distribution. (Under these facts, the contingent remainder is descendible.) If C died thereafter, survived by B and E, the contingent remainder in E would "fail by its own terms." By way of contrast, if B died thereafter, survived by C and E, the contingent remainder in E would be transformed into a possessory fee simple absolute in E and A's reversion in fee would be displaced altogether ("divested") by the vesting in possession of E's interest.

For purposes of properly representing others in the preparation, interpretation, or litigation of dispositive documents, it is desirable, then, to keep in mind that classification of a future interest at its creation is frequently no more than a point of departure. Although occasionally critical in itself (a contingent future interest is void at its creation under the Rule Against Perpetuities in orthodox form if it might vest, if at all, at a remote time), initial characterization of an interest is much more often a matter preliminary to solving a problem, not a solution to a problem.

§ 9.3 **Using Future Interests.** Future interests permit a donor to extend his control over property through time, and even the unlettered know this. Usually it is some variation of the life estate-and-remainder, or income interest for life-with power of appointment that appears in dispositive instruments. However, relatively simple limitations cause legal problems at times. If the decedent's will reads "to my wife for life, then to my children for their lives, principal to my grandchildren," and his wife and several children survive him, he has violated no rule of law. Because children of the testator are identifiable persons at his death, the gift of principal by will is a gift to persons whose parent or parents are alive at the testator's death, or whose parent or parents predeceased the testator, and therefore the gift of principal by will to grandchildren of the testator does not violate the Rule Against Perpetuities in orthodox form even though it includes grandchildren unborn at the testator's death. If the donor's irrevocable trust (as opposed to his will) reads "to my wife for life, then to my children for their lives, principal to my grandchildren" (the same words as those used in the will just described), the gift of principal violates the Rule Against Perpetuities in orthodox form when "children" is given its customary construction "children whenever born." (The trust takes effect at its creation, and includes secondary gifts of income to unborn children of the settlor. Those gifts are valid under the Rule. But the gift of principal, including as it does a gift to an "unborn child of an unborn child" is bad under the "unit rule" of Leake v. Robinson (1817)—a gift bad as to some members of the class is bad as to all.)

Although relatively simple limitations creating future interests can and do create legal problems, future interests that are free from legal defects can nonetheless create other kinds of problems. A owns land in fee simple absolute and devises it "to B for life, remainder to C" (B being A's widow, and C being A's son who survives A). B takes a

present, possessory life estate, and C takes an
indefeasibly vested remainder. But from the fact
that it is easy to create future interests, it does not
follow that it is wise. A life estate may prove to be
inadequate for B's support (and if the inadequacy
of the life estate is demonstrated years after the
right to elect has ceased to exist, it will be profit-
less to point out that B could have elected to take
against the will). Furthermore, the matter of the
adequacy of a life interest aside, splitting ownership of land between B and C inhibits sale of the
fee simple. Even though the interests of both are
alienable, either the life tenant or the remainderman may be reluctant to sell. ("Dad wanted it this
way, and I think we should leave things as they
are.") Statutes facilitating sale may offer relief in
this connection, but requiring a beneficiary to seek
statutory relief is a poor substitute for thinking
through the consequences of a disposition of property before it is made.

But we live in a time of successive marriages,
and often the testator fears that after his or her
death the surviving spouse will find a new spouse
who perforce will enjoy the testator's bounty.
Therefore the absolute gift of the entire estate to
the surviving spouse is dismissed by the testator as
inadvisable, and instead the survivor is given an
absolute gift of a fraction of the estate, or, alternatively, a life estate or an income interest for life,
with future interests created in children of the
testator. If the testator is a person of substantial
wealth, so that the limited gift to the surviving

spouse is adequate under the circumstances, the arrangement is both common and defensible.

If an income interest for life for the surviving spouse in itself appears to be inadequate, it can be made both more attractive to the beneficiary and more defensible as a dispositive device by making it a part of a trust in which the trustee has adequate powers to invade corpus of the trust for the proper support of the income beneficiary. Unquestionably persons at times may reasonably differ on what is proper by way of support. Nonetheless, giving a trustee power to invade provides some assurance that the requirements of a primary object of the testator's bounty are met, while at the same time the estate is protected from foolish dissipation. Here again, even in the absence of powers to invade bestowed on the trustee, statutes may afford relief to the income beneficiary who finds income inadequate for proper support. Availability of statutory relief does not relieve the lawyer of the obligation to suggest to the testator that powers to invade corpus might, in an appropriate case, be created by the dispositive instrument.

Contingencies or conditions can be attached to future interests, and they often are. A devises "to B for life, remainder to C provided he attains 35" (C not having attained thirty-five at A's death). Sometimes the conditional nature of the gift is emphasized by the explicit creation of an alternate gift: "to B for life, remainder to C provided he

attains 35, and if he does not, then to D." The gift
on condition involving who takes should be distin-
guished from the gift to which a Claflin-type restraint on possession is attached: "to B for life,
principal to C, payable in the following manner,
namely, one-third plus accumulated income on
that share on his 25th birthday, one-third plus
accumulated income on that share on his 30th
birthday, and the remaining one-third...." Claflin v. Claflin (1889). Even if C fails to attain the
prescribed ages, his successor in interest takes (C's
interest is alienable, devisable, and descendible).

The lawyer who writes "to B for life, remainder
to C provided he attains 35, and if he does not,
then to D," has made the conditional nature of the
gift to C clear. If he writes "to B for life, then to C
at 35," he invites controversy. Must C attain
thirty-five in order to qualify for the intended gift?
Or is there a gift to C with possession or payment
merely withheld until C reaches thirty-five?
There is nothing to be said for creating gifts that
invite construction of the dispositive instrument,
for the costs of construction frequently diminish
the subject matter of the intended gift.

§ 9.4 The Language of Class Gifts. The language of class gifts is well established, but it is not
altogether precise. That a class "closes" at a particular times tells us that a person born after that
time cannot share. Suppose that at the execution
of his will, A has a son B, and B has several
children. A's will says: "I leave my farm to the

children of my son B." The class is "open" between the time of execution of the will and the
time A dies to admit other children born to B, but
the class "closes" at A's death. A child conceived
by B after A's death and born alive does not share
in the gift. (The rule of construction need not
have worked out that way, but it did.) Had A's
will read: "I give $100,000 to such of the children
of my son B as attain 21" and B, having four
children, survives his father, the class closes at A's
death if a child of B alive at A's death has attained
twenty-one at A's death. Closing the class at A's
death permits ascertaining the maximum number
of children who will share, and distributing a share
to the child of B who meets the description of the
donee of the gift. Closing the class does not necessarily tell us the ultimate or final number of the
shares. If a child of B alive at A's death is under
twenty-one, such child might or might not attain
the prescribed age. If only one of B's four children
is twenty-one at A's death, such child is entitled to
his one-fourth share of $100,000 (that is, $25,000)
absolutely. He also has a vested interest in the
balance of the gift ($75,000), subject to possible
complete divestment.

A class gift is called "postponed" when it follows
a "particular estate." A, survived by his son B,
devises "to B for life, remainder to the children of
B." The class gift is a future interest—a postponed
gift. (If a child of B is in existence at A's death,
that child has a vested interest subject to possible
partial divestment by the birth of further children
to B. The class closes at B's death.) Suppose that
A's will says: "I leave my farm to the children of

my son B." If children of B are alive at A's death,
they take, and they take to the exclusion of a child
conceived by B after A's death—the gift is an
"immediate" gift, rather than a postponed gift, and
the class closes at A's death. (If B is childless at
A's death, all children of B, whenever born, share.
The first child born to B takes "by way of executory devise." In this instance, it is true that
there is no "particular estate" at the testator's
death to support calling the gift of the future
interest a "postponed" gift, but it is certainly postponed in the sense that it is not possessory—there
is no ascertainable taker.)

§ 9.5　How Class Gifts Work. The substantive
law on class gifts consists of rules of construction
that have developed to give effect to the presumed
intention of the transferor. Because the rules of
construction were not created all at the same time,
and because they reflect ideas that are inconsistent
with each other, they at times work at cross purposes. Some of the rules of construction that are
now well established might have been formulated
in a different way, but they were not. Of course it
is true that once the general operation of the rules
of construction has been grasped, one can speculate
on how the rules might work in a similar, but
nonetheless different kind of case, but one should
not assume that the method of operation one has
"reasoned" to on the basis of "general" operation
coincides with the rule worked out by established
precedent. The precedent might well take a different tack because it reflects a different competing
principle.

For example, if A devises "to B for life, remainder to the children of B," and B and several of his children survive the testator, children conceived by B after the death of the testator, and born alive, share in the gift of the remainder. Here there is no compelling reason to "close" the class at the testator's death to afterborn children of B, although one could argue that A "intended" only children known to him to share. Although B has children alive at A's death, they are in no position to call for an immediate distribution because there is an outstanding life estate in B. So the class remains "open" at A's death to admit afterborn children of B on the assumption that A intended that as many as possible of the children of B share. (The class "closes" at B's death when the life interest in B ceases, and the remainder becomes a possessory interest.)

By way of contrast, if A devises "to the children of B," and B and several of his children survive the testator, children conceived by B after the death of the testator, and born alive, do not share in the devise. The class "closes" at A's death. Again, one could argue that A "intended" that all children of B, whenever born, should share, but the well established rule of construction worked out otherwise. Closing the class at A's death fixes the number of children who share, and permits an immediate distribution to objects of the testator's bounty who in every respect meet the description of the intended beneficiaries of the gift. Closing the class facilitates sale of the subject matter of the gift (an "indefeasibly vested" interest in property is more likely to be attractive to a buyer than a "vested interest subject to open" is). Ironically, if A devises "to the children of B," and B survives A but has never had a child, all children of B, whenever born, share under the "rule" of Weld v. Bradbury (1715). (Here, the subject matter of the intended gift might have been given in its entirety to the first-born child of B, to the complete exclusion of children born to B thereafter, but the rule of construction worked out otherwise.)

If A devises "to B for life, remainder to such of the children of B as attain 21," and B and several of his children survive the testator, the class is open at A's death even though a child of B has attained twenty-one at A's death. (That child cannot call for immediate distribution because there is an outstanding life estate.) The class closes at B's death. Even at B's death the final or ultimate number of shares might not be determinable because a child or children of B then alive might not as yet have attained twenty-one. Should they attain twenty-one, they share.

Suppose that A bequeaths "$10,000 apiece to each child of B." The only other dispositive clause of A's will is a residuary devise and bequest to C. Both B and C survive the testator. If B has five children at A's death, each takes $10,000. Children conceived by B after A's death, and born alive, do not take. To permit afterborn children to take precludes distributing the residuary estate before B dies because it is not possible to determine before then how much of the estate to set aside to pay $10,000 legacies to each of the children of B. It is presumed, therefore, that the testator would exclude afterborn children of B from the gift.

Whether the death of a member of a group precludes his sharing in a class gift depends upon the words of the gift. If A devises "to B for life, remainder to the children of B," and B and several of his children survive A, the class is open at A's death. If a child of B alive at A's death predeceases B, he nonetheless shares. At A's death the remainder vests "subject to open" in the children of B then alive. A child of B alive during the life tenancy has an alienable, devisable, and descendible interest in the remainder. If such a child predeceases B, and has not transferred his interest during his lifetime, it passes to his devisee by will, or his successor under the intestacy act. When B dies, the person who then owns that interest has a share of the possessory interest.

By way of contrast, if A devises "to B for life, remainder to such of the children of B as survive B," a "condition of survivorship" is attached to the gift in remainder. If a child of B alive during the life tenancy predeceases B, he simply never takes an interest at all. Only those children of B who survive B are objects of A's bounty.

The class-closing rules are referred to as "rules of convenience"—they facilitate administration of the estate of the testator, and permit beneficiaries to take absolute interests in the subject matter of the gift at the earliest appropriate time. A potential taker who is excluded from sharing by the operation of the rules understandably does not view them as a "convenience."

Because the rules of construction on class gifts are just that—rules of construction, not "rules of property" or "rules of law," they give way to expressions of contrary intent. Suppose that a prospective testator is considering a devise "to the children of B," and B is a person alive at the execution of the will who might still be alive at the testator's death. The testator does not wish the class to "close" at his death if B is then alive. If so, the lawyer preparing the will might write "I give my farm to such of the children of B as are alive at my death, and are born at any time thereafter, share and share alike." Under this language, children of B born after the testator's death share. (Children of B alive at the testator's death have a fee simple, subject to possible partial divestment.) Persons might reasonably differ on the wisdom of a gift of this kind. The point here is that if the rules of construction are distasteful, they can be avoided by drafting.

§ 9.6 Drafting. Because natural objects of a donor's bounty occur in groups, it is natural, and at times desirable, to use group language in identifying beneficiaries. But group language should be used with care. For example, A, owning property absolutely, may have four children—C, D, E, and F.

A devises the property to his surviving spouse, B, for life and "then to my children, C, D, E, and F, or the survivor or survivors of them." If C, D, E, and F (as well as B) all survive A, but both C and D die before B, both survived by a child or children, do E and F have possessory interests at B's death to the complete exclusion of the successors in interest of C and D? What did A mean by "my children, C, D, E, and F, or the survivor or survivors of them"? Although the substantive law on construction of limitations and class gifts, including anti-lapse statutes, may shed some light on these questions, the careful lawyer should not rely on construction to effect intention. Rather, he or she should ascertain intention, and express it. Ascertaining intention may not be easy. Expressing intention is often time consuming and difficult.

If it is A's intention that his children be required to survive only A himself (as opposed to surviving both A and B), the lawyer might write: "To B for life, remainder to my children," or (making explicit what is implicit under the substantive law on class gifts) "to B for life, remainder to such of my children as survive me," or (anticipating birth or adoption of a child) "to B for life, remainder to such of my children now alive and born to or adopted by me hereafter as survive me."

But a child of the testator may have died before the execution of the will, survived by a child or children who survive the testator. Or a child of the testator who was alive at the execution of the will may predecease the testator, survived by a child or children who survive the testator. If the lawyer has used the language of the preceding paragraph in creating limitations, such surviving grandchildren clearly are not entitled to share under the description given to the beneficiaries, for they are not children of the testator. Whether or not under any of the limitations a gift by substitution exists under an anti-lapse statute is a matter of local law. For example, if the words of A's will are "to B for life, remainder to my children," and C and D, children of A alive at the execution of the will, both predecease the testator, survived by a child or children who survive the testator, an anti-lapse statute may create a gift by substitution in such grandchildren of A. Thus, if A were survived by his widow B and his two other children, E and F, the fee simple on B's death (E and F and the above-mentioned grandchildren surviving her) would be in E, F, and A's grandchildren, namely, the children of C and D. (If E, or F, or the above-mentioned grandchildren predeceased B, their respective successors in interest—whoever they are— would take.)

It is said that states usually apply their anti-lapse statutes to class gifts where a member of the class dies after the execution of the will, and before the testator dies. And the last sentence of Section 2–603 of the Uniform Probate Code (the anti-lapse section) provides that one who would have been a devisee under a class gift had he survived the testator, is treated as a devisee whether his death occurred before or after the execution of the will.

Nonetheless a testator interested in achieving substantial equality of gifts to issue should not rely on an anti-lapse statute. Determining that an anti-lapse statute applies to a particular set of facts might require a lawsuit. To provide explicitly for the surviving child or children of a child of the testator who is alive at the execution of the will but who might predecease the testator, the limitations might be worded in this way: "to B for life, remainder to such of my children now alive and born to or adopted by me hereafter as survive me, provided, however, should a child of mine now alive, or born to or adopted by me hereafter, predecease me, survived by a child or children who survive me, such grandchild or grandchildren of mine shall take the share his or their parent would have taken had such parent survived me."

Just as the lawyer should avoid "my children, or the survivor or survivors of them" when describing beneficiaries of a future interest after a life estate, so too he should forgo "my children or their descendants." If the intention is both to require survivorship (under some circumstances) and to achieve equality among children and the representatives of deceased children, the lawyer might use this language: "to B for life, remainder to such of my children now alive and born to or adopted by me hereafter as survive me, in equal shares; provided, however, should a child of mine now alive, or born to or adopted by me, predecease me, survived by a child or children who survive me, such child or children shall take the share his or their

parent would have taken had such parent survived
me; and provided, however, should a child of mine
now alive, or born to or adopted by me, survive me,
but predecease my wife, survived by a child or
children, such child or children shall take the
share his or their parent would have taken." Under this language, if A is the testator, and his child
C (alive at the execution of the will) predeceases
him, C being survived by a child or children who
survive A, such child or children of C take an
indefeasible share of the subject of A's gift. If A is
also survived by his spouse B (the life tenant) and a
child E, E takes a vested interest in A's gift subject
to possible divestment should E die during B's
lifetime survived by a child or children. Should E
die during B's lifetime not survived by a child or
children, E's vested interest in A's gift becomes
indefeasible. The draftsman might sensibly make
this explicit: "... and should a child of mine now
alive, or born to or adopted by me, survive me, but
predecease my wife, not survived by a child or
children, such child's share in my farm shall thereupon be indefeasibly vested in such child." The
entire paragraph might be cast as follows: "I devise my farm to B for life, remainder to such of my
children now alive and born to or adopted by me
hereafter as survive me, in equal shares; provided,
however,

> (a) should a child of mine now alive, or born to
> or adopted by me, predecease me, survived by
> a child or children who survive me, such
> child or children shall take the share his or

their parent would have taken had such parent survived me; and

(b) should a child of mine now alive, or born to
or adopted by me, survive me, but predecease
my wife, survived by a child or children, such
child or children shall take the share his or
their parent would have taken; and

(c) should a child of mine now alive, or born to
or adopted by me, survive me, but predecease
my wife, not survived by a child or children,
such child's share in my farm shall thereupon
be indefeasibly vested in such child."

If, then, A had a wife B, and four children, C, D, E,
and F, alive at the execution of the will, and C and
D both predeceased A, survived by a child or children who survived A, such child or children of C
and D, respectively, take from A the shares C and
D would have taken. If B, E, and F survive A, and
E dies during B's lifetime, survived by a child or
children, such child or children of E take from A
(by way of divesting gift) what E would have taken.
If F dies during B's lifetime, survived by no child
or children, F's share in A's gift then vests indefeasibly in F. (And if F survives B, his share in A's
gift vests indefeasibly in him—his dying thereafter
survived by a child or children is irrelevant. If B
predeceases A, the limitations take effect as if the
intended gift for B had not been attempted.)

Just as the drafting lawyer may make explicit
what is implicit in a class gift to which an anti-
lapse statute is applied, so too the lawyer may

avoid the impact of an anti-lapse statute if that is consistent with intention. Within broad limits, a testator is free to do as he wishes with his property at death. Anti-lapse statutes reflect presumed intention. It is conceivable that a testator may wish to give only to living descendants in the first generation. If it is A's intention that only such of his children (if any) as survive both him and his wife share, the lawyer might write: "to B for life, then in fee simple to such of my children, C, D, E, and F as survive both me and my wife, and if none of my children survive both me and my wife, then in fee simple to...." If A anticipates birth or adoption, the lawyer might write: "to B for life, then in fee simple to such of my children now alive and born to or adopted by me hereafter as survive both me and my wife, and if...." To make avoidance of the anti-lapse statute explicit, the lawyer might write: "Section _____ of the statutes of _____ (the anti-lapse statute), as said section exists at the date of my death, shall not be applied to the above gift of my _____."

Drafting to anticipate contingencies that are likely to occur is tedious, time-consuming, and ill-paid. Therefore lawyers rely on the substantive law on construction of limitations, class gifts, lapse, the acceleration of remainders, and on the operation of anti-lapse statutes to achieve what can be achieved through drafting.

§ 9.7 The Basic Language of Powers. The language used with respect to powers is fairly well developed, but it is changing. It is conventional to class powers as "general" or "special." A general power permits the holder of the power (called—not too helpfully—the "donee" of the power) to appoint to anyone, including himself or his estate. A special power permits appointment to a class, not including the holder of the power or his estate. Because of the importance and impact of the Internal Revenue Code, the classification of powers into "general" and "special" may give way to "general" and "non-general," because those are the descriptive words associated with the Code, and lawyers and writers tend to use the language of the Code itself in order to assure conformity to the Code.

If a power is exercisable during the lifetime of the holder, it is an "inter vivos" power. If exercisable only by will, it is a "testamentary" power. (A power can be both "inter vivos" and "testamentary": "to such person or persons as B by deed or will appoints.") Persons taking by the exercise of a power are called "appointees" (prior to appointment, they are "objects of the power"). The subject matter of a power is the "appointive property" or "property subject to the power," as opposed to "owned" assets of the donee. The person who creates a power is the "donor" of the power.

One intended to have a power of appointment may refuse to take it—he or she "renounces" or "disclaims" the power. A holder of a general power of appointment of any kind can extinguish the power by a "release." The distinction between renunciation (with the consequence that one never has a power) and release (destruction of an existing power) is important. For example, under the Federal Gift Tax, release of a general power to appoint by deed or will results in a gift from the holder of the power to that person or those persons benefiting from the release. By way of contrast, renunciation of such a power (like renunciation of a devise or bequest under a will) does not result in the making of a gift. A special power of appointment is releasable unless it is a power in trust.

Although much of the law on powers of appointment is judge-made law, some jurisdictions have a statutory system of powers. Even a state without a statutory system may have a statute defining the kinds of powers, or a statute dealing with a particular matter arising under the law of powers, such as whether a residuary clause in the will of the donee of a testamentary power of appointment exercises the power where it has not been otherwise expressly exercised. For example, Colorado Revised Statutes of 1987, 15–2–303 provides as follows:

No power shall be considered to be exercised by the provisions of the residuary clause of the will of the donee of the power unless said clause expressly exercises such power.

A donee intending to avoid the impact of this statute might provide in his residuary clause as follows: "All the rest, residue and remainder of my estate, including gifts that fail through lapse or otherwise, I give, devise, and bequeath to ..., and all property over which I have a power of appoint-

ment under the will of my father, I hereby appoint
in its entirety to...."

§ **9.8 The Origin of Powers.** The power of
appointment originated in the English system of
"uses" (the old counterpart of the modern trust).
Prior to the enactment of the Statute of Wills, the
power to devise freehold interests in land was
denied at Common Law. But proper manipulation
of the "use" permitted substantially the same
thing to be accomplished. If A, the owner in fee
simple, enfeoffed "B and his heirs to the use of A
for life and thereafter to such person as A should
by last will appoint," B on A's death could be
compelled in Chancery to convey to A's appointee,
who took by way of a "shifting use." Although
such circumvention of the rules of the Common
Law was unnecessary after the Statute of Wills of
1540, the possibilities of the "power" continued to
be recognized, and powers are frequently created
today. For example, suppose that A by his will
creates a testamentary trust of his residuary estate
and directs that the trustee "pay the net income to
my wife B for life, and at her death to pay principal to such person or persons as my wife B by deed
or will appoints, and in default of appointment, to
pay principal to such of my children as survive me,
in equal shares." A is survived by B and by
several children. A as "donor" has created a "general" power of appointment in B the "donee"—a
power under which B can lawfully create ownership of the principal in any person, including B
herself, by making an effective "appointment."
(For death tax purposes, mere possession of such a
power by B at her death is treated as the equiva-

lent of ownership of the trust corpus at death. Internal Revenue Code § 2041.) A has also created an "express gift in default of appointment" in those of his children who are alive at his death. (To the extent that B does not effectively appoint principal, principal is in such children.)

§ 9.9 **What Motivates the Creation of Powers?** A power consists of words through which a donor projects control over wealth after a particular event has prima facie spent itself, and, perhaps, after the donor himself has died. But the power differs from other future interests devices in that an owner of property who creates a power of appointment often gives to another a discretion to direct the devolution of wealth in the light of events that occur after the power is created. Thus, if the testator devised "to B for life, remainder to such of the children of B as survive B," all the children of B who survive him are treated equally. But if the testator devises "to B for life, remainder to such of the children of B surviving B, to one or more to the exclusion of others, and in such shares and proportions, as B in his absolute discretion by last will appoints," B may favor those of his children who are diligent, or impecunious, or ill. B is in a sense making a will for the donor at a time when the donor himself can no longer act.

One who owns property may make an inter vivos transfer of the property, either in trust or not, and "reserve" to himself a power of appointment with respect to the property transferred, or some part of it. But the most useful power of appointment is not one retained by the original owner of the property subject to the power, but one created in someone other than the original owner, as described in the paragraph immediately above. A general power or a special power created in someone other than the original owner of the property may be exercisable years after the original owner has died, under circumstances which he could not foresee. Shifting interests in income or principal in accordance with the needs of beneficiaries as they exist from time to time is the most important work of the power.

Although the creation of powers is customarily justified on the ground that powers permit flexibility, achieving flexibility does not always motivate creation of powers. A decedent who leaves property to his or her surviving spouse absolutely or by another qualifying form of disposition may claim a "marital deduction" for Federal Estate Tax purposes. A life estate given to the spouse coupled with a general power of appointment given to the spouse over the remainder is a qualifying form of disposition for marital deduction purposes. In the absence of statute, creditors of the holder of a general power cannot reach the subject matter of the power merely because the holder can, if he wishes, make the appointive property his own. (If the holder of a general testamentary power exercises his power by will, and dies insolvent, his creditors can subject appointive property to their claims after first exhausting owned assets of the holder of the power.) If A dies devising his estate to his surviving spouse B for life, "remainder to such person or persons as B by deed or will appoints, and in default of appointment, to such of my children as survive me, share and share alike," A in some instances may be morally certain that his estate can effectively claim a marital deduction with respect to the testamentary transfer for the benefit of his surviving spouse, that through the power his wife has substantial "property" available to her should she require it, though it is beyond the reach of her creditors, and that in all probability his undiminished estate will pass to his children after the death of his wife because she will never exercise the power. Here, "flexibility" in the usual sense does not motivate creation of the power.

§ 9.10 How Powers Work. Because a general power of appointment so closely approximates ownership of the appointive property, the substantive law on general powers is less strict than the law on special powers. The contrast is pointed up, although not very accurately, by reported cases in which the holder of a special power is called a "trustee." By way of example, if A, owning land in fee simple absolute, grants or devises it "to B for life, remainder to such person or persons as B by will appoints," and B executes a will purporting to appoint the remainder in its entirety to his daughter X, who predeceases B, it is conceivable that a gift by substitution as a result of statute exists in X's issue who survive B. An anti-lapse statute that makes no reference to testamentary gifts by way of appointment may be construed to cover this kind of case because the general power in B so closely approximates ownership that it can be treated for purposes of an anti-lapse statute (as it is for death tax purposes) as the equivalent of ownership of the appointive property. Likewise, if a holder of a general testamentary power purports by his will to "blend" the appointive property with "owned" assets for purposes of disposition to a person who in fact predeceases the holder of the power (and no gift by substitution is possible under an anti-lapse statute), or if the holder of a general testamentary power purports by his will to make an appointment by way of trust and the appointment is ineffective, the appointive property is said to be "captured" for the benefit of the estate of the holder of the power. After all, he could have appointed directly to his estate.

Because a power is historically an ability in the holder to effect a shift in property rights from one person to another through exercise of a power (the happening of an event), it is part of the accepted substantive law of powers that an appointee taking property as a result of an exercise of a power takes from the creator of the power (the "donor") rather than the holder of the power. For example, suppose that A, owning land in fee simple absolute, grants it "to B for life, remainder to such of the children of B, to one or more to the exclusion of others, and in such shares and proportions, as B in his absolute discretion by deed or will appoints." Because A has created merely a life estate and a special power to appoint, A has a reversion in fee. If B appoints the remainder in its entirety to his

daughter X, the appointment displaces A's reversion. (Had A in his deed made an express gift in
default of appointment, such as, "and in default of
appointment, to my son C," B's appointment to X
displaces the remainder in C.) And X takes from
A, the donor, not B, the donee.

The notion that the appointee takes from the
donor and not from the donee has not been pushed
to the extreme. Suppose that A by deed creates a
life estate in B and a special power to appoint, as
just described, and suppose that thereafter A dies,
survived by B and several children of B, including
X. B executes a will purporting to appoint the
remainder in its entirety to X. X predeceases her
father B. B dies and his will takes effect. Is his
appointment to X effective because X takes from
the donor, not the donee, and X was alive when A
died? Long ago it was decided that here the intended appointment fails. Exercise of the power is
indeed an "event," but when appointment is by
will, the appointee must survive the donee in order
to take. (The power in this case being a special
power, no gift by way of substitution is created by
an anti-lapse statute, for to create such a gift is to
permit an appointment to a non-object of the power.)

§ 9.11 **Drafting.** Because the power of appointment is an unusual device, problems encountered in connection with powers are many. A
lawyer creating powers or exercising powers cannot reasonably be expected to anticipate all prob-

lems, but he or she can anticipate some. In the case stated in the paragraph immediately above, when B executes his will purporting to exercise the special power created by A, B can create an alternate appointment to take effect should his daughter X predecease him, just as B can create a gift in the alternative should an intended beneficiary of a testamentary gift of B's "owned" (as opposed to "appointive") property predecease B: "and with respect to the land situated at ... over which I have a power of appointment under a deed recorded in ..., I appoint such property in its entirety to my daughter X; if my daughter X does not survive me, I appoint such property in its entirety to my daughter Y."

Similarly, encounters with the law on "powers in trust" and "illusory appointments" can be avoided by making an express gift in default of appointment, and by making explicit the right of the holder of a special power to prefer one or more of several objects of the power to others to whom an appointment might be made. For example, suppose that A devises land "to B for life, remainder to such of the children of B, to one or more to the exclusion of others, and in such shares and proportions, as B in his absolute discretion by deed or will appoints, and in default of appointment, remainder to C." Suppose that B, survived by his children X, Y, and Z, by will appoints the land in the following shares: one-half to X, three-eighths to Y, and one-eighth to Z. Can Z effectively complain that the appointment to him is "illusory," and that A intended that all the children of B were to take "substantial" shares by way of appointment? No, because this special power in B is clearly "exclusive" or "exclusionary." The lawyer drafting the power has precluded effective use of the "illusory" appointment notion. (B could have excluded Z altogether.) Now, suppose that again B died survived by his children X, Y, and Z, and that B never attempted to exercise his power. A power of appointment is said to be "personal" to the donee— when he dies, the power ceases to exist. Can X, Y, and Z effectively argue that B's power was "in trust," and that in the absence of an effective exercise of the power by B, X, Y, and Z take a gift by implication? No, because there is an express gift in default of appointment, and furthermore, the power is "exclusive" or "exclusionary." When B dies without having exercised the power, that express gift in default becomes a fee simple absolute in C. The lawyer has precluded effective use of the "power in trust" notion.

When can "illusory appointments" or "powers in trust" be argued? Suppose that A devises land "to B for life, remainder among the children of B as B by deed or will appoints." B, survived by his children X, Y, and Z, by will appoints the land in the following shares: one-half to X, three-eighths to Y, and one-eighth to Z. Alternatively, B dies, survived by his children X, Y, and Z, and B has never attempted to exercise the power. These are circumstances under which "illusory appointments," on the one hand, or "powers in trust," on the other, might come up.

Suppose that A creates a trust to pay the net income "to B for life, principal to such of the children of B to one or more to the exclusion of others, and in such shares and proportions as B in his absolute discretion by deed or will appoints, and in default of appointment, principal to the children of B in equal shares." There is a vested remainder subject to open at the creation of the trust if a child of B is then alive. If B's children, X, Y, and Z are alive during the time that the income interest in B exists, and B dies without having exercised the power, X, Y, and Z take corpus of the trust in equal shares as beneficiaries of the express gift in default of appointment, and this is true even if one or more of them fail to survive B (the gift in default is not conditioned on a remainderman's surviving the income beneficiary, although it is subject to diminution by birth of children to B during the time the income interest exists, and subject to diminution or complete extinguishment by the exercise of the power by B). Now suppose that B did exercise the power to this extent: By will he appointed one-half the corpus of the trust to X, who along with Y and Z survive B. Does X take not only by appointment, but also as one of the takers in default? If a creator of a power wishes to preclude X from taking both as an appointee and as a taker in default in this kind of case, he can anticipate the problem by providing as follows:

No child of B to whom an appointment is made by B may share in the gift in default of appointment unless the property appointed to him is added to the property to be distributed in default of appointment.

In the case just put, X would not, of course, want to contribute because his gift by way of appointment is larger than that which he would receive were he to contribute. The clause set out is called a "hotchpot" clause.

It bears emphasis, then, that in creating powers, as well as in exercising or "executing" powers, a lawyer should use the same care that he uses in drafting a devise or bequest in a will. If the creator of the power has required that exercise be made in a formal fashion, formality in exercise should be adhered to. And in particular, exercise or non-exercise of the power, as the case may be, should be explicit: "And with respect to the property over which I hold a testamentary power of appointment under the will of my father, I expressly refrain from exercising the power by this my last will, and any reference to my estate or my residuary estate or my property in this my last will does not refer to property over which I have merely a testamentary power of appointment."

CHAPTER 10

USING PRIVATE EXPRESS TRUSTS; CHARITABLE TRUSTS

§ 10.1 **Trusteeship versus Guardianship.** As a means of making gifts of real or personal property, the trust is especially useful where the intended beneficiary or beneficiaries are persons who cannot wisely manage property (because of demonstrated indifference to the consequences of their conduct), or who cannot under law actively manage property (because of minority or other legal disability), or who simply are not interested in property management (because of the "responsibility" entailed in sensibly arranging and reviewing ownership of property). Suppose that A, married to B, is a relatively young man with several minor children. A's assets are not of great value, and he has no prospect of inheriting any. A has insurance policies on his life that name B as primary beneficiary, if B survives A, and their children as contingent beneficiaries if she does not. A's will leaves all of his estate to B if she survives him, and all of his estate to their children if she does not.

Suppose that B in fact predeceases A, and that A dies thereafter survived by several children, and some of them are minors. That part of A's probate estate passing to his minor children, and that part

of proceeds of life insurance payable to minor beneficiaries, will be managed by a guardian. (A
guardian, unlike a trustee, does not have title.
Title is in the minor, but he is under legal disability to convey, to encumber, or to devise.) The
guardian may be a person nominated by A himself
in his will, or (if A has made no nomination, or his
nominee cannot serve, or does not choose to serve)
the guardian may be a person chosen by the court.

If a minor child of A acquires assets on A's
death, as just described, and such minor child dies
thereafter during his minority, his estate may be of
a size sufficient to require administration, and that
entails expense. Alternatively, if a minor child of
A acquires assets on A's death and thereafter attains his majority, he is entitled to manage his own
affairs, and that includes managing his own property, regardless of kind, or value, or vulnerability
to loss in the hands of an inexperienced person.

If A wishes to avoid these possible consequences
of passing property outright to a young child either
through the insurance device or by will, he can use
the inter vivos trust-"pour-over" will combination.
A creates an inter vivos trust for the benefit of his
children. The dispositive provisions of the trust
instrument include a "gift over" of the interest
passing to a young beneficiary if he survives A, but
dies thereafter before attaining twenty-one: "...
and if any child of mine dies under the age of 21,
his or her share shall thereupon be added to the
shares of such of his brothers and sisters as survive

him or her...." (The existence of the gift over prevents a young beneficiary from initially acquiring an interest that is outright or absolute.) The dispositive provisions of the trust instrument also include a clause postponing possession of a child's share (or perhaps just a part of it) until a child attains a prescribed age (say, twenty-five) that is greater than the age of majority. By giving the trustee of the inter vivos trust appropriate powers, A provides for a beneficiary's support, care, and education in the interval between A's death and the time that a beneficiary comes into actual possession of property, free from trust. (At this point one might infer, and properly so, that A's inter vivos trust is to be of substantial importance only if B predeceases A, and A dies thereafter survived by a young child or children.) In connection with the creation of the inter vivos trust, A executes a will that leaves all of his estate to his wife B if she survives him, and that contains a "pour-over" clause leaving all of his estate to the trustee of his inter vivos trust if B does not survive A. A makes B the primary beneficiary of his life insurance, if she survives him, and he makes the trustee of his inter vivos trust the contingent beneficiary if B does not survive A. Under these arrangements, if B predeceases A, and A dies thereafter survived by a young child or children, the trustee under powers bestowed by A provides for the young beneficiary until such time (if at all) as the interest intended for him is turned over to him free from trust.

The use of the inter vivos trust-"pour-over" will combination by the person of little property is facilitated in some jurisdictions by statutes that validate the inter vivos trust even though assets in the trust are only "nominal." Such statutes are of critical importance to a young person who must rely on insurance to create an "estate" if he or she dies at an early age before having the opportunity to accumulate property through earnings. Where such statutes exist, the inter vivos trust is a tentative arrangement that is intended to come into full play and achieve flexibility in the disposition of property only if there is no surviving spouse.

The matter of flexibility with respect to a minor beneficiary's interest aside, trusteeship as an administrative device with respect to property is generally superior to guardianship.

State statutes tend to give to trustees greater administrative powers than are given to guardians. Consequently, an act lawfully performed by a trustee without a court order may require a court order if performed by a guardian. Because the private express trust is a means of making gifts, the creator of a trust is free within broad limits to enlarge the administrative powers accorded to a trustee by statute or judge-made law. The ability of a testator to enlarge the administrative powers of the person he or she nominates as guardian of an estate of a minor or an incompetent may not be clear in the particular jurisdiction.

Guardians ordinarily must furnish bond, and must ordinarily act only on court order. Acting on court order requires representation by an attorney. Both guardians and trustees customarily are paid for their services, but furnishing bond and requiring legal services on a regular basis usually make guardianship more expensive than trusteeship. (The trustee of an inter vivos trust is not under court supervision unless he or she petitions for instructions, or the trust in some other way becomes the subject of litigation. On the other hand, the trustee of a testamentary trust must "account" periodically to the probate court.)

Because statutory investment powers of guardians may be more restrictive than the statutory or judge-made rules governing the making of investments by trustees, property or funds managed by a guardian may be subject to more erosion through inflation than property or funds managed by a trustee. Of course neither the guardian nor the trustee is an insurer of the continuing value of the property or funds that he manages. (Both are under a duty to insure against loss of property by such hazards as fire or theft.) Under either guardianship or trusteeship, property managed by the fiduciary may simply decline in value because of conditions beyond the control of the property manager, and the manager may be altogether free from fault. If so, the loss falls on the owner of the beneficial interest, and cannot be shifted to the manager. But to this hazard that is a part of life whether property is managed by a fiduciary or managed by an owner, an element of additional risk exists where a trust instrument gives a trustee sweeping powers to invest that permit the trustee to subject the trust estate to greater risks than it otherwise could lawfully be subjected to as a matter of state law. A power in a trustee to treat trust property substantially as if it were the trustee's own is a power to destroy. That kind of power, if bestowed at all by the creator of a trust, should be given only after considerable thought.

§ 10.2 **"Keogh" Trusts and Individual Retirement Accounts.** Because employees under "qualified" pension plans were afforded tax benefits (such as "deferring" income) not available to self-employed persons, Congress in 1962 enacted the Self–Employed Individuals Tax Retirement Act (commonly called the Keogh Bill). Under the terms of the Act, the Internal Revenue Code was amended to permit self-employed persons to create "qualified" retirement plans that afford to self-employed persons tax benefits roughly comparable (but not identical) to those that theretofore had been available to only employees under "qualified" plans. If a self-employed person uses the trust device when creating a "qualified" plan in accordance with the law, the trust is sometimes called a "Keogh" trust. The Keogh trust is used by self-employed persons who want to achieve some retirement security on roughly the same tax terms that are afforded to groups with traditionally more political clout.

By the Pension Reform Act of 1974 (Employee Retirement Income Security Act or "ERISA"), and

later legislation, Congress created the Individual
Retirement Account ("IRA"). Under limits set by
law, sometimes deductible contributions to an Individual Retirement Account can be put into one or
more of a number of permissible forms of investment. Both employed and self-employed persons
can create IRAs. Tax benefits available under
IRAs are comparable to those available under
"qualified" pension plans and Keogh plans. A
contributor to an IRA who has a non-employed
spouse can create an IRA for the spouse, and take
a larger deduction than he or she would otherwise
be entitled to. (This permits the creation of a
pension plan for both the employed spouse and the
non-employed spouse.)

§ 10.3 **Marital Deduction Trusts.** Section
2056 of the Internal Revenue Code allows a deduction, called the "marital" deduction, for some kinds
of dispositions of property to the surviving spouse
of a decedent. To qualify for the marital deduction, property passing to the surviving spouse must
pass absolutely, or by another qualifying form of
disposition, so that the property might be exposed
to the Federal Estate Tax when the surviving
spouse dies. (Because the surviving spouse might
be empowered to dispose of all such property during his or her lifetime in such a way that the
Federal Estate Tax does not apply to the lifetime
disposition of such property by the surviving
spouse, there is no assurance that the Estate Tax
will in fact apply to such property at the death of
the surviving spouse. Furthermore, where proper-

ty is disposed of by way of trust in such a way that the disposition unquestionably qualifies for the marital deduction, the trustee might be empowered to make payments of corpus from time to time to the surviving spouse. If so, trust corpus might be exhausted long before the surviving spouse dies, and again, the property qualifying for the marital deduction would not be exposed to the Estate Tax on the death of the surviving spouse.)

One way to qualify a disposition to the surviving spouse for the marital deduction is to create a "marital deduction" trust. For example, A might by his will direct that his estate pass to a trustee, in trust, the net income to be paid to his wife B for life, the principal to be paid to such person or persons as B by deed or will appoints, and in default of appointment, the principal to be paid to the children of A and B. A dies, survived by his wife B and their children C, D, and E. The corpus of this testamentary trust qualifies for the marital deduction because the combination of the income interest given to B for life and the general power of appointment given to B is treated as equivalent to an absolute transfer to B for purposes of the Federal Estate Tax. Such a qualifying trust is commonly called a "marital deduction" trust or a "marital" trust. A qualified terminable interest property trust ("Q–TIP trust") is a trust that can be used to take advantage of the marital deduction.

Because a revocable trust that is still revocable at the death of the creator is treated as testamentary for purposes of the Federal Estate Tax, a

revocable trust under the terms of which the surviving spouse of the creator acquires property absolutely, or by another qualifying form of disposition,
qualifies for the marital deduction under the Federal Estate Tax. For example, A, married to B,
creates a revocable trust by which net income is
payable to A himself for life, then to B for life,
with principal being payable to such person or
persons as B by deed or will appoints. A dies,
survived by his wife B, the trust being unrevoked.
Corpus of the trust qualifies for the marital deduction under the Federal Estate Tax at A's death
because the combination of the income interest
given to B for life and the general power of appointment given to B is treated as equivalent to an
absolute transfer to B, and the revocable trust is
treated as equivalent to a will. Such a qualifying
trust also is called a "marital deduction" trust or a
"marital" trust even though the trust was created
during A's lifetime.

As opposed to giving the surviving spouse under
a trust the net income for life, with a general
power of appointment over principal, the donor
spouse might give the surviving spouse the net
income for life, with principal being payable to the
estate of the surviving spouse. This combination
qualifies for the marital deduction (although it is
not commonly used). Such a "marital deduction"
trust is also referred to as an "estate" trust because corpus of the trust becomes a part of the
estate of the surviving spouse (and is administered
as a part of his or her estate).

Although it is not difficult to create an interest in the surviving spouse that qualifies for the marital deduction under the Federal Estate Tax, it bears emphasis that the requirements of the Code must be observed if the desired deduction is to be achieved.

§ 10.4 Revocable Trusts under Forced Share Statutes.

In many states a surviving spouse is entitled by law to a distributive share of the estate of the deceased spouse, and the surviving spouse cannot be deprived of his or her distributive share by the will of the deceased spouse. The surviving spouse who is dissatisfied with the provision, if any, made for him or her by the will of the deceased spouse might elect under statute to "take against the will" of the deceased spouse, and thereby acquire a distributive share in the estate.

Suppose that A, while married to B, transfers property irrevocably to a trustee in trust to pay the net income to A for life, and on A's death, to pay the principal to C. A dies leaving a will that makes no provision for B. B and C survive A. The corpus of the irrevocable trust is not a part of A's estate for probate purposes, and it is not viewed as a part of A's estate should B elect under statute to take against A's will. (The corpus is includible in A's "gross estate" for Federal Estate Tax purposes under Section 2036 of the Internal Revenue Code because A has made an inter vivos transfer with a "retained life estate.")

Suppose that A, instead of creating the irrevocable trust as described in the paragraph above, creates a revocable trust with beneficial interests identical to those just described. A dies leaving a will that makes no provision for B. B and C survive A. The corpus of the revocable trust is not a part of A's estate for probate purposes. Corpus is includible in A's gross estate for Federal Estate Tax purposes under Section 2036 (transfers with a retained life estate) and under Section 2038 of the Internal Revenue Code. (The revocable trust for Federal Estate Tax purposes is viewed as a will substitute.) Whether corpus is viewed as a part of A's estate should B elect under statute to take against A's will turns on state law. In some states the revocable trust is viewed as testamentary for purposes of the "elective share" statute, and corpus of the revocable trust is viewed as a part of the estate of the deceased spouse should the surviving spouse elect to take against the will. In other states the revocable trust is not viewed as a will substitute for purposes of the elective share statute. In such states, the revocable trust might be used to insulate property from the claims of a surviving spouse who might be dissatisfied with the provisions of the will of the deceased spouse. Even if the law of one's state of domicile treats the revocable trust as testamentary for purposes of the elective share statute, one might during his lifetime insulate property from claims under the elective share statute by creating a revocable trust in a neighboring state where the revocable trust is not so viewed, fixing the administration of the trust by the trust terms in that neighboring state, and making that neighboring state the situs of the trust. However, in this connection it bears emphasis that protecting the surviving spouse against disinheritance is a matter of policy having a long history. If a decedent during his lifetime transferred some of his property to a neighboring state in such a way that it is there insulated from the claims of his surviving spouse under an elective share statute, his having made such a transfer might be taken into account by the court in the decedent's state of domicile when determining the amount to be awarded from domiciliary property to the surviving spouse who has elected to take against the will of the decedent.

§ 10.5 **Charitable Trusts.** A trust is "charitable" if created to support religion or education, to promote health, to relieve poverty, or to perform an act that the general government itself might perform (such as building a bridge for public use). Although individuals can and do benefit from charitable trusts, such trusts are both condoned and encouraged because the general public benefits from them. A characteristic common to charitable trusts is the absence of personal profit—charitable trusts exist to promote the general good, not to enrich the individual. It does not follow at all that the charitable trust device (or the non-profit charitable corporation) has never been abused. On the contrary, there are numerous reported cases on the misuse of the charitable trust. But it has worked reasonably well over several centuries, and it gives a diversity to American life and law that would be missed were it unlawful to create charitable trusts.

Listing generally accepted charitable purposes such as "supporting religion" or "promoting health" fails to reveal the wide range of purposes that judges have found to be "charitable." It is true that a valid charitable trust could be established by a simple testamentary statement: "I leave all of my estate in trust for charity." But only an extensive (and not very profitable) examination of cases gives one an appreciation of what is "charitable" for legal purposes. Although there is much general agreement on the matter, it is hardly surprising that once outside the solid area of general agreement, one finds that an activity deemed charitable in one state is viewed differently in another, or that what is charitable for purposes of applying "cy pres" is not necessarily charitable for purposes of tax exemption.

Much of the law applying to trusts applies across the board to private express trusts, charitable trusts, trusts for unincorporated associations, and even "honorary" trusts. (An honorary trust is not a trust at all, in the usual sense. Rather, it is a device by which a donor achieves a purpose not considered altogether anti-social, such as providing maintenance for a pet for some reasonable length of time after the owner's death.) The law on fiduciary administration applies to all trustees, although there is evidence that it is relaxed with respect to trustees of charitable trusts. Just as there can be no private express trust unless there is identifiable trust property, there can be no charitable trust unless there is identifiable subject matter of the trust. (Many a testamentary intention is frustrated altogether because the property of the decedent is consumed in paying his debts.)

But there are some differences in doctrine. An individual or individuals are beneficiaries of a private express trust, whereas the beneficial interest of a charitable trust is in the public. Individuals enforce private trusts. The Attorney General enforces charitable trusts (and as a consequence, enforcement tends to be lax). However, individuals affect enforcement of charitable trusts in this way: If the stated charitable purpose of a charitable trust ceases, and the donor lacked a general charitable intent, there is a resulting trust for the successors in interest of the donor (heirs, next of kin, or residuary devisees and legatees, as the case may be). Because the original purpose of a charitable trust may cease, a prudent lawyer should anticipate failure of the original purpose, and provide for a secondary gift to another charity: "To Charity B, and if Charity B ceases to exist, to Charity C." Although the common law Rule Against Perpetuities applies to contingent gifts to charity that might vest, if at all, at a remote time, an exception to the Rule is made for a gift over from one charity to another charity that might take effect, if at all, beyond the perpetuities period. Because costs of litigation over trusts are frequently borne by the trust fund itself, it is important that litigation be discouraged by anticipating events that might lead to a lawsuit. To the extent that costs are payable from trust assets, the donor's gift (whether for private or public purposes) is diminished.

The indirect enforcement of charitable trusts by heirs, next of kin, or residuary devisees and legatees of the donor has its counterpart with respect to trusts for unincorporated associations and honorary trusts. A disappointed heir who believes (and perhaps with reason) that the amount set aside by the decedent for the care of his race horses is excessive, might attack the disposition either at the time of the decedent's death or thereafter.

Unlike a private express trust, a charitable trust may lawfully endure forever. A trust for an unincorporated association may by its terms lawfully endure beyond the perpetuities period provided that it is so created that it is terminable within the perpetuities period. Honorary trusts must be so created that their duration is limited to the perpetuities period. (For example, the lawyer might explicitly set the term of the honorary trust at fifteen years from the death of the testator.)

However, just as the donor creating a private express trust should not ordinarily push the duration of the trust to its outermost permissible limits, so too the creator of the charitable trust (or the trust for an unincorporated association, or an honorary trust) should consider the purpose of the gift, and limit the life of the trust accordingly. Wealth should not be tied up for an appreciable length of time unless there is a persuasive reason for taking it out of commerce. Furthermore, pushing doctrine to its limits tends to antagonize the natural objects of the donor's bounty. It is one thing to attach a spendthrift restraint to the beneficial interest of a child or grandchild known to the donor to lack judgment. It is another to attach it to beneficial interests of the unborn. A beneficiary who might not otherwise attack a trust may be goaded into doing so by the existence of restraints on possession that appear to him to be unreasonable, or a directed trust duration that serves little purpose other than indulging the donor.

Although as a matter of the traditional substantive law on charitable trusts, a great variety of activities have been deemed charitable under state law, there is currently a factor at work that unquestionably affects both the language by which gifts to charity are created, and the characteristics attached by donors to such gifts. Under the Federal Income, Gift, and Estate Taxes, deductions are available to donors with respect to charitable gifts. The income of charitable trusts and foundations may not be subject to income taxes. Under state law, property tax exemptions may be available to charities. Donors are aware that just as the general law of trusts (and nonprofit corporations) favors the gift to charity, the tax laws encourage gifts to charity. If a tax deduction is available to a donor, the donor normally wants it. If his charitable gift can be enhanced by freedom from income and property taxes, he normally expects that the gift will be constructed in such a way that all available tax benefits are taken advantage of.

Here it bears emphasis that what is charitable for purposes of state law is not necessarily charitable for purposes of Federal tax law. Unquestionably there is great overlap, but the Internal Revenue Code has its own general descriptions of the charitable donee, and its own requirements for tax benefits. For example, an organization does not qualify as charitable for purposes of Federal tax deductions if a "substantial part" of its activities is "carrying on propaganda, or otherwise attempting, to influence legislation." And under the Tax Reform Act of 1969, the language creating the gift at times is critical. If a donor creates a remainder for charity in property other than a farm or residence property, he must create it by a "charitable remainder annuity trust" or a "charitable remainder unitrust" or through a "pooled income fund" if the gift of the remainder is to qualify for the charitable deduction.

§ 10.6 Mortmain Acts. A number of states have had statutes called "mortmain" acts intended to affect an attempted testamentary disposition to charity. Testamentary gifts to charity, particularly by a will executed within a relatively short period before the death of the testator, were thought by state legislatures to be made at the expense of the heirs of the decedent. The mort-

main acts were not uniform. Some have been
repealed or declared unconstitutional. Nonetheless, they are still of interest to persons tracing
title to property over time, and Idaho Code § 15–2–
615 still invalidates testamentary gifts to charity
unless the will was executed at least 120 days
before the death of the testator. Idaho's mortmain
act is complemented by Idaho Code § 15–2–616
restricting testamentary gifts to nursing home or
residential home operators if the testator was a
resident in the home within one year before death.

§ 10.7 **Community Foundations.** It is not
unusual for a donor to attempt to achieve a charitable purpose with inadequate resources. The testatrix in Lippincott Estate (1959), left her residuary estate in trust to use the annual income "for
the purpose of paying entrance fees into homes and
institutions for the blind or other homes in ...
Pennsylvania, of persons qualified as hereinafter
provided...." The trustees were authorized by
the will to advertise periodically for applicants and
were directed to notify "all organizations within
... Pennsylvania interested in ... relief of the
blind as to the function of the Fund...." Income
not expended in paying entrance fees was to be
used to start the blind in business. As an incident
to an accounting proceeding, a trustee of the Lippincott trust petitioned for discharge, appointment
of a substitute trustee, and modification of the
terms of the trust. In disposing of the petition, the
court said:

> When we consider the many responsibilities
> placed upon the trustees in administering this
> small trust, its impracticability comes into sharp

focus. The average income which this fund can be expected to produce is approximately $750 a year. The trustees' joint compensation for administering the trust would be about $37.50 annually. With these miniscule earnings, and for this negligible compensation, they are expected to carry out the ambitious program defined by testatrix.

The trust intended by the testatrix in *Lippincott Estate* was impracticable from its inception. In some localities there are "community foundations" or "community trusts"—usually nonprofit corporations created for the express purpose of receiving property and channelling it to charities. A donor wishing to make a charitable gift, but lacking either adequate resources or a particular charitable purpose (or both) might sensibly turn to the community foundation as a means of carrying out his charitable intent, and lawyers should be aware of the fact that such a facility for making charitable gifts exists. Making gifts through the community foundation helps to assure effecting charitable intention at a reasonable administrative cost. Because a community foundation or community trust is itself a charity, making gifts through such a facility does not jeopardize the charitable deduction.

CHAPTER 11

THE RULE IN SHELLEY'S CASE; THE DOCTRINE OF WORTHIER TITLE; THE RULE AGAINST PERPETUITIES; THE RULE AGAINST ACCUMULATIONS

§ 11.1 The Rule in Shelley's Case and the Doctrine of Worthier Title. Two notions that are feudal in origin may affect the work of a property lawyer today. They are the Rule in Shelley's Case and the Doctrine of Worthier Title.

If A owns land in fee simple absolute and his conveyance reads "to B for life, remainder to the heirs of B," applying the Rule in Shelley's Case to the intended remainder results in treating A's deed as if it had read "to B for life, remainder to B and his heirs." (The remainder intended by A for B's heirs is by operation of a rule of law changed into a remainder in B himself.) If A owns land in fee simple absolute and his conveyance reads "to B for life, remainder to my [A's] heirs," applying the Doctrine of Worthier Title to the intended remainder results in treating A's deed as if the intended future interest had been omitted from the instrument altogether. (A himself then has a reversion in fee by implication.)

Simes' statement of the Rule in Shelley's Case is in part as follows:

> If a life estate in land is conveyed or devised to [B], and by the same conveyance or devise, a remainder in the same land is limited, mediately or immediately, to the heirs of [B], ... and the life estate and remainder are of the same quality, then [B] has a remainder in fee simple.... Simes, Future Interests 45 (2d ed. 1966).

The Rule in Shelley's Case applies only to remainders (legal or equitable) in land.

Gulliver's statement of the Doctrine of Worthier Title is:

> A provision for the intestate successors of the transferor is void if it would give them the same interest as they would take if the provision were omitted from the instrument and the interest remaining in the transferor as a result of such omission passed to them by intestacy. Gulliver, Cases on Future Interests 98 (1959).

Note that Gulliver's statement suggests a hypothetical situation: Imagine that the intended future interest were omitted from the deed or instrument of trust. If immediately thereafter the grantor or settlor were to die intestate, would the retained interest passing to his heirs be the same as that which they were intended to take under the deed or instrument of trust? If so, this is the kind of limitation to which the Doctrine of Worthier Title can be applied. Although the Doctrine is applicable to both legal and equitable interests, in realty or personalty, it is not confined to remainders.

To the extent that it exists today in the United States, the Doctrine of Worthier Title (unlike the Rule in Shelley's Case) is a rule of construction. That is, applying it is said to turn on the intention of the transferor. The Rule in Shelley's Case, being a rule of law, or a rule of property, applies irrespective of intention. Statutes in many jurisdictions have abolished the Rule in Shelley's Case. Sometimes the status in a jurisdiction of the Doctrine of Worthier Title is unknown because there is neither a statute on the Doctrine nor an authoritative judicial decision dealing with it. The state of New York, commonly credited with resurrecting the Doctrine in the United States, abolished it in 1966.

Where the Doctrine of Worthier Title exists, it creates a rebuttable presumption that a provision in a deed or trust instrument purporting to create an interest in the "heirs" or "next of kin" or "personal representative" of the transferor does not in fact do so. The presumption can be overcome by evidence of a "contrary intent." (The transferor not only wrote a limitation down, but also meant it.) Identifying evidence of contrary intent that is invariably persuasive is just as difficult as one would expect it to be. The decided cases on this matter are unmanageable.

If the presumption created by the Doctrine of Worthier Title is not overcome, the transferor has a retained interest by way of reversion or resulting trust. He might or might not still possess that interest at his death. If he does possess it at death, it might or might not pass by intestacy to his heirs.

A lawyer does not use the Rule in Shelley's Case or the Doctrine of Worthier Title in the same sense that he uses (say) powers of appointment. Rather, being aware of them, he takes account of them. Applying the Doctrine of Worthier Title rationally requires reading "heirs" of the transferor to mean "such person or persons who would be the successors in interest of the transferor at his death were he to die intestate still owning the subject matter of the transfer." This ordinary meaning of "heirs" can be avoided by drafting: "to B for life, and then to that person or those persons who would be my heirs, or would have been my heirs, as the case may be, were I to die, or had I died, when B dies." Under this language, the identity of the takers of the future interest is fixed at B's death (not before B's death, even though the transferor happens to predecease B, and not after B's death, even though the transferor happens to survive B).

The matter of drafting aside, both the Rule in Shelley's Case and the Doctrine of Worthier Title are relevant in connection with such matters as analyzing limitations to determine what property interests are created, identifying beneficiaries of property interests, determining creditors' rights with respect to property interests, and taxing transfers of property interests. Both the Rule and

the Doctrine are feudal in origin, but their impact
has been a continuing one that has not altogether
disappeared from the law.

§ 11.2 The Rule Against Perpetuities. The
Rule Against Perpetuities (in orthodox or wait-and-
see or cy pres form) regulates the creation of future
interests. The Rule Against Accumulations regulates directed accumulations of income. Both rules
are "rules of law" or "rules of property"—they
apply irrespective of intention. In operation they
are intent-defeating.

Under the Rule Against Perpetuities in orthodox
form, an interest is invalid unless it is so created
that it must vest, if it vests at all, within a period
measured by some life in being at the creation of
the interest and twenty-one years.

A lawyer engaged in trusts and estates work
should know enough about the Rule Against Perpetuities to avoid violations of the Rule in drafting
instruments, and to recognize violations of the
Rule when examining instruments drawn by others. In both connections, he or she should be
informed on relevant statutory or judge-made
changes in the Rule that have occurred during the
past forty years, but the lawyer should not assume
that modification of the Rule in orthodox form
appreciably affects the matter of drafting. Regardless of modification, the prudent lawyer drafts to
conform limitations to the requirements of the
Rule in orthodox form. It is true that a limitation
that is bad under the Rule in orthodox form may

be saved under a "wait and see" or "cy pres" version of the Rule, but demonstrating validity under a relaxed form of the Rule may require litigation.

For purposes of the Rule, "interest" means future interest, and includes the contingent remainder, the contingent executory interest, and the vested remainder subject to open.

Note that the Rule does not require that an interest be so created that it is certain to vest within the perpetuities period. Rather, the Rule requires that an interest be so created that a contingency with respect to it will be resolved within the perpetuities period (a life in being at the creation of the interest and twenty-one years). The Rule says "vest, if at all"—a valid interest may fail by its own terms within the perpetuities period rather than vest. If A dies survived by B and C, devising "to B for life, then to C if C survives B," the contingent remainder in C is good under the Rule Against Perpetuities. (The contingent remainder is so created that it must vest, if it vests at all, within the lifetime of either B or C, and both B and C are "lives in being" at A's death, when his will "speaks.") But C may ultimately predecease B. If so, the contingent remainder simply fails.

To determine whether a deed, an instrument of trust, or a will violates the Rule Against Perpetuities in orthodox form, one first goes back in time to the date that the instrument took effect for perpe-

tuities purposes: the time of delivery, in the case of
a deed; the time of execution, in the case of an
irrevocable trust; the date of death, in the case of
a will; and the date of the settlor's death, in the
case of a revocable trust. (For perpetuities purposes, a revocable trust is treated as if it were a
will.)

Next, one examines the instrument to see if it
creates any future interests. (The Rule does not
apply to present interests.) If there is a future
interest, one classifies it according to the customary rules of construction. To classify properly
requires knowing relevant facts: Who is alive at
the effective date of the dispositive instrument? If
attaining a prescribed age is a condition precedent,
has the age already been attained at the effective
date of the dispositive instrument? For example,
suppose that at the execution of A's will, his son B
has a child C who is three years of age. A's will
says: "I devise my farm to B for life, remainder to
C if C attains 35." Suppose that at A's death, he
still owns the farm and he is survived by B and by
C, now fifteen. Because the intended gift of the
future interest to C is subject to an express condition precedent of attaining the age of thirty-five, it
is contingent, but it is a contingent remainder that
does not violate the Rule. (Viewed as of the time
that A dies, it will vest, or not, within C's own
lifetime, and C is a "life in being" at A's death. It
will also vest, or not, within B's lifetime and twenty-one years, and B is a "life in being" at A's death.
Because C is already fifteen at A's death, the

contingent remainder will also vest, or not, within the "period in gross" of twenty-one years.) Alternatively, suppose that at A's death, he still owns the farm and he is survived by B and by C, now forty. Under these facts, the intended gift of the future interest to C is an indefeasibly vested remainder, an interest to which the Rule Against Perpetuities does not apply.

If classification of a future interest demonstrates that it is a reversion, a possibility of reverter, a right of entry for condition broken, an indefeasibly vested remainder, a vested remainder subject to divestment, or a vested executory interest, there is no perpetuities problem because these interests are not subject to the Rule. If the interest is a contingent remainder, a contingent executory interest, or a vested remainder subject to open, it is subject to the Rule and must be examined for possible violation of the Rule. (The matter of powers of appointment, and appointments themselves under the Rule Against Perpetuities, requires separate treatment, and is not considered at this point.) Examination of an interest for possible violation of the Rule Against Perpetuities in orthodox form proceeds in the following way:

Although the Rule invalidates an interest that might vest, if at all, at a remote time, one identifies a violation of the Rule by attempting to demonstrate the validity of a questioned limitation and being unable to do so. For example, if A devises "to B for life, remainder to that child of B who first attains 35," and B, a person who has never mar-

ried, survives A, the contingent remainder is bad
under the Rule Against Perpetuities in orthodox
form because it is impossible to demonstrate validity. The only appropriate "life in being" at A's
death that one might use to attempt to demonstrate validity is B. Now it is true that a child
born to B after A's death might attain thirty-five
within a period measured by B's lifetime and twenty-one years (indeed, such a child might attain
thirty-five within B's lifetime—without adding on
the twenty-one year period). But the requirements
of the Rule are not met merely because a child of B
might attain thirty-five within the perpetuities period of a life in being and twenty-one years. The
test for validity under the Rule in orthodox form is
a possibilities test, not an actualities test. Viewed
as of the time that A dies, it must be certain that a
child of B will attain thirty-five, or not, within the
perpetuities period. Put shortly, it must be clear
with respect to the gift intended for B's child that
the contingency will be resolved within the period.

If the validity of a questioned limitation can be
demonstrated by an acceptable method, that is
sufficient to save the limitation from the Rule.
Suppose that A devises "to B for life, remainder to
C if C attains 35." Both B and C survive A, but C
is fifteen at A's death. The validity of the contingent remainder in C can be demonstrated in three
ways, any one of which is in itself sufficient to save
the limitation from invalidity under the Rule in
orthodox form. C will attain thirty-five, or not,
within his own lifetime, so C's life can be used as

the "life in being" at A's death to demonstrate
validity. Because C is already fifteen at A's death,
C will attain thirty-five, or not, within B's lifetime
and twenty-one years, so B's life (with the twenty-
one year period) can be used to demonstrate validity. Last, C will attain thirty-five, or not, within
the "period in gross" of twenty-one years, so the
period in gross can be used to demonstrate validity.
(If C were only five years of age at A's death, the
only method of demonstrating validity is to use C's
life—he will attain thirty-five, or not, within his
own lifetime.)

Occasionally the limitation is such that it is
demonstrably valid although there is no such thing
as "the" life in being for demonstration purposes.
Suppose that a testator had five children at the
execution of his will, that two more children were
born to him before his death, and that he dies
survived by four children. His will reads: "I leave
all of my estate to such of my children who survive
me as attain the age of 40." No child of the
testator who survives him is forty at his death.
But the contingent future interest is unquestionably valid under the Rule in orthodox form because
a child alive at the testator's death will attain
forty, or not, within that child's own lifetime.
Here, there is not "the" life in being at the testator's death, but "lives in being," and each life is
used to demonstrate validity under the Rule.

§ 11.3 The "Perpetuities Period". The Rule
includes the expression "some life in being at the

creation of the interest and twenty-one years."
"Perpetuities period" is a short-hand way of describing the time within which a questioned interest must "vest, if at all" if it is to be valid or
"good" under the Rule Against Perpetuities in
orthodox form. Because it is permissible for a
lawyer to provide explicitly for the so-called "measuring lives," it is conventional to say that the
perpetuities period consists of any reasonable number of lives in being at the creation of the interest
and twenty-one years. For example, A, survived
by several children and grandchildren, might provide by his will as follows: "$100,000 to such of my
grandchildren as are alive twenty-one years after
the death of the survivor of X, Y, and Z." X, Y,
and Z are very young persons known to A, and all
three survive A. The intended gift is unquestionably valid under the Rule Against Perpetuities in
orthodox form. However, lawyers do not habitual-
ly provide explicitly for "measuring lives," and
therefore one must ordinarily determine for one's
self what the "perpetuities period" is in the particular case by casting about for a relevant "life in
being" at the creation of the questioned interest
that is appropriate for purposes of demonstrating
validity under the Rule.

§ 11.4 Class Gifts Under the Rule. Under
the Rule Against Perpetuities in orthodox form, a
"unit rule" applies to a gift to a class: If the
interest of any member of the class might vest, if
at all, at a remote time, the class gift is bad in its
entirety.

For example, suppose that A devises "to B for
life, then to B's children for their lives, remainder

to the grandchildren of B." At A's death, B, several children of B, and several grandchildren of B are alive. "Children" is construed to mean "children of B whenever born," and "grandchildren" is construed to mean "grandchildren of B whenever born." Under these facts, the intended gift to grandchildren of B is a vested remainder "subject to open" to admit grandchildren of B born after A's death. It is bad in its entirety under the Rule because the ultimate or final number of grandchildren sharing in the gift is not certain to be fixed or determined within the perpetuities period. After A's death, B might conceive a child who is born alive. That after-born child of B might be the survivor of B's children, and that after-born child of B might conceive a child born alive more than twenty-one years after the death of the survivor of all relevant "lives in being" at A's death. Because there is no persuasive reason for "closing" the class of grandchildren until all of B's children have died, there is the possibility that this "unborn child of an unborn child" of B might enter the class of grandchildren at a remote time. The possibility that the ultimate number of grandchildren of B sharing in the gift might not be known until a remote time makes the intended gift to grandchildren bad in its entirety.

Similarly, if A devises "to B for life, remainder to such of the children of B as attain 25," the intended gift to the children of B is bad in its entirety under the Rule if B is alive at A's death, and "children" is construed to mean "children of B

whenever born." The gift is bad even though a
child or children of B alive at A's death have
already attained twenty-five at A's death. Under
these facts, the vested remainder is "subject to
open." After A's death, B might conceive a child
who is born alive less than four years before B
himself dies. The test for validity under the Rule
Against Perpetuities in orthodox form is a possibilities test, not an actualities test. In actual fact,
the after-born child of B might die within twenty-
one years after B's death, so that the ultimate or
final number of children sharing in the gift would
be fixed or determined within the perpetuities period. But viewed as of the time A dies, it is possible
that an after-born child of B who is not excluded
from the class (because he is born during the life
tenancy while the class is "open") might attain
twenty-five at a time beyond a period measured by
B's life and twenty-one years. Therefore the intended gift to children of B who attain twenty-five
is bad in its entirety.

The effects of the unit rule on class gifts are
mitigated by the exceptions of Cattlin v. Brown
(1853), and Storrs v. Benbow (1853), and by the
operation of "class-closing" rules, as well as the
application of "cy pres." But it bears emphasis
that limitations like those in *Cattlin* and *Storrs* are
not common, and the application of cy pres (reformation of the instrument so that it complies with
the requirements of the Rule) is a matter of judicial discretion invoked through a lawsuit. The
unit rule on class gifts is an ever-present threat to

dispositions in trusts and wills that are in no sense unusual.

Limitations like those of Cattlin v. Brown escape the harsh effects of the unit rule on class gifts. *Cattlin* involved a gift to a class of sub-classes, and under the "rule" of Cattlin v. Brown, a gift to a particular sub-class is valid under the Rule Against Perpetuities in orthodox form even though the gift to another sub-class is remote. For example, suppose that A creates a testamentary trust to pay the net income "to B for life, then to the children of B for their lives, and on the death of the survivor of the children of B, to pay that proportionate share of principal represented by a child of B to his issue, per stirpes." At A's death, B and several of his children are alive. "Children" is construed to mean "children of B whenever born." More children are born to B after A's death. Under the rule of Cattlin v. Brown, the life of B is used to demonstrate that the number of shares into which principal is initially divided is determinable at a time within the perpetuities period, namely, at B's death. B is a life in being at A's death, and the number of children B has is fixed at his death (plus an actual period of gestation). The life of a child of B alive at A's death is used to demonstrate that the number of his issue sharing in that part of principal represented by such child of B is determinable within the perpetuities period, namely, at the death of such child of B alive at A's death. Under the rule of Cattlin v. Brown, the gifts of principal are good under the Rule with respect to grandchildren of B whose parent is alive at A's death, but bad under the Rule with respect to grandchildren of B whose parent is an "afterborn" child of B. Gifts of principal that are bad under the Rule are separated from those that are good, and the latter are permitted to stand. Note in connection with the rule of Cattlin v. Brown that if B (the primary income beneficiary of the trust) is A's child, applying the rule of *Cattlin* might result in unequal treatment of persons related to the testator in the same degree, because in a particular case, one or more children of B are in fact after-born children. This inequality resulting from a violation of the Rule is different from the inequality intended by the testator himself when he creates sub-classes. (Taking on a per stirpes basis by sub-classes might (but not necessarily would) result in inequality.)

The "rule" of Storrs v. Benbow shows how the class-closing rules preclude a violation of the Rule. Suppose that A bequeaths "$1,000 apiece to each child of B who attains 30." B is alive at A's death and has several children. If a child of B whenever born were a permissible legatee under A's will, the intended gift as to such afterborn child of B is bad under the Rule Against Perpetuities in orthodox form because an afterborn child of B might attain thirty, if at all, at a time beyond the period measured by B's life and twenty-one years. The "class-closing" rule precludes after-born children of B from taking at all, the matter of attaining the prescribed age aside. The class closes at A's death, and only children of B alive at A's death are permitted to qualify for the legacy. The intended legacies are valid under the Rule as to children of B alive at A's death who have not then attained thirty, because any child of B alive at A's death who is then under thirty will attain thirty, or not, within that child's own lifetime.

Note that the class-closing rule as applied in Storrs v. Benbow also precludes a gift to an after-born child that would not violate the Rule at all: Suppose that A bequeaths "$1,000 apiece to each child of B who attains 21." If B is alive at A's death, any after-born child of B would attain twenty-one, or not, within a period measured by B's life and twenty-one years. Even so, such after-born child is precluded from qualifying for a legacy by the class-closing rule.

§ 11.5 **Powers and Appointments under the Rule.** Both powers of appointment and interests that result from the exercise of powers fall within the ambit of the Rule Against Perpetuities in orthodox form.

A general power to appoint by deed or will that is acquired by the holder contemporaneously with its creation is exempt from the Rule. (Because a general power to appoint by deed or will is comparable to ownership of the property subject to the power, acquiring a general power to appoint by deed or will when the power is created is like acquiring an indefeasibly vested remainder, and the indefeasibly vested remainder is exempt from the Rule.)

A general power to appoint by deed or will that is not acquired at its creation is nonetheless good under the Rule in orthodox form if the power is so created that it must be acquired, if acquired at all, within the perpetuities period. For example, if A creates a testamentary trust "to pay the net income to B for life, and then to pay the principal to such person or persons as B's widow by deed or will appoints," and B is an unmarried person at A's death, the general power is good under the Rule because any person later qualifying for the power as B's widow is identifiable, if at all, at B's death, and B is a "life in being" at A's death, when A's will takes effect.

A general testamentary power of appointment, or a special power of appointment, is void ab initio under the Rule Against Perpetuities in orthodox form if it is so created that it might be exercised at a remote time. It follows that to be valid under the Rule, a general testamentary power or a special power that is intended for a person unborn at the time the dispositive instrument takes effect must be so described that exercise beyond the perpetuities period is impossible. For example, if A creates a testamentary trust "to pay the net income to B for life, and then to pay principal to such of my grandchildren, namely, X, Y, and Z, as B's first-born son appoints," the special power is good under the Rule even though B, who along with X, Y, and Z survives A, is a person who has never married. Although the special power is intended for a person unborn at A's death (when A's

will takes effect), an effective appointment is confined to persons alive at A's death. Therefore the
power cannot be exercised beyond the perpetuities
period.

In summary, then, if acquiring a general power
to appoint by deed or will might be deferred to a
time beyond the perpetuities period, the power is
bad under the Rule Against Perpetuities in orthodox form. A general testamentary power of appointment or a special power of appointment is bad
under the Rule if it is so created that it might be
exercised at a remote time.

Because holding a general power to appoint by
deed or will is comparable to owning the subject
matter of the power (and is so treated for Federal
Estate Tax purposes), the validity under the Rule
of appointments made by the exercise of a general
power to appoint by deed or will is determined by
computing or measuring the perpetuities period
from the time of the exercise of the power. Suppose that A creates a testamentary trust of which
his widow B is the sole income beneficiary. The
trust terms give B a general power to appoint
corpus of the trust by deed or will. (Because the
life estate-general power of appointment combination closely approximates an absolute interest, this
"marital trust" qualifies for the marital deduction
under the Federal Estate Tax.) The general power
itself is exempt from the Rule because it is acquired by B at its creation at A's death. B appoints principal by will to C for life, remainder to

C's children. C survives B, but C is a person unborn at A's death. The appointment is nonetheless valid under the Rule Against Perpetuities in orthodox form because C is a person in being when the power is exercised at B's death, and the number of children of C who share in the remainder is determinable within the life-time of C. For purposes of determining the validity of the appointment made by B, the perpetuities period "runs" from the time of B's death.

To determine the validity under the Rule of an appointment made by the exercise of a general testamentary power or a special power, one "reads back" or interpolates the appointment into the instrument creating the power, and computes or measures the perpetuities period from the time that the power was created. In this connection, perpetuities law simply reflects the traditional notion that exercise of a general testamentary power or a special power is an event upon the happening of which the subject matter of the power passes from the creator of the power (the "donor") to the appointee. (The appointee takes from the creator of the power, the "donor," not from the holder of the power, the "donee.") Nonetheless, facts existing at the time the appointment is made are taken into account when determining the validity of the appointment (this is referred to as taking a "second look" at the facts). For example, suppose that A leaves his entire estate in trust "to pay the net income to B for life, and then to pay principal to such of the children of B, to one or more to the exclusion of others, on such conditions, and in such shares and proportions, as B by will appoints, and in default of appointment, to pay principal to such of B's children as survive him, share and share alike." B survives A. B has never married. The special power created in B is good under the Rule Against Perpetuities in orthodox form because it is exercisable only by B, a person alive when A dies and his will takes effect. (The contingent remainder in default of appointment is also good under the Rule because it will vest, if at all, at B's death.) Suppose that B by will appoints principal in its entirety "to such of my [B's] children as attain 25." B is survived by several children, namely, C, D, and E, the youngest of whom is four years of age. B's appointment is valid under the Rule because "read back" into A's will it is as if A's will had read: "to pay the net income to B for life, and then to pay principal to such of the children of B as survive B and attain 25 no later than twenty-one years after B's death." The children of B who do in fact attain twenty-five are identifiable within twenty-one years after B's death, and B is a person in being at A's death when the special power was created, and the perpetuities period began to run. Because B's youngest child is four years of age at B's death, the final or ultimate number of children of B sharing in the appointment is determinable within B's lifetime and twenty-one years.

§ 11.6 Drafting under the Rule. Taking account of the statement of the Rule, and keeping in mind both the "perpetuities period" and the complexities involved in applying the Rule to powers, and appointments made by the effective exercise of powers, the lawyer can construct these caveats with respect to the preparation of dispositive documents:

(1) Because the Rule applies only to future interests, do not create future interests unless they are essential to the plan of disposition. Generally speaking, persons of modest means have no occasion to create anything other than the outright devise or bequest, free from future interests, powers of appointment, or trusts, and the lawyer preparing the dispositive instrument in some circumstances is obligated to point that out to the client.

(2) Do not create gifts extending to the third generation unless the testator is willing to treat like kinds of persons in an unequal way. Suppose that A has a child B and devises "to B for life, then to B's children for their lives, remainder to the grandchildren of B." "Children" is construed to mean "children whenever born," and "grandchildren" is construed to mean "grandchildren whenever born." If B survives A, the gift to grandchildren of B is bad under the Rule Against Perpetuities in orthodox form even though B has a child or children, as well as grandchildren, alive at A's death. (The gift is a gift to a class that includes an unborn child of an unborn child of B. Under the "unit rule" on gifts to a class, a gift bad as to some members of the class is bad as to all members of the class.) The secondary gift of income to chil-

dren of B is good under the Rule although it
includes an unborn child of B. (The interest of
that child will vest, at the latest, at B's death.)
The gift to grandchildren is good if the lawyer
writes "to B for life, then to B's children for their
lives, remainder to grandchildren of B alive at my
[A's] death and born thereafter to a child or children of B alive at my [A's] death." (Under this
language, the parent of a grandchild of B qualifying to share in the remainder might be born during
the interval between the execution of the will and
the time that A dies.) The gift to grandchildren is
also good if the lawyer writes "to B for life, then to
B's children for their lives, remainder to grandchildren of B alive at my death and born thereafter
during the lifetime of the survivor of B's children
alive at my death." (Under this language, the
parent of a grandchild of B qualifying to share in
the remainder might be born after the death of A.)
But limitations of the kind just suggested might
result in inequality of treatment with respect to
A's great-grandchildren, depending on the turn of
events. The inequality would not result from a
"per stirpes" distribution among the grandchildren
of B; rather, it would originate in excluding some
grandchildren of B from sharing at all.

(3) Do not condition gifts on attaining an age
beyond twenty-one unless the gift is to a person or
persons specifically identifiable by the express
words of the dispositive instrument at the time
that the dispositive instrument takes effect for
perpetuities purposes. Suppose that A devises "to

B for life, remainder to such of the children of B as attain 25." B survives A, and "children" is construed to mean "children whenever born." The remainder is bad under the Rule Against Perpetuities in orthodox form even though a child of B has attained twenty-five at A's death. (Because the class is "open" at A's death, and does not "close" until B's death, a child may be born to B within four years of B's death and attain twenty-five beyond the perpetuities period.) By way of contrast, had A intended to give only to children of B known to him, the devise might have read "to B for life, remainder to such of X, Y, and Z as attain 25." Suppose that A is survived by B, and by X, Y, and Z, none of whom is twenty-five. The lives of X, Y, and Z can be used to demonstrate the validity of the contingent remainder under the Rule. Or had A intended to give only to children of B alive at A's death, the devise might have read "to B for life, remainder to such of the children of B alive at my [A's] death as attain 25." Children of B alive at A's death are specifically identifiable persons whose lives can be used to demonstrate the validity of the remainder under the Rule.

(4) Because the Rule Against Perpetuities applies only to a narrow category of cases, do not create an interest that raises perpetuities questions of the more difficult kind where that serves no purpose. Suppose that A has a child B, and that B has three children, X, Y, and Z. Suppose that the lawyer learns that A wishes to create a life estate in B and a future interest in such of X, Y, and Z as

survive B and attain twenty-one. He could write
"to B for life, remainder to such of the children of
B as survive B and attain 21." Suppose that A
dies, survived by B and by X, Y, and Z, none of
whom is twenty-one. Although the facts at the
execution of the will may be such that the gift of
the future interest must be confined as a matter of
construction to such of X, Y, and Z as attain
twenty-one, the use of "children" invites treating
the future interest as a gift to a class that is
"open" at A's death to admit a child or children of
B born after A dies. (The gift is good under the
Rule, even so.) The validity of the future interest
under the Rule is arguably more obvious if the
lawyer writes what the testator intended: "to B for
life, remainder to such of X, Y, and Z as survive B
and attain 21." (The lives of X, Y, and Z can be
used to demonstrate the validity of the contingent
remainder under the Rule, and one need not consider the "opening" and "closing" of a gift to a
class.)

(5) A special power of appointment that is exercisable beyond the perpetuities period is void ab
initio under the Rule Against Perpetuities in orthodox form. Before professional trustceship
passed from individuals to trust companies, this
aspect of the Rule may not have been the danger
that it is today. "Sprinkling," "spraying," and
"discretionary" trusts involve special powers, and
frequently the power is intended by its creator to
permit an appointment among a class that includes
persons unborn when the perpetuities period be-

gins to run. Where a special power is given to an identified natural person, it cannot be exercised beyond the perpetuities period because it is personal to him. But if a special power is created in a corporate trustee to appoint among a class including the unborn, the power is intended to be exercisable at a time that might be remote. Do not create a special power in a corporate trustee unless exercise of the power is limited either explicitly or implicitly to the perpetuities period (for example, confine permissible appointees to persons alive when the testator creating the testamentary trust dies).

(6) When testing the validity of an appointment made by the exercise of a special power or a general testamentary power, the appointment must be "read back" or interpolated into the instrument creating the power, and the perpetuities period is measured from the time the power was created (the appointee takes from the donor, not the holder of the power). In exercising a special or a general testamentary power, the lawyer should reconstruct the instrument creating the power so that it contains the contemplated appointment, for only in this way can the effectiveness of the appointment be determined. If A by will created a life estate in B, with a general testamentary power of appointment in B, and the draft of B's will purporting to exercise the power reads in part "I appoint to my children for their lives, remainder to my grandchildren," the contemplated appointment might in part be bad under the Rule. For "read

back" into A's will, the appointment takes this form: "to B for life, then to B's children for their lives, remainder to the grandchildren of B." The appointment to B's children will be good, because all of B's children are identifiable within B's lifetime, and B is in being at A's death. But the attempted appointment to B's grandchildren will be bad if a child born to B after A's death survives B.

(7) Either expressly limit the duration of a private express trust to the perpetuities period, or include a "perpetuities savings clause" in the dispositive document. The former requires that a trust end by its own terms within the perpetuities period. The latter directs restructuring of limitations in order to avoid an alleged violation of the Rule.

§ 11.7   Reforming the Rule. Reforming the Rule Against Perpetuities in orthodox form has taken two principal forms: (1) adopting a "wait and see" version of the Rule or (2) authorizing "cy pres" to reform a limitation that violates the Rule. (Some jurisdictions have adopted a combination of "wait and see" and "cy pres.")

A state that adopts "wait and see" abandons the possibilities test for validity of a questioned limitation under the Rule, and instead tests validity by the actualities test: Does the questioned limitation in fact vest within the perpetuities period? If so, it is valid or "good" under the Rule Against Perpetuities in "wait and see" form. If it does not vest within the perpetuities period, it is void or "bad," even under "wait and see." For example, suppose that A devises "to B for life, remainder to such of the children of B as attain 25." B survives A, but no child or children of B are alive at A's death. "Children" is construed to mean "children whenever born." If such of B's children as attain twenty-five in fact do so within B's lifetime and twenty-one years, the future interest is valid under the Rule in "wait and see" form.

A state that authorizes "cy pres," first uses the possibilities test of the orthodox Rule to check the validity of a questioned limitation under the Rule, and if a violation exists, reforms the limitation (if possible) so that it will not violate the Rule. For example, suppose that A devises "to B for life, remainder to that child of B who first attains 25." B, a person without children, survives A. Under the Rule Against Perpetuities in orthodox form, it is possible that the child (if any) of B who first attains twenty-five might do so at a time later than the period measured by B's life and twenty-one years. The intended contingent remainder is therefore void ab initio under the Rule in orthodox form. By "cy pres" it is reformed to read "remainder to that child of B who first attains 21."

The Uniform Statutory Rule Against Perpetuities, enacted in a number of states, sets out the Rule in orthodox form, but also provides both a ninety-year "wait and see" period and "cy pres" reformation of an interest that violates the Rule in its less rigorous "wait and see" form.

§ 11.8   The Rule Against Accumulations.   If a private express trust requires that income be accumulated for a period beyond the perpetuities period, the directed accumulation is void ab initio in its entirety under the common law Rule Against Accumulations.

A mandatory accumulation of income for charity may endure indefinitely, but it is subject to control by a court (and it follows that the direction will be ignored if circumstances so warrant).

Under the Rule Against Accumulations, the perpetuities period is used as a measuring device, just as it is with respect to the duration of the indestructible trust.   A directed accumulation that by the terms of the trust instrument will last no longer than the life of an identified person at the effective date of the instrument and twenty-one years is a permissible accumulation under the common law.   Some states have statutes on directed or mandatory accumulations, and here, as in other connections, one should check for the existence of a statute.   Both common law and statutory versions of the rule against accumulations are little known. Because an occasional donor is taken with the notion that a dream impossible of immediate fulfillment may be realized ultimately through the miracles wrought by compound interest or shrewd investment policy, lawyers preparing trusts, and lawyers examining dispositive documents, should be aware that a directed or mandatory accumulation of income may fall afoul of a rule of law.

If the law of the jurisdiction governing the dispositive document does not include a rule against accumulations, a lawyer should not conclude that it is safe to direct an accumulation for a private purpose for the perpetuities period. There is an undercurrent of antipathy toward the directed or mandatory accumulation of income (just as there is toward the Claflin-type restraint on possession). Therefore, if an accumulation of income is to be required at all, the period should be kept as short as possible consistent with attaining the objective of the donor. An accumulation that is required to last for the perpetuities period might, indeed, be upheld as valid. But if a shorter period is acceptable to the donor, it might not arouse the antagonism of those in a position to raise questions about validity after the donor has died and is no longer in a position by his existence alone to discourage assaults on his dispositive schemes.

CHAPTER 12

SOME ASPECTS OF FIDUCIARY ADMINISTRATION

§ 12.1 **Contract and Tort Liability of the Fiduciary.** A lawyer who never becomes a trustee of an inter vivos or a testamentary trust may nonetheless advise or represent a trustee. A lawyer who never becomes a trustee may administer the estate of a decedent as executor or administrator. Trusteeship and executorship are not identical. A private express trust is ordinarily intended to last for an appreciable period of time. (A charitable trust may be so created that it will endure indefinitely.) An estate is ordinarily administered over a relatively short period of time (a year or two) and then "closed."

But trustees, executors, and administrators of estates are fiduciaries. They hold and administer property that belongs to others. Although the substantive law on trustees, executors, and administrators is not identical in every respect, it has a common core. A lawyer aware of the dangers to both the lawyer and the client posed by the substantive law on (say) trusteeship, is prepared in a general way to cope with problems arising out of administration of an estate.

For purposes of Federal Income Taxation a trust or an estate of a decedent may be an "entity," but

traditionally the view was, and largely still is, that
neither the trust nor the estate of a decedent is an
artificial person. Traditionally a person who con-
tracted with a trustee dealt with the trustee as an
individual, not as a representative of others. If a
tort was committed by a trustee during the administration of the trust, the trustee was personally
liable to the injured person. Of course if a trustee
properly entered into a contract for the benefit of
the trust, and was held individually liable on the
contract, the trustee could lawfully shift the ultimate burden of liability to the trust (that is, in a
sense, to the beneficiaries of the trust) through the
right of indemnity. Similarly, if a trustee was held
liable for tort committed during administration of
the trust, the trustee at times could shift the
ultimate burden of liability to the trust. For example, suppose that A is sole proprietor of a thriving business. A dies, devising his entire residuary
estate, including the business, to his friend T, in
trust. A's will expressly authorizes T to continue
operating the business. As operator of the business, T enters into a contract with P. Viewed from
the standpoint of the beneficiaries of the trust, the
making of the contract is within T's powers and is
appropriate or "prudent" as it is sometimes said.
Performance of the contract does not proceed
smoothly, and P sues T as an individual for breach
of contract, and secures judgment against T. Because the contract was properly entered into by T,
and because it was made for the benefit of the
trust, the burden of the judgment should not be

borne by T personally or individually. Through
T's "right to indemnity," he can shift the burden
from himself by paying the judgment from trust
assets in the first instance (the right to "exoneration") or by reimbursing himself from trust assets
after having paid the judgment (the right to "reimbursement"). If he wishes to avoid judgment
against himself as an individual, T at the outset of
the lawsuit by P, can petition to be "exonerated"
from personal liability by having any judgment be
against him as trustee, that is, be against him in
his representative capacity only.

That a fiduciary may have a right to indemnity
may be small comfort to the fiduciary in a particular case. If a trustee is entering into an authorized
contract for the benefit of the trust, the trustee
sensibly contracts to avoid personal liability altogether. In this connection it is foolish for the
trustee to rely on the designation "trustee" in the
contract. That may be brushed off in litigation as
"descriptio personae" or "surplusage." Rather,
the contract should be more explicit: "T, as trustee
of the XYZ Trust, in his representative capacity,
and not as an individual," or "The XYZ Trust, by
T, trustee, in his representative capacity and not as
an individual." Further, the contract should state
explicitly that the other contracting party looks
solely to trust assets for satisfaction of any claim
arising out of the contract, and not to the trustee.

Viewed from the standpoint of one contracting
with the trustee, it might seem that it is always

preferable to contract in such a way that the
trustee is personally liable on a contract that it is
within the trustee's powers to make, and that is
prudently made, for then one might in an appropriate case secure a judgment against the trustee as
an individual, or "personally" as it is said. But
that assumption may be ill-founded. It might be
the case that trust assets are ample, but that the
trustee personally has little property out of which
to satisfy a judgment were a contract claim asserted against the trustee personally. Under such
circumstances, if a judgment were secured against
the trustee personally, satisfaction of the judgment
would depend upon gaining access to trust assets
through the trustee's right to indemnity. Gaining
access to trust assets might occur through action
by the trustee or by a proceeding in equity brought
by the unpaid judgment creditor.

One who contracts with the trustee only in the
trustee's representative capacity, and who expressly agrees to look only to trust assets for satisfaction
of any contract claim, does not reach trust assets
through the trustee's right to indemnity, because
the trustee is not personally liable on such a contract. Not relying on the right to indemnity is
important not only where the trustee personally
has little property, but also where the trustee has
committed a breach of trust in connection with
some other transaction.

Traditionally, a trustee's right to indemnity is
affected by the state of accounts between the trust-

ee and the trust. For example, the trustee might be liable to the beneficiaries for a breach of trust that has no connection whatever with the contract the trustee has made. If so, the right to indemnity in connection with contract claims is diminished or even extinguished altogether, as the case may be. Suppose that T, the trustee of a private express trust, has committed a breach of trust by using trust assets to pay his personal creditors. For the breach of trust, he is liable in money damages to the beneficiaries of the trust. As a matter of administering the trust, T prudently enters into a contract with P that is within T's trust powers. Performance of the contract does not proceed smoothly, and P sues T as an individual for breach of contract, and secures judgment against T. The traditional view is that T's right to indemnity with respect to P's judgment is diminished to the extent that he is liable to the beneficiaries for breach of trust for using trust assets to pay his personal creditors. Because P's rights with respect to reaching trust assets are in these circumstances traditionally viewed as derivative in nature (that is, dependent upon T's right to indemnity), satisfaction of P's judgment is jeopardized. In some jurisdictions, the traditional view of the right to indemnity is rejected, and P may resort to trust assets to satisfy his claim regardless of the state of accounts between the trustee and the trust. Nonetheless, the traditional view still has substantial support.

With respect to tort liability and the right to indemnity, the trustee should take account of the

fact that this is an age of insurance. Just as it
may be a part of the duties of a trustee to procure
insurance against loss of trust assets by fire, it may
be a part of the duties as trustee to procure insurance against depletion of trust assets resulting
from tort claims against the trustee. Put briefly,
the right of indemnity may be extinguished or
diminished because the trustee failed in the obligation to procure liability insurance. For example,
suppose that A is sole proprietor of a thriving
business. A dies, devising his entire residuary
estate, including the business, to his friend T, in
trust. A's will expressly authorizes T to continue
operating the business. T as trustee uses due care
in selecting B as an employee for the business. In
the course of his employment, B negligently injures
P in both his person and his property. P sues T on
a respondeat superior basis, and secures a judgment against T. Because T used due care in selecting B as an employee, and is liable to P only on a
respondeat superior basis, the burden of the judgment prima facie ought not to be borne by T, but
by the trust. But if as a matter of prudent trust
administration, T should have procured liability
insurance to protect trust assets from depletion
through tort claims, T is not entitled to indemnity
as to the amount of insurance that he should have
obtained, and failed to obtain.

In connection with tort liability, as with contract
liability, it is the traditional view that the trustee's
right to indemnity is affected by the state of accounts between the trustee and the trust. And

again, in some jurisdictions, the traditional view is rejected, and the injured third person may resort to trust assets to satisfy the tort claim regardless of the state of accounts between the trustee and the trust.

§ 12.2 **The Duty of Loyalty.** The duty of loyalty is not well known or understood, and in application it often comes as a shock to the unsuspecting trustee. The duty of loyalty has been called "the most fundamental duty" owed to the beneficiary by the trustee. The trustee is not permitted to put himself or herself in a position where self-interest conflicts with a duty to the beneficiaries of the trust.

The duty of loyalty is violated if a trustee sells a trust asset to the trustee as an individual, or if the trustee buys the trustee's own property for the benefit of the trust. In this connection it is irrelevant that the price is the same as it would have been had the trustee in each instance dealt with a stranger rather than the trustee as an individual. The transaction in either case is voidable by the beneficiaries.

Enforcing the duty of loyalty leads to harsh results. A trustee in good faith uses trust funds to buy personally owned securities for the benefit of the trust. The securities are within the "legal list" of trust investments, and would be viewed as "prudent" trust investments had the purchase been made from a stranger. The securities suddenly plummet in value because of unforeseeable changing economic conditions. The beneficiaries then discover the breach of trust, repudiate the purchase, and demand that the trustee restore to the trust fund the monies used to purchase the now worthless securities. Had the securities been purchased from a stranger, the loss in value would have to be borne by the beneficiaries, for a trustee is not a guarantor of the continued existence of the trust fund. In this instance, the loss is borne by the trustee because the trustee unknowingly violated the duty of loyalty.

The duty of loyalty crops up in both simple and complicated cases. For example, the decedent in Jubinville v. Jubinville (1943), was the sole owner of a licensed liquor package store that passed to plaintiff Zenaide Jubinville on decedent's death. During the last years of the decedent's life, his health failed, and his son Antonio frequently conducted the business on behalf of his father, and in the words of the court, Antonio "occupied a relation of trust and confidence to his father." After the decedent's death, Antonio conducted the business under a license to himself (and later to himself and his wife). Zenaide Jubinville was held entitled to an injunction requiring defendant Antonio to surrender the license for cancellation, and to refrain from attempting to prevent issuance of a license to Zenaide or her nominee. Antonio as a fiduciary could not lawfully seek a license for his own benefit to continue the business that his father had owned, because his duty as a fiduciary conflicted with his self-interest.

Suppose a more complicated case. T is a professional trustee, and as such T administers numerous trusts. As a matter of prudent trust administration, it is desirable that one trust administered by T acquire a particular kind of security as an investment and that another trust administered by T divest itself of that particular kind of security. T, as trustee of the one trust buys the security from himself as trustee of the other trust. Thereafter the purchased security plummets in value because of unforeseeable changing economic conditions. Is T liable for breach of trust, specifically, for breach of the duty of loyalty? Here T is not purchasing from himself as an individual. If the transaction was fair to both trusts, there is no breach of trust and therefore no liability. But to avoid having "fairness" established through a lawsuit, this kind of "self-dealing" can be anticipated by the donor when creating the trust:

I hereby authorize the trustee hereinafter named, and any successor thereto, to enter into any transaction authorized by this article with the trustee or trustees of any other trust in which any beneficiary hereunder has a beneficial interest although such trustee is, or such trustees include, the trustee hereinafter named, or any successor thereto.

This clause is directed to meeting a particular problem that might arise in trust administration. The duties of a trustee are numerous. Clauses in trust instruments directed to meeting particular kinds of problems arising during trust administration are sometimes supplemented by an "exculpatory" clause:

Neither the trustee hereinafter named, nor any successor trustee, shall be liable for loss to the trust estate or to any beneficiary of this trust unless the loss was caused by the willful neglect or default of the trustee.

Judges considering the effectiveness of exculpatory clauses have by no means given them an unqualified indorsement. A paid fiduciary who tries to have it both ways may find a judge to be altogether unsympathetic to attempts to avoid liability by resort to exculpatory language in the dispósitive instrument. The fiduciary may be overcome by an overriding notion of "public policy." It does not follow that it is either improper or unwise to insert exculpatory language into a document. Rather, a trustee ought not to assume that exculpatory language will inevitably prove to be effective.

§ 12.3 **Trust Investments.** Because the trustee of a private express trust is holding and managing property that in equity belongs to the beneficiaries of the trust, the trustee is subject to judge-made or statutory duties. Some of these duties are what one would expect. The duty to preserve and protect trust property, for example. Others are what one might expect on reflection. Because a trust ordinarily lasts an appreciable period of time, the trustee is much more than a mere custodian.

He is under a duty to make the trust property productive. Making trust property productive often includes making investments.

By decision, or court order, or statute (or some combination of them) trustees are restricted or limited to certain kinds of investments. The "prudent man" rule on investments that was established by judicial decision is highly generalized:

All that can be required of a trustee to invest, is, that he shall conduct himself faithfully and exercise a sound discretion. He is to observe how men of prudence, discretion and intelligence manage their own affairs, not in regard to speculation, but in regard to the permanent disposition of their funds, considering the probable income, as well as the probable safety of the capital to be invested. Harvard College v. Amory, (1830).

A statute on trust investments may be much more explicit: Trustees are limited to investing in obligations of the United States, obligations of the state enacting the statute, notes secured by first mortgages on real property, bank deposits insured by the Federal Deposit Insurance Corporation, and so on. Statutes of this kind are called "legal lists." It bears emphasis that from the fact that (say) a kind of bond or note is listed in a "legal list," it does not follow that investment of trust funds in a bond or note of the listed kind is appropriate in the particular case. For example, the legal list might include "bonds issued by municipalities in this state." Although the City of X is a "municipality in this state," investment of trust funds in bonds being issued by the City of X might be improper as a matter of fiduciary administration because the economic and fiscal history of the City of X indicates that the City of X might encounter difficulty in meeting bond payments as they fall due.

The "prudent man" rule on trust investments allows the trustee some flexibility with respect to investments because the rule is couched in general terms. A trustee investing in accordance with a statutory "legal list" or a court order may find himself with little or no flexibility on investments. Because a trustee is under a duty to make the trust property productive, and because income beneficiaries, in particular, are likely to find investment practices of the trustee unsatisfactory, the trustee working under any rule on trust investments often finds himself in an unenviable position. In the case of In re Trusteeship Under Agreement with Mayo (1960), a beneficiary of inter vivos trusts created in 1917 and 1919 sued the trustees and sought court orders permitting the trustees to invest in corporate stock, a prohibited form of investment under the trust instrument. The petitioner emphasized decrease in value of the trust corpus because of inflation. The Supreme Court of Minnesota authorized deviation from the terms of the trust. By way of contrast, where the testator in Toledo Trust Co. v. Toledo Hospital (1962), created a charitable trust and directed that all investments be in "interest bearing securities issued by the United States of America or by any state of the United States of America or by any governmental subdivision of the state of Ohio," the Supreme Court of Ohio refused to allow deviation from the restrictive provision of the will despite changing economic conditions and general inflationary factors.

Because judge-made or statutory rules on trust investments make investment practice hazardous, a person or a corporation considering taking on the burden of trusteeship may condition acceptance of the job on being freed from the application of restrictions on the making of investments that would otherwise apply. Freeing the trustee from the restriction that would otherwise apply is allowed because the trust is a means of making gifts, and a donor within broad limits can fashion the gift. The donor can withhold possession of an indefeasibly vested equitable gift, or can make a gift of a future interest, rather than a present interest. In most states the donor can in some way insulate the gift from the claims of the beneficiary's creditors. Similarly, the donor wishing to do so can expose the gift to hazards greater than it otherwise would be exposed to. The donor by the trust instrument may, for example, free the trustee from judge-made or statutory rules on investment that otherwise would apply. The donor desiring to do this should not rely on something as vague as "hold, manage, lease and care for said property and collect the income therefrom all in accordance with his best judgment and discretion." That kind of language invites litigation. (The trustee would not sensibly put much faith in it.)

§ 12.4 **Administrative Powers.** Administration of a decedent's estate is frequently concluded in a year or so after the decedent's death, whereas a private express trust normally lasts some appreciable period of time, such as twenty years, or the lifetime of the income beneficiary. The personal representative of the decedent (executor or administrator) finds and assembles the assets of the decedent, preserves them during the time that creditors' claims are being considered and paid, and death tax liability (if any) is being determined, and ultimately distributes the net probate estate to the devisees and legatees under the decedent's will, or to the decedent's successors in interest under the statute of descent and distribution.

By way of contrast, the trustee of a private express trust ordinarily knows at the creation of the trust precisely what the subject matter of the trust is, and throughout the period of trust administration, the trustee's only contact with creditors may be with creditors of the beneficiaries of the trust (as differentiated from creditors of the creator of the trust). More importantly, the trustee's duties with respect to the subject matter of the trust often go beyond mere conservation. The trustee ordinarily has the duty of making the trust property productive. And the trustee frequently finds himself making distributions to beneficiaries throughout the term of the trust, as well as at the termination of the trust. Put briefly, administration of the estate of a decedent tends to be a short-term process, with ultimate distribution to the beneficiaries of the estate; administration of a private express trust tends to be a long-term process, with periodic distributions to beneficiaries of the trust.

Nonetheless, executors or administrators of decedents' estates, and trustees of private express trusts, do work that is substantially the same in many respects. Therefore it is convenient to consider at the same time the administrative powers of both kinds of fiduciaries.

Administrative powers exist in fiduciaries as a matter of state law, and that law is not uniform in the United States. Administrative powers that fiduciaries hold as a matter of state law can be enlarged by the testator in the will, or by the settlor in the instrument of trust. Because state law on fiduciary administration is often in an unsatisfactory state, it is common to find provisions in wills and trusts on fiduciary administrative powers. Even if state law on fiduciary administrative powers is relatively satisfactory, a lawyer may nonetheless insert in a will or a trust instrument powers in addition to those given by law because the nature of the property to be administered and the family circumstances of the donor make additional powers desirable, and the lawyer might also insert in the instrument the powers given by law because that assists the fiduciary in his work with persons who are unfamiliar with the general law on administrative powers.

Administrative powers included in wills and trusts reflect the fact that the law on fiduciary administration varies somewhat from state to state, and that the property and family circumstances of individual donors often require powers tailored to meet particular client needs. Nonetheless, there are certain matters with respect to which there is fairly common agreement that the powers given to the fiduciary by law are inadequate, and should ordinarily be displaced or supplemented.

Language introducing the administrative powers given to an executor by will might read as follows:

In addition to and not by way of limitation of such powers as executors and administrators have by common law or by statute, I give to my executor hereinafter named, and any successor executor, the following powers, all of which may be exercised without application to any court.

The language "all of which may be exercised without application to any court" frees the executor from securing a court order that otherwise might be required under state law to perform an administrative act.

State law regulating administration of assets by fiduciaries tends to require conservatism. If a fiduciary is trustworthy, and a person of good judgment, it is ordinarily advisable to give the fiduciary powers that permit using judgment for the benefit of the estate:

> To retain any property, real or personal, that he receives as a part of my estate, even though such property by reason of its kind, amount, or proportion to the total amount of my estate, would otherwise be considered inappropriate. To sell, exchange, lease, partition, give options upon, or otherwise dispose of any property, real or personal, in my estate, at public or private sale or otherwise, for cash or credit, upon such terms and conditions, and at such prices as he thinks fit.

Because a personal representative may need cash (to pay taxes, or routine expenses of administration), and a forced sale of assets to yield cash might be inadvisable, the representative should be empowered to borrow, and to use property in the estate as security for loans:

> To borrow money, and to mortgage or pledge any property in my estate, real or personal, as security therefor.

To facilitate transfer of property, it may be desirable that title to property be held in a form other than the customary fiduciary form (Estate of X, by Y, executor):

> To keep any property in the name of the executor or in the name of a nominee without disclosure of the fiduciary relationship in any instrument of ownership, or in bearer form.

The decedent may have been engaged in controversy at death, or controversy with respect to the
estate may arise after death. Claims both by and
against the estate may exist or arise. Power in the
executor to exercise judgment with respect to such
matters, and to compromise rather than litigate, is
ordinarily desirable:

> To collect, pay, contest, compromise, settle, re-
> new, or abandon claims by or against my estate,
> wherever situated, on whatever terms he finds
> advisable.

An executor should be empowered to employ
others without being subject to the charge of improper delegation of authority:

> To employ attorneys, accountants, bankers, bro-
> kers, and investment counsel, and to rely on
> their advice without making further inquiry, and
> to hire agents, custodians, and depositaries.

Actual distribution of the net probate estate is at
times made easier by according some discretion to
the executor:

> To distribute my estate among beneficiaries in
> cash or in kind, or both, in divided or undivided
> interests, and in proportionate or disproportion-
> ate shares, at such values as my executor deems
> appropriate, with such valuation to be final and
> conclusive to the distributees.

The function of the executor or administrator of
the estate of a decedent tends to be short-term.
The function of the trustee of a private express

trust tends to be long-term, and ordinarily involves investing and reinvesting trust assets. Because state law on investments tends to restrict the trustee to conservative kinds of investments, the creator of the trust may enlarge investment powers:

> To invest and reinvest the trust estate in any property, real or personal, including securities of domestic and foreign corporations, common stocks, preferred stocks, bonds, mortgages, mortgage participations, investment trusts, mutual funds, and common trust funds, irrespective of any common law or statutory rule on investments by trustees, and irrespective of any common law or statutory rule requiring diversification of investments by trustees.

Inserting language in a trust instrument that affects the function of the trustee has its dangers. It bears emphasis that the line dividing administrative powers from dispositive powers is often a thin one. Creation of a power thought to be administrative by the lawyer may carry adverse Federal tax consequences because that dividing line for tax purposes has been crossed. Or the creator of an inter vivos trust by the trust instrument may deprive the trustee of powers otherwise available to such an extent that the trust is thereafter attacked as a "sham." In short, varying the powers of the trustee should be given some thought, just as exempting a fiduciary from the requirement of furnishing bond should be a matter of informed choice, not a matter of routine.

CHAPTER 13

THE FEDERAL ESTATE
AND GIFT TAXES

§ 13.1 **Introduction.** The Federal Estate Tax
is a tax on transfers of property at death, and on
transfers treated for tax purposes as in substance
taking effect at death. The tax, of course, covers
transfer of the net probate estate from the decedent to his successors (whether by will or by intestacy). It sensibly covers transfers by familiar will
substitutes (for example the revocable inter vivos
trust, and the joint tenancy with the incident of
survivorship). It may also catch the payment of
proceeds of insurance on the life of the decedent
(although under the current provisions of the Internal Revenue Code, avoidance of this aspect of
the tax is invited). And a number of devices that a
layman might think to be not testamentary at all
(a survivor annuity, for example) may fall within
the ambit of the tax. Acquiring familiarity with
the Federal Estate and Gift Taxes consists in large
part of determining how ordinary contractual and
property devices are treated for tax purposes.

The Federal Gift Tax is a tax on inter vivos
transfers that complements the Estate Tax. Under the Tax Reform Act of 1976, the two taxes are
integrated. Tax rates for lifetime and deathtime
transfers are the same. Internal Revenue Code

§§ 2001, 2502 (the words "Internal Revenue Code" are omitted hereinafter in citing sections of the Code). At death, the Estate Tax is determined by applying the rate schedule to the cumulative lifetime and deathtime transfers, and then subtracting the gift taxes payable on the lifetime transfers.

A unified credit is allowed against the Federal Gift and Estate Taxes. The unified credit of $30,-000 in 1977 gradually rose to $192,800 in 1987 and thereafter. The credit is a dollar-for-dollar reduction in the tax owed. (Prior to the Tax Reform Act of 1976, there was a $30,000 "lifetime" exemption under the Gift Tax and a $60,000 exemption under the Estate Tax. For decedents who died in 1987 and thereafter, the credit of $192,800 is equivalent to an exemption of $600,000—the "unified credit exemption equivalent.")

Prior to the Tax Reform Act of 1976, a gratuitous lifetime transfer of property occurring within the three years preceding the date of death of the decedent was presumed to be in contemplation of death, and if the Estate Tax were to be avoided, the personal representative of the decedent was required to demonstrate that the presumption should not apply. Under the Tax Reform Act of 1976, a gratuitous transfer of property that was unquestionably complete for Gift Tax purposes during the lifetime of the donor was nonetheless treated as testamentary for Estate Tax purposes if it occurred within the three years preceding the date of death of the decedent. In this connection, the Federal Estate Tax was not being applied to a conventional will substitute (such as the revocable inter vivos trust). Rather, as a matter of policy, a lifetime transaction that might in fact have been a "deathbed" transfer was treated under § 2035 as if it were a deathbed transfer.

Under the Economic Recovery Tax Act of 1981, the impact of § 2035 was softened, and many gifts made within the three years preceding the date of death of the decedent are not includible in the gross estate. But the three-year rule of § 2035 still applies to some transactions (for example, transfer by the decedent of a policy of life insurance on his life).

The arithmetical sum of the values assigned for Federal Estate Tax purposes to property transferred by the decedent at death (or treated as if it in substance passed at death) constitutes the gross estate of the decedent. The gross estate, therefore, includes not only the value of the probate estate of the decedent, but also the value of property passing to beneficiaries of the decedent by way of will substitutes and other arrangements treated as transfers at death for tax purposes. The gross estate less certain allowable deductions constitutes the taxable estate of the decedent. § 2051. Because of the relatively generous unified credit and the existence of deductions with respect to most estates, only a very small proportion of the population is affected by the Federal Estate Tax.

Many states levy "death" taxes—either estate taxes (taxes on disposition of property by the decedent) or inheritance taxes (taxes on acquisition of property from the decedent). Although the theory of the death tax affects the tax paid, the tax, regardless of name, falls in fact in some manner on the successors in interest of the decedent (heirs, devisees, legatees), and collection is assured by making the personal representative of the decedent responsible for the tax, and by paying the tax from the estate of the decedent. Although the Federal Estate Tax is indeed an estate tax, who takes is important in connection with the deduction allowed for property passing outright (or by another qualifying form of disposition) to a surviving spouse (the marital deduction) and the deduction allowed for property given to charity (the charitable deduction). A limited credit is allowed under the Federal Estate Tax for state death taxes paid. § 2011. (Under the Federal Estate Tax, deductions reduce the amount of property that is taxable, credits reduce the amount of the tax itself.)

Neither gift taxes nor death taxes are major sources of government revenue. Because of the unified credit, the marital deduction, and the charitable deduction, few estates are affected by the Estate Tax. Because of the unified credit and the $10,000 per donee annual exclusion, as well as the marital deduction, the charitable deduction, and the split-gift provision of the Gift Tax, few lifetime transfers are affected by the Gift Tax. To the extent that either tax applies, it tends to apply to the well-to-do and the wealthy.

§ 13.2 Using Lifetime Transfers to Avoid or Minimize Taxes. Even if a prospective donor might be affected by the Gift Tax or the Estate Tax, or both, the donor can avoid tax, or minimize it. Suppose that a person has three children and twelve grandchildren. By taking advantage of the $10,000 per donee annual exclusion he can give $150,000 each year to his children and grandchildren ($10,000 to each child and grandchild) without incurring a Gift Tax. §§ 2503(b), 2504(b). If the donor's spouse consents to join in making gifts (under the split-gift provision of the Gift Tax § 2513), the donor can double the value of tax-free transfers per year. Such tax-free transfers are permissible even though the donor (and the donor's wife, if she joins in making the gifts) has exhausted his unified credit under the Gift Tax, for the unified credit and the exclusion are mutually exclusive.

If the donor is in a high Income Tax bracket and members of his family are in lower brackets, the family (viewed as a unit) may reduce Income Tax by completed gifts of income-producing property from the donor to family members in Income Tax brackets lower than his (income from the transferred property is then taxable to the donee, not the donor). Where substantial lifetime gratuitous transfers are made, the tax motive (if any) may be Income Tax saving, not death tax avoidance. A saving on Income Tax recurs year after year once the transfer has been effected.   The Gift Tax is paid but once.

If a Gift Tax is paid on a lifetime transfer that occurs more than three years before the date of death of the donor, the amount of the tax paid is removed from the donor's estate (where it would be taxed at the highest applicable bracket), and the Gift Tax payable is taken into account in computing the Estate Tax payable on the donor's death. (If a Gift Tax is paid on a lifetime transfer that occurs within three years of the date of death of the donor, the amount of the tax is includible in the donor's gross estate under § 2035.)

Nonetheless, despite the existence of the annual exclusion, the unified credit, the split-gift provision, and the marital and charitable deductions under the Gift Tax (to say nothing of the possibility of Income Tax saving), there is little evidence that the well-to-do or the wealthy strip themselves of property during their lives to avoid or minimize taxes.   Regardless of means, persons appear to hold onto property until death, and of the two Federal transfer taxes, the Estate Tax is by far the more important.

§ 13.3   **What Is a Gift for Federal Tax Purposes?**   The Internal Revenue Code does not define a gift for Gift Tax purposes.   Whether a lifetime transfer is viewed as a gift for Gift Tax purposes is determined by drawing on such sources as the Internal Revenue Code itself, the Regula-

tions, reported decisions, Revenue Rulings, and
Common Law notions of gifts.

Because the Gift Tax is a transfer tax, there is
no gift for Gift Tax purposes unless there is a
transfer of property. Refusal to accept a devise or
bequest under a will is not a transfer of property
by the intended beneficiary under the will to that
person or those persons (successors in interest of
the decedent) who benefit from the refusal.
§ 2518. One does not transfer what he himself
does not have. Such disclaimer of a devise or
bequest is to be differentiated from the consequence of destroying an ability to shift property
from one person to another: Release of a power to
revoke or modify a trust is a method of making
gifts for Gift Tax purposes.

Although the Gift Tax is a tax on the transfer of
property, the tax is measured by the value of the
property transferred. In order that there be a
taxable transfer, there must be a transfer of property, not services. And there must be a present
transfer of property, not a transfer of a promise to
transfer property. A gift of the donor's own written promise to pay money (that is, the donor's own
promissory note) is not a gift for Gift Tax purposes.
If one pays a debt owed by another, he has indirect-
ly made a gift to the debtor of the sum paid, and
although the consequence is not so obvious, the
same is true if a creditor forgives a debt. (There
has been a gratuitous transfer of an economic
benefit from creditor to debtor, and that constitutes a gift for Federal Gift Tax purposes.)

So long as one has the right to reclaim the
subject matter of an intended gift, there is no gift.
If A, solely with his own funds, establishes a bank
account on which either A or B may draw, there is
no gift from A to B for Gift Tax purposes until B
makes a withdrawal without obligation to account
to A for part of the proceeds. If A, solely with his
own funds, buys a United States Savings Bond in
"coownership" form "A or B," there is no gift from
A to B until B cashes the bond without any obligation to account to A.

On the other hand if, A, solely with his own
funds, purchases certificates of stock in the names
of himself and B in survivorship form, the purchase in itself constitutes a gift from A to B for
Gift Tax purposes.

If A creates a trust reserving to himself the
power to revoke or modify, he makes no gifts for
Gift Tax purposes when he establishes the trust
(although there are gifts as rights to payment to
beneficiaries—other than A himself—accrue from
time to time after creation of the trust). The
power to revoke or modify is the power to reclaim
the subject matter, and there is therefore no gift on
creation of the trust. If A creates an irrevocable
trust, designating B as beneficiary of net income
for life and C as beneficiary of principal, there are
completed gifts to B and C when the trust is
established. There is a gift to B of the present
value of B's income interest. The value of corpus
less the value of B's income interest is the value of

the gift of principal to C. (A has gratuitously
transferred the subject matter of the trust at creation of the trust, irrespective of the division of
gifts between B and C. But there is only one gift
of a present interest—the gift of income to B—so
only one $10,000 per donee annual exclusion can
be claimed. Section 2503(b).)

A transfer of property in exchange for a release
by the transferee of his or her marital property
rights (as opposed to the right to support) is not a
transfer for an "adequate and full consideration in
money or money's worth" under the Gift Tax (and
is therefore a gift) even though made pursuant to
an antenuptial or postnuptial agreement that is
enforceable between the parties under state law.
But transfers to settle marital property rights
made pursuant to a divorce decree, being involuntary transfers, are not gifts under the Gift Tax.
Harris v. Commissioner (1950). In connection with
transfers between spouses in settlement of marital
or property rights, § 2516 of the Gift Tax provides
that if such transfers are made pursuant to a
written agreement, and divorce occurs within the
three-year period beginning on the date one year
before such agreement is entered into, the transfers are deemed made for a full and adequate
consideration in money or money's worth (and are
therefore not gifts) irrespective of whether the
agreement is approved by the divorce decree.
Here, the Code takes a commonly recurring set of
circumstances and indicates what the tax consequence is. Section 2516 does not preclude a find-

ing of a nongratuitous transfer in cases falling outside its terms. If A and B, husband and wife, enter into a written agreement relative to their marital and property rights, and divorce occurs more than two years thereafter, transfers made pursuant to a decree incorporating the agreement are still involuntary transfers, not subject to taxation as gifts.

§ 13.4 The Unified Credit and the Annual Exclusion. The $10,000 per donee annual exclusion is allowed only with respect to the gift of a present interest, not a future interest. The unified credit may be drawn on by the donor with respect to either kind of gift.

The $10,000 per donee annual exclusion is just that: It is available each year with respect to a donee, but it cannot be cumulated. If A gives only $10,000 to B in a single year, that gift to B is excluded from A's gross gifts. If A gives only $1,000 to B in a single year, and only $15,000 to B in the next succeeding year, the $1,000 gift to B is excluded from A's gross gifts in the year made, but only $10,000 of the $15,000 gift to B is excluded from A's gross gifts in the next succeeding year—A cannot "save" any or all of an available exclusion in one year and add it to the exclusion in a subsequent year. Nor may a donor shift the "unused" part of the exclusion from one donee to another. If A gives $1,000 to B in a single year and $19,000 to C in the same year, the $1,000 gift to B is excluded from A's gross gifts, and the first $10,000 of the

$19,000 gift to C is excluded from A's gross gifts. Had A given $10,000 each to B and C, both gifts would be excluded in their entirety from A's gross gifts.

Unlike the exclusion, the unified credit is available in any year (to the extent that it has not been allowable). If in a single year A gives B $30,000 and he has not drawn on his unified credit, the first $10,000 of the gift to B is excluded from A's gross gifts for the year. If A wishes to do so, he may avoid payment of Gift Tax by drawing on his unified credit with respect to the tax payable on the $20,000 taxable gift.

§ 13.5 Present and Future Gifts for Purposes of the Exclusion. The $10,000 per donee annual exclusion is allowed only for a gift of a present interest, not for a gift of a future interest. From the fact that a gift is viewed as an immediate or present gift for purposes of state property law, it does not follow that it will be so viewed for purposes of the Federal Gift Tax. Suppose that A irrevocably transfers $100,000 in trust, to accumulate the income until B (age 30) attains the age of 40, or sooner dies, and on B's attaining 40, to pay the principal and accumulated income to B, or, should B die before attaining 40, to pay the principal and accumulated income to B's estate. At the creation of the trust, B has an indefeasibly vested interest in the subject matter of the trust, subject to a restraint on possession, and no other person has an interest. Nonetheless, the gift to B is a gift of a future interest for purposes of the Federal Gift

Tax, and no part of the gift is excluded under the
annual exclusion.

By way of contrast, suppose that A irrevocably
transfers $100,000 in trust, to pay the net income
to B (age 30) for life, and at B's death, to pay the
principal to B's estate. Again, no one other than B
has an interest in the trust. But A has made two
gifts to B—a gift of income that is a present interest for purposes of the annual exclusion, and a gift
of principal that is a future interest.

If A irrevocably transfers $100,000 in trust, to
pay the net income to B (age 30) for life, and then
to pay the principal to C, A has again made a
gratuitous transfer of $100,000. The present value
of the income interest is a gift of a present interest
to B with respect to which the exclusion may be
claimed. $100,000 less the present value of the
remainder interest is the value of the gift to B.
The gift to C is a future interest for purposes of
both state property law and the Gift Tax.

The annual exclusion applies even though the
present interest may be affected by the exercise of
a power, provided the power is exercisable only in
favor of the beneficiary of the present interest. If
A irrevocably transfers $100,000 in trust, to pay
the net income to B for life, and then to pay the
principal to C, with the trustee empowered to invade corpus for the benefit of B, the first $10,000 of
the present value of the gift of income to B is
excluded from A's gross gifts.

§ 13.6 The Annual Exclusion and Gifts to Minors. For purposes of the annual exclusion, one must differentiate between gifts to minors (persons who have not attained the age of 21) and gifts to adults. A gift disqualifying for the exclusion under the Gift Tax because it is deemed "future" when made to an adult, may qualify for the exclusion when made to a minor because it is a "present" gift under § 2503(c) of the Internal Revenue Code. Suppose that A irrevocably transfers $100,000 in trust, to pay so much of the income and the principal to B (age 4), or for B's benefit, as the trustee in his uncontrolled discretion sees fit, and to pay the principal and any accumulated income to B on his attaining 21, and if B dies before attaining 21, to pay the principal and any accumulated income to B's estate. The gift to B is a present interest under § 2503(c) of the Code, and the first $10,000 of the $100,000 gift is excluded from A's gross gifts.

Section 2503(c) was enacted in 1954 to facilitate claiming the annual exclusion with respect to transfers for the benefit of minors of a commonly recurring kind. Section 2503(c) is in this respect comparable to § 2516 of the Code, enacted in the same year to free from the Gift Tax transfers in settlement of marital or property rights of a commonly recurring kind. Like § 2516, § 2503(c) is not exclusive—a gift for the benefit of a minor may qualify for the exclusion even though it does not fall under § 2503(c).

A gift to a custodian on behalf of a minor complying with the requirements of a state Gift to

Minors Act falls under § 2503(c) and qualifies for the exclusion. The general enactment of such statutes makes it easy indeed to make a gift to a minor that qualifies for the exclusion.

§ 13.7 Split Gifts; The Marital Deduction. The split-income provision of the Income Tax, the split-gift provision of the Gift Tax, and the marital deduction of the Gift and Estate Taxes became parts of the tax law in 1948 as a consequence of an effort to put taxpayers in common law states and community property law states on a rough parity.

California, Arizona, New Mexico, Texas, Louisiana, Nevada, Washington, and Idaho are community property states. Wisconsin's version of the Uniform Marital Property Act, based on community property principles, became law in 1986. (Michigan, Nebraska, Oklahoma, Oregon, and Hawaii were community property states briefly.)

In a common law state, if A, married to B, by his earnings amasses personal property valued at $400,000, B has no interest in the personalty during A's lifetime. If A dies, B surviving, the entire $400,000 worth of personalty is a part of A's gross estate for Federal Estate Tax purposes. Should A by will attempt to disinherit B, such protection as is afforded to B as a surviving spouse is a matter of state law, with variation from jurisdiction to jurisdiction.

In a community property state, if A, married to B, by his earnings amasses property valued at $400,000, B becomes the owner of an undivided

one-half of the property as it accumulates. If A
dies, B surviving, only one-half of the "community"
property is included in A's gross estate for Federal
Estate Tax purposes. The other one-half of the
community property was B's property before A
died, and B does not "take" it from A on A's death.
With respect to his undivided one-half of the community property, A has an absolute right of testamentary disposition—he may, if he wishes, effectively ignore B as a beneficiary of his will.

In a community property state, property brought
to the marriage by a spouse, and property acquired
after marriage by a spouse through gift, devise,
bequest, or inheritance, is the separate property of
the spouse. With respect to such separate property, a spouse in a community property state has an
absolute right of testamentary disposition, just as
the spouse does with respect to an undivided one-
half of community property. Separate property is
included in a decedent's gross estate.

The protection afforded a spouse in a community
property state when marriage is dissolved by death
or divorce originates in his or her being the owner
of an undivided one-half of community property as
it accumulates. The disparity in Gift Tax treatment of taxpayers in common law states and community property states (prior to Congressional efforts at affording relief) had the same origin: In a
common law state, if A, married to B, earns $100,-
000 and gives half of his earnings to B, he has
made a gratuitous transfer of $50,000 for Federal

Gift Tax purposes. In a community property state, if A, married to B, earns $100,000, half of his earnings belong to B as they are earned. The earnings of a spouse are viewed as attributable to the efforts of both. If A and B give community property to C, each spouse is a donor of half the value of the gift.

The marital deductions under the Gift Tax, § 2523, and under the Estate Tax, § 2056 (along with the "split-gift" provision of the Gift Tax, § 2513) were created to put taxpayers in common law states on a rough parity with taxpayers in community property states. Before 1982 there were limits on the marital deductions. For example, under the Tax Reform Act of 1976, the Estate Tax marital deduction was limited to the greater of $250,000 or one-half of the value of the adjusted gross estate. Under the Economic Recovery Tax Act of 1981, the limits on both the Gift Tax marital deduction and the Estate Tax marital deduction were eliminated, and the marital deduction, like the charitable deduction, is now an "unlimited" deduction. (The 1981 Tax Act included a transitional rule with respect to trusts and wills executed before September 12, 1981, which direct that the surviving spouse receive the maximum amount of property qualifying for the marital deduction that is allowable under Federal law.)

§ 13.8 The Orphan's Deduction. By § 2057 of the Estate Tax, the Tax Reform Act of 1976 introduced a deduction called the "orphan's deduction." The orphan's deduction was repealed by the Economic Recovery Tax Act of 1981 with respect to estates of decedents dying after December 31, 1981.

§ 13.9 Property Qualifying for the Marital Deduction. If A, married to B in a community property state, accumulates $400,000 through his earnings, and dies thereafter, B surviving, only one-half of the $400,000 in community property is included in A's gross estate for Estate Tax purposes. The other undivided one-half of the property was B's prior to A's death, and if B dies owning that one-half, it is included in B's gross estate.

In order that the marital deduction in a common law state serve roughly the same purpose as denominating property "community" property serves in a community property state, it is essential that property passing to the donee spouse from the donor spouse pass absolutely (or by another qualifying form of disposition) so that it might be exposed to a death tax in the hands of the donee spouse. Because of the inherent characteristics of some kinds of property interests, they do not qualify for the marital deduction. If A dies possessed of a fee simple absolute and devises it to his surviving spouse B for life, the life interest in B does not in itself qualify for the marital deduction because it is a "nondeductible terminable interest"—it ceases at B's death. If the life estate in B is coupled with a general power in B to appoint the remainder, the combination qualifies for the marital deduction because B in substance has the economic equivalent of a fee simple absolute, and the combination

is so treated for both Gift and Estate Tax purposes.
Furthermore, under the terms of the Economic
Recovery Tax Act of 1981, if A uses the property to
create a qualified terminable interest property
trust (a "Q–TIP" trust) for the benefit of his surviving spouse B for life, with remainder payable to
their children C and D, the property qualifies for
the marital deduction. (Although B is not the
beneficiary of the remainder, the value of the property in the trust at B's death is includible in B's
gross estate for Estate Tax purposes.)

Property included in the gross estate of the decedent that passes (or has passed) absolutely to the
surviving spouse (or by another qualifying form of
disposition) and qualifies for the marital deduction
may pass in a variety of ways: by will, by intestacy, by election to take against the will, by exercise
of a general power of appointment, by survivorship
(where property is held during marriage in survivorship form), by revocable trust, and through fulfillment of an insurance contract, to name some of
them.

§ 13.10 "Survivorship" Clause and the Marital Deduction. A testator may prefer that a
beneficiary of his will be disqualified for a devise or
bequest unless the beneficiary survives the testator
by a period of time sufficient to permit the beneficiary to enjoy the gift personally. And the testator
may wish to avoid taxation of the same property
twice within a very short period of time. To
achieve these objectives, the testator conditions his
gift by a "survivorship clause": "I give my resi-

dence, located at _____, together with furniture
and furnishings not otherwise specifically be-
queathed above, to my sister Martha provided she
survives me by sixty days." A devise or bequest to
a surviving spouse that otherwise qualifies for the
Estate Tax marital deduction is not disqualified by
such a survivorship clause provided the period of
required survivorship does not exceed six months:
"I leave all of my estate to my wife Mary provided
she survives me by one hundred and twenty (120)
days." One hundred and twenty days being less
than six months, this required period of survivorship does not disqualify the testamentary gift to
the spouse for the marital deduction.

In order that the Estate Tax marital deduction
be properly claimed, it is essential that the spouse
in fact survive the decedent. In the event that the
decedent and his spouse die simultaneously, the
marital deduction may nonetheless be used if the
will provides a presumption that the donee spouse
survived: "My wife Mary shall be presumed to
have survived me if the order of our deaths cannot
be established by evidence."

§ 13.11 **Property Qualifying for the Estate
Tax Marital Deduction.** Property that passes (or
has passed) to the surviving spouse must be included in the gross estate of the decedent to qualify for
the Estate Tax marital deduction. If no property
included in gross estate of the decedent passes (or
has passed) absolutely to the surviving spouse (or
by another qualifying form of disposition, such as
the life estate-and-remainder, or the life estate-
and-general power combination), no marital deduc-

tion is available. Furthermore, the marital deduction is limited by the net value of the qualifying property that passes (or has passed) to the surviving spouse. The value of property includible in the gross estate that passes (or has passed) to the surviving spouse is affected by the deductions for expenses, indebtedness, and taxes under § 2053, losses under § 2054, and appropriate charges against the marital interest, such as death taxes payable out of the interest either by direction of the decedent or as a matter of applicable state law (in the absence of direction by the decedent). To prevent taxes from depleting the marital deduction, the decedent may direct that death taxes be paid from property that does not qualify for the marital deduction.

In a community property state, if A, married to B, died prior to 1977, B surviving, and his gross estate included only community property, no marital deduction was allowed. If the estate included separate property, the marital deduction was available, measured by the separate property. In this latter case, either community property of the decedent or separate property of the decedent passing absolutely to the surviving spouse (or by another qualifying form of disposition) satisfied the marital deduction gift. Under the Tax Reform Act of 1976, if A, married to B, died after 1976, B surviving, and his gross estate included only community property, a partial marital deduction was available to the extent that the $250,000 minimum marital deduction exceeded the decedent's share of the community property. Under the Economic Recovery Tax

Act of 1981, the marital deduction is an unlimited
deduction, and either community property of the
decedent or separate property of the decedent included in the gross estate of the decedent that
passes (or has passed) absolutely to the surviving
spouse (or by another qualifying form of disposition) qualifies for the marital deduction.

§ 13.12 **The Gross Estate.** Included in the
decedent's gross estate is the value of his probate
estate—interests owned by the decedent at death
subject to administration by the probate court—
and the value of interests treated by the Internal
Revenue Code as in substance passing from the
decedent at death. This non-probate category of
transfers includes some transactions that are fully
completed during the decedent's lifetime. For example, suppose that the decedent created an irrevocable inter vivos trust, reserving to himself the
net income for life, and directing that at the settlor's death, the trustee pay the principal to B if
then alive, or if B be then dead, to pay the principal to C. If the settlor dies thereafter, the then
value of the corpus of the trust is includible in his
gross estate under § 2036 (transfers with a retained life estate). Although at the creation of the
trust the decedent made an irrevocable gift of a
future interest (the gift of principal), the future
interest becomes possessory at the settlor's death.
(If B dies during the settlor's lifetime, nothing with
respect to the trust is includible in B's estate
because B's interest "fails by its own terms" when
B dies. If C dies during the settlor's lifetime, B
surviving, the value of C's interest is includible in

C's estate for Federal Estate Tax purposes under § 2033 because C's interest—unlike B's—is conditioned only on B's failure to survive the settlor.) The great variety of lifetime transactions, property or contractual, that fall within the ambit of the Federal Estate Tax explains the number and complexity of the sections of the Federal Estate Tax devoted to them. In addition to § 2035 (transfers within three years of death) and § 2036 (transfers with a retained life estate), there is § 2037 (transfers taking effect at death), § 2038 (revocable transfers), § 2039 (survivor annuities), § 2040 (joint tenancies and tenancies by the entirety), § 2041 (general powers of appointment), and § 2042 (life insurance). Arriving at the arithmetical figure that is the gross estate of a decedent requires reviewing events during the decedent's lifetime and at death to determine which transfers, if any, fall within the ambit of §§ 2033 through 2042 of the Code.

§ 13.13   Survivorship Interests. For purposes of the Gift Tax and § 2040 of the Estate Tax ("joint interests") it is essential to differentiate among tenancies in common, joint tenancies with the right of survivorship, and tenancies by the entirety.

If A, solely with his own funds, purchases real property, and A and B take title to the real property as tenants in common, A has made a gift to B for Gift Tax purposes of one-half the purchase price of the real property acquired. (A might claim the $10,000 per donee annual exclusion with respect to the gift.) If A dies, B surviving, the

value of A's undivided interest is includible in A's
gross estate under § 2033 because it is a part of A's
probate estate. B takes no part of A's undivided
interest at A's death, unless B is an heir, a devisee,
or a spouse who effectively claims an elective share
of A's estate as a matter of state law. In short, if B
takes from A, B does not take by "survivorship."
(B at A's death already owns an undivided share of
the property as a tenant in common.) If A and B
in the supposed case are husband and wife, and A
solely with his own funds purchased the land, A
has made a gift to B of one-half the purchase price
of the land, but with respect to this gift to a spouse,
A might claim both the annual exclusion and the
unlimited marital deduction.

If A and B purchase property in survivorship
form ("to A and B, and to the survivor of them"),
and A dies thereafter, B surviving, it is said as a
matter of property law that A's interest ceases at
A's death, and B is thereafter the sole owner as
survivor under the instrument of transfer. For
Federal Estate Tax purposes, the property law
view of survivorship interests is modified: Under
§ 2040, the full value of the property subject to a
right of survivorship is includible in the gross
estate of the decedent, but the decedent's executor
or administrator may demonstrate that some or all
of the value should be excluded because it "originally belonged to [the survivor and had never been
received or acquired by the survivor from the dece-
dent] for less than an adequate and full consideration in money or money's worth. ..." If B contrib-

uted from B's separate funds one-fourth of the acquisition cost of the jointly owned property, one-fourth of the value of the property at A's death (or the alternate valuation date) is excluded from A's gross estate.

However, if the purchasers of the property in the preceding example are husband and wife holding title as tenants by the entirety, one-half of the value of the property is includible in the gross estate of the first to die, irrespective of disproportionate contributions toward acquisition.

Because of lapse of time between the date of acquisition of survivorship property and the date of death, the right to exclude from the gross estate of the decedent the value of the property proportionate to the contribution of the survivor may be illusory. The burden of showing the contribution of the survivor is on the personal representative of the decedent, and evidence essential to proving contribution may be unavailable.

Although both the Gift Tax and the Estate Tax build on state law characteristics of survivorship interests, the taxes stress the economic origin of survivorship interests, and the economic consequences of holding property in survivorship form. With respect to survivorship interests, it is helpful to ask the following questions: What is the subject matter of the interest? (Real property? Bank account? United States Savings Bond? Certificate of stock?) Who are the joint owners? (Brother and sister? Husband and wife?) If the joint owners are husband and wife, do they hold as tenants by the entirety? How was the joint ownership acquired? (By purchase? By gift?) If joint ownership with the right of survivorship originated in purchase, what proportion of the cost of acquisition was attributable to each owner? How was the tenancy terminated? (By severance? By gift from one tenant to the other? By death?) Answers to questions of this kind are best demonstrated by a few examples.

If A and B are brothers, and A and B purchase land, taking title in survivorship form, and A contributes three-fourths of the price and B contributes one-fourth of the price, A makes a gift to B for Gift Tax purposes to the extent that his contribution exceeds the value of his retained interest. Because a joint tenancy at Common Law is "severable" (either A or B can destroy the right of survivorship by a conveyance to X), A's retained interest for Gift Tax purposes is only one-half the value of the real property acquired.

Consistent with the basic principle under the Gift Tax that a fully revocable gift is no gift at all, if A, solely with his own funds, opens a bank account in the form "A or B and the survivor of them," there is no gift for Gift Tax purposes until B makes a withdrawal without obligation to account to A for part of the proceeds. If A purchases a United States Savings Bond in "coownership" form, there is no gift to the coowner until the coowner cashes the bond without obligation to account to A for part of the proceeds. The entire balance in the bank account at A's death, B surviving, is includible in A's gross estate under § 2040. The value of the uncashed United States Savings Bond is includible in A's gross estate at his death, B surviving, under § 2040, and these consequences follow irrespective of the fact that under state law (with respect to the bank account) and under Federal law (with respect to the bond), B is the sole owner at A's death.

Certificates of stock may be acquired in survivorship form. If A, solely with his own funds, purchases stock and takes title in the form "A and B as joint tenants with right of survivorship and not as tenants in common," A has made a gift to B of one-half the value of the stock because a joint tenancy in stock is "severable" by assignment. If A dies, B surviving, the value of the stock in its entirety is includible in A's gross estate.

A survivorship interest can be terminated by events other than "severance" or death of a joint owner. If A, solely with his own funds, purchases stock and takes title in the names of himself and B in survivorship form, he makes a gift to B. If the stock is sold thereafter and all of the proceeds of the sale are kept by B, A has made a second gift to B.

Property is frequently acquired and held in survivorship form. Putting property in survivorship form is defensible both as a matter of convenience and as a means of avoiding probate. But survivorship interests carry no tax advantage, and they may have an unexpected and disagreeable tax consequence.

§ 13.14 Transfers within Three Years of Death. If A owns property absolutely and makes complete gratuitous transfers of that property more than three years before his death (retaining no interests, powers, or "strings" with respect to it), the property is not a part of A's estate at death for Estate Tax purposes even though unquestionably made in contemplation of death. If a complete gratuitous transfer is made within three years of the donor's death, the Estate Tax consequence turns on the nature of the interest transferred. For example, if A gives $50,000 in cash to B within the three years preceding A's death, the transfer does not fall within the ambit of § 2035. But if A gives a policy of life insurance on his life to B within the three years preceding A's death, the full value of the proceeds is includible in A's gross estate under § 2035.

The sweep of § 2035 is broad. For example, A creates a revocable trust, designating B as beneficiary of net income for life and C as beneficiary of principal. Within the three years preceding his death, A relinquishes the power to revoke. Although destruction of the power results in completed gifts for Gift Tax purposes, relinquishment of the power is within the terms of both § 2035(a) and § 2038(a) for Estate Tax purposes.

Suppose that six years before his death A procures a $30,000 policy of life insurance on his own life, designating his wife B as beneficiary. A immediately assigns all of the incidents of ownership to B, but nonetheless pays all of the annual premiums on the policy until his death. A dies, B surviving. Although half of the premiums paid on the policy were paid during the three years preceding A's death, no part of the proceeds of the policy is includible in A's gross estate. Revenue Ruling 71–497.

§ **13.15 Sections 2036, 2037, and 2038.** Although the titles commonly associated with §§ 2036 ("Transfers with Retained Life Estate"), 2037 ("Transfers Taking Effect at Death"), and 2038 ("Revocable Transfers") describe the coverage of these sections of the Estate Tax in a general way, it bears emphasis that the sweep of these sections is wide.

For example, suppose that A transfers property in trust to pay the net income to B for life, and then to pay the principal to C, with a reserved power in A to revoke the trust at any time. If A dies possessed of the power to revoke, the value of the corpus of the trust is includible in A's gross estate under § 2038 as a "revocable" transfer—a transfer essentially testamentary for death tax purposes. By way of contrast, suppose that A creates an irrevocable trust of property, designating himself as trustee, to accumulate income for B (age 5) until B reaches 21, when accumulated income is payable to B, and to pay the net income to B thereafter, and to pay principal to B when B reaches 25; should B die before attaining 25, the corpus and any accumulated income are expressly made payable to B's estate. Under the trust instrument, A has the power to terminate the trust at any time and pay over the corpus and any accumulated income to B. If A dies possessed of the power to terminate, the value of the corpus of the trust is includible in A's gross estate even though A could not reclaim for himself any part of the gift to B.

In order that a power be a "taxable power" under § 2038 (that is, in order that the value of the subject matter of the power be includible in the decedent's gross estate), the power must relate to property transferred by the decedent himself during his lifetime (in this respect differing from a § 2041 power), and the power must be exercisable by the decedent at his death. Suppose that A creates an irrevocable trust to pay the net income to his wife B for life, with a power in A, after B's death, to appoint net income among their then living children, and with principal being payable to C. A dies thereafter, possessed of the power, and survived by B, C, and several children. Nothing is includible in A's gross estate under § 2038 because the power in A is not exercisable until after B's death.

If a reserved power in the decedent to allocate income or principal to persons other than himself is exercisable only in accordance with a "determinable, enforceable, objective, external standard" (or,

as it is sometimes said, if the power is "ministe-
rial"), the power is not a taxable power under
§ 2038. Litigation has demonstrated that a power
to invade the corpus of a trust for the "best interests" of the beneficiaries, or for their "comfort and
happiness," or as "circumstances ... require" is
not a power exercisable only in accordance with a
determinable, enforceable, objective, external standard. It is stated in Old Colony Trust Co. v.
United States (1970), that "[t]he trust provision
which is uniformly held to provide an ascertainable standard is one which, though variously expressed, authorizes such distributions as may be
needed to continue the beneficiary's accustomed
way of life."

On the other hand, an otherwise taxable power
in the decedent does not fall outside the ambit of
§ 2038 just because it is exercisable only with the
consent of a person or persons having "adverse
interests"—for example, beneficiaries of a trust
whose interests would cease were the power to be
exercised. Although the person whose consent is
required might indeed consistently refuse to give it
(and thereby make the power a nullity), beneficiaries of trusts are often members of the settlor's
family. For Estate Tax purposes, no inquiry is
made into the probability that consent to exercise
of a power will not in fact be given.

Like § 2038, § 2036 encompasses not only the
kind of transaction falling within the literal terms
of the section, but also the kind of transaction

treated for death tax purposes as intended to be covered by the section. If A, owning land in fee simple absolute, transfers it to B reserving to himself a life estate, the value of the land at A's death is includible in A's gross estate under § 2036 ("Transfers with Retained Life Estate") because B's indefeasibly vested remainder becomes a possessory interest at A's death. But the coverage of § 2036 is not confined to this simple kind of case. If A transfers property irrevocably in trust to pay the net income to his wife B for life, and thereafter to himself for life, and then to pay the principal to their children C and D, the value of the corpus of the trust, less the value of B's income interest, is includible in A's gross estate if A dies, B surviving. It is not essential for purposes of § 2036 that the decedent be receiving or enjoying the reserved life interest at his death; it is sufficient that he made a transfer of property and retained the life interest.

The value of property transferred by the decedent during his lifetime may be includible in his gross estate under § 2036 even though the "life estate" is not one in the decedent himself. A creates an irrevocable trust to pay the net income to his wife B for life "for her support and maintenance," and to pay the principal to C. A dies, B surviving. Section 2036 applies. If income is required to be used to discharge the decedent's legal obligation to support B, it is as if A had received the income and used it to support B.

Under either § 2036 or § 2038, administrative or managerial powers in the decedent are to be differentiated from taxable powers. It is not unusual for a decedent to create a trust of which he is trustee or co-trustee. Because state law on fiduciary administration tends to be strict and inhibiting, settlors frequently free trustees from state law that is otherwise applicable by inserting in the trust instrument enlarged administrative powers. If a power is properly described as "administrative" for Estate Tax purposes, possession of such a power by the decedent at death does not make the subject matter of the power includible in his gross estate.

Section 2037 ("Transfers Taking Effect at Death") requires including in the gross estate the value of property transferred during the decedent's lifetime under such circumstances that the "possession or enjoyment of the property" could be obtained only by surviving the decedent, and the decedent retained a "reversionary interest" exceeding in value 5 per cent of the value of the property immediately before the death of the decedent.

Suppose that A transfers property to a trust company to pay the net income to B for life, and then to pay the principal to C if C survives A. Under the law of property, A has created an income interest in B for life, and an equitable contingent remainder in C—contingent because it is expressly conditioned on C's surviving A, the transferor. Because C might not survive A, A has an equitable reversionary interest in the property—an interest by way of "resulting trust." A dies sur-

vived by B and C. Because C survived A, A's
reversionary interest does not exist after A's death
(it is divested by the vesting of C's contingent
remainder), and therefore nothing is includible in
A's gross estate under § 2033. But enjoyment of
C's interest is dependent on C's surviving A, and if
the value of A's reversionary interest exceeded 5
per cent of the value of the property just before A's
death, § 2037 applies. The value of the corpus of
the trust, less the value of B's income interest, is
includible in A's gross estate.

Suppose that A owns land in fee simple absolute
and he creates a fee simple determinable in B ("to
B and his heirs so long as the land is used for
school purposes"). In most states, A has a possibility of reverter "by operation of law." (That is, by
implication—A, having a fee simple absolute, did
not convey a fee simple absolute). If A dies possessed of the possibility of reverter, its value is
includible in A's gross estate under § 2033. Here
A's "reversionary interest" persists after A's death,
unlike the reversion in A in the paragraph above
which ceased at A's death. If A creates an inter
vivos trust to pay the net income to B for life, and
then to pay the principal to such of B's children as
survive B, and A dies survived by B, the value of
A's resulting trust is includible in A's gross estate,
but again under § 2033. A's reversionary interest
is one which persists after A's death, and the
condition of survivorship attached to the gift to the
children of B requires that they survive B, the

income beneficiary, not A, the settlor. Therefore
§ 2037 has no application.

In short, if limitations under a deed or trust
instrument are such that § 2037 might apply, the
"reversionary interest" in the transferor is valued
just before his death to see whether the "5 per cent
test" is met, and if it is, the reversionary interest is
thereafter ignored and attention is directed to the
interest "taking effect" at the transferor's death,
the value of which is includible in his gross estate.
The includible interest is valued just after the
transferor's death. If A transfers property to a
trust company to pay the net income to B for life,
and then to pay the principal to C if C survives A,
and A dies survived by B and C, in applying
§ 2037, one in substance views the transfer to C (as
opposed to the interest in B) as a testamentary one:
"I give to C if he survives me." Under the facts, C
survives, and C takes.

Suppose that A transfers property to a trust
company to pay the net income to a designated
charity for A's life, and on A's death, to pay the
principal to such of the children of A as survive A,
and if no child of A survives A, to pay the principal
to such person or persons as A by will appoints,
and in default of appointment, to pay the principal
to B. Under § 2037(b)(2) the power in A is viewed
as a "reversionary interest" in A, and if A dies
intestate survived by a child or children, and the
power in A meets the "5 per cent test" just prior to
A's death, the value of the entire corpus of the

trust is includible in A's estate under § 2037. If
no child or children of A survive A, the intended
gift for A's children "fails by its own terms" and
there is no interest in them to value after A's
death. But § 2037 does apply to the gift to B—it
vests indefeasibly at A's death. And the value of
the corpus of the trust is includible in A's gross
estate under § 2038 because A possessed an exercisable power at his death over property transferred by him during his lifetime.

§ **13.16 Annuities.** The coverage of § 2039 is
not confined to annuities. It extends to death
benefits payable to the survivor of the decedent by
virtue of his death. If A, solely with his own
funds, procures an annuity payable in monthly
installments to himself for his life, and then to his
wife B for her life, if she survives him, the value of
B's interest is includible in A's gross estate under
§ 2039 if A dies, B surviving. Likewise, if under
A's contract of employment a sum is payable to A
on his retirement, or is payable to his spouse B if A
dies before retirement, B surviving, the sum is
includible in A's gross estate under § 2039 if A dies
before retirement, B surviving. Even though the
fund out of which a survivor annuity or lump sum
is paid originated wholly or in part in contributions made by the decedent's employer, the contributions made by the employer are attributed to the
decedent for purposes of § 2039.

Like § 2040, § 2039 makes allowance for contribution by the survivor toward acquisition of an
annuity. If A, married to B, purchases a "surviv-

orship annuity," and B from her own funds contributes one-half of the acquisition cost, only one-half of the value of B's interest is includible in A's gross estate on his death, B surviving.

A joint and survivor annuity under a "tax qualified" plan qualifies for the marital deduction provided no one other than the spouse has any rights prior to the death of the surviving spouse.

§ 13.17   Life Insurance. Since 1954 the "incidents of ownership" test (as opposed to the "premiums payment" test) has been used for purposes of determining whether the proceeds of insurance on the life of the decedent that are payable to a beneficiary other than the estate are includible in the gross estate. For example, if A procures a $50,000 policy of life insurance on his own life and designates his wife B as beneficiary, and A dies, B surviving, the proceeds of the policy are includible in A's gross estate under § 2042 if A at death possessed an "incident of ownership" with respect to the policy. Incidents of ownership include the right to change the beneficiary, the right to surrender the policy to the insurer for cash, the right to pledge the policy as collateral for a loan, the right to assign the policy, and the right to designate the mode of payment under a settlement option.

To avoid includibility of the proceeds of insurance on his life in his gross estate, the owner may during his lifetime assign all rights in the policy to another. As indicated above in connection with § 2035 (transfers within three years of death), if the assignment is made more than three years before the death of the assignor, no part of the proceeds is includible in the assignor's gross estate at his death. Revenue Ruling 71–497.

If A, married to B, with B's consent procures a policy of life insurance on B's life, and the insurance is in force at A's death, B surviving, the value of the policy at A's death is includible in his estate under § 2033 because A is the owner of the policy at his death. And if B, with A's consent, procures a policy of insurance on A's life that designates B as beneficiary, and the insurance is in force at A's death, B surviving, no part of the proceeds is includible in A's estate because A was not the owner of the policy at his death. In short, § 2042 is concerned with a policy of insurance on the life of the decedent (1) the proceeds being payable to the estate of the decedent or (2) the proceeds being payable to a beneficiary other than the estate, the decedent having an incident of ownership at death.

Section 2042 permits a person of modest means to create an estate at death that passes to his beneficiaries free from Federal Estate Tax even though the decedent paid the costs of maintaining the policy from procurement until death. Like creation in 1948 of the split-gift provision of the Gift Tax, and the marital deduction under both the Gift Tax and the Estate Tax, the enactment of § 2042 was a boon to the taxpayer and a loss for the Treasury.

§ 13.18 **Powers of Appointment.** Under both the Gift and Estate Taxes, a general power of appointment is a power to appoint to one's self, or one's creditors, or one's estate, or the creditor's of one's estate. If X transfers property to a trustee to pay the net income to B for life, and then to pay the principal to C, with a power in A to appoint the principal by deed or will to such persons as A selects, A has a general power for purposes of both § 2514 of the Gift Tax and § 2041 of the Estate Tax. If A exercises the power during his lifetime by appointing the principal to D, A has made a gift to D under § 2514 because exercising the power is treated as the equivalent of A's owning the subject matter of the power and transferring it gratuitously to D. (On A's appointment, C's future interest ceases and D becomes the equitable remainderman under X's trust instrument.) Alternatively, if A dies possessed of the power, the value of the future interest subject to A's power is includible in A's estate if the power is a post–1942 power.

An intended donee of the power need not accept the power—he may disclaim it. Disclaimer of a general power (like disclaimer of a bequest under a will) does not result in a gift under the Gift Tax to that person or those persons who benefit from non-acceptance of the power. But release of an existing general power is equivalent to exercise for tax purposes. In the example in the paragraph above, if A releases his general power, he has extinguished a condition attached to the gift of principal to C, namely, non-exercise of the power by A, and A has in substance made a gift to C.

A power of appointment that would otherwise be a general power is non-general for tax purposes if

its exercise is limited by an ascertainable standard
relating to the health, education, support, or maintenance of the holder of the power. Nor is a power
that would otherwise be general treated as a general power if it is exercisable by the holder only with
the consent of the creater of the power, or only
with the consent of a person having a substantial
interest in the property subject to the power which
is adverse to exercise of the power in favor of the
holder. If a general power of appointment is exercisable only with the consent (say) of one other
person not having an adverse interest, the holder
is deemed to have a general power with respect to
half the property subject to the power. For example, if X transfers property to a trustee to pay the
net income to B for life, and then to pay the
principal to C, with a power in A, with B's consent,
to appoint the remainder to such person as A
selects, and A dies possessed of the power, B and C
surviving, half of the value of the future interest is
includible in A's estate under § 2041 of the Estate
Tax.

Although the Code and Regulations on powers of
appointment are complex, they in general more
faithfully reflect the economic consequences of the
existence of powers as a property device than does
the traditional substantive law of general powers
in a non-tax context. Generally speaking, the Federal Gift and Estate Taxes treat exercise, release,
lapse, and non-exercise of powers as equivalents,
and that similarity in function is one that can be

remembered when the detail of the tax law has been forgotten.

§ **13.19** **The** **Charitable** **Deduction.** Although the Federal Gift and Estate Taxes are assessed to the donor, identity of donees is important with respect to both the charitable and the marital deductions under both taxes.

The charitable deduction is an unlimited deduction under both the Gift and Estate Taxes. For example, if A, owning realty in fee simple absolute, gratuitously transfers it to a qualified charity, no Gift Tax is payable. Section 2522. If the entire gross estate of a decedent passes (or has passed) absolutely to a qualified charity, the transfer is tax-free under the Estate Tax. Section 2055. The unlimited charitable deduction demonstrates the indulgence given to charitable transfers in the United States under both Federal and state law. What is now an unlimited marital deduction under the Economic Recovery Tax Act of 1981 originated in an attempt to put taxpayers in common law states and community property states on a rough parity. In order that either the charitable or the marital deduction be properly claimed under the Estate Tax, the property with respect to which the deduction is sought must be included in the gross estate of the decedent. For example if the decedent during his lifetime creates a revocable trust with net income payable to himself for life, remainder to a qualified charity, the value of the corpus of the trust is includible in the decedent's gross estate

at death under both §§ 2036 and 2038. Because
the gift to charity vests indefeasibly at the decedent's death, the estate may effectively claim the
charitable deduction with respect to it.

To qualify for a charitable deduction under the
Federal Income, Gift, and Estate Taxes, a gratuitous transfer by the donor must be to a qualified
charity—that is, an organization listed in §§ 170,
2055, and 2522, of the Internal Revenue Code. It
bears emphasis that an organization that is "charitable" under state law for purposes of (say) applying the cy pres doctrine is not necessarily charitable for purposes of Federal tax law. Although in
this connection there is of course great overlap, a
lawyer representing a donor who expects to claim a
charitable deduction as a result of making a gratuitous transfer must ascertain that the recipient of
the gift is a qualified donee under the tax law.

Although an inter vivos or testamentary transfer
to a qualified charity need not be a present interest
to entitle the donor to the charitable deduction,
gifts of qualifying future interests ("charitable remainders") following "income" interests in non-
charities are hedged about with restrictions.
Apart from charitable remainders in farms or resi-
dences, charitable remainders qualifying for the
charitable deduction under the Gift and Estate
Taxes must be created by a charitable remainder
unitrust, a charitable remainder annuity trust, or
a pooled income fund.

Consistent with treating a general power in the donee (the holder of the power) as the equivalent of ownership of the appointive property under §§ 2514 and 2041, respectively, of the Gift and Estate Taxes, appointment to a qualified charity by the donee is treated under both taxes as a gratuitous transfer by the donee himself (rather than by the creator of the general power), and the donee is entitled to claim the charitable deduction. Similarly, release or non-exercise of a general power that results in an indefeasible vesting of an interest in a qualified charity may entitle the donee to claim the charitable deduction. Suppose that a decedent devises a life estate in his residence to his surviving spouse for life, remainder to a qualified charity, but with a power in A to appoint the remainder by deed or will to such person or persons as A selects. Because the testamentary gift to charity is subject to a general power in A, the decedent's estate cannot effectively claim a charitable deduction under the Estate Tax for the gift of the future interst to charity. If A releases his power during his lifetime, he has himself made a gift to charity for Gift Tax purposes, and if A dies not having exercised or released the power, he has in substance made a testamentary transfer to charity because the charitable gift is no longer subject to defeasance by the exercise of A's power.

§ 13.20 Generation–Skipping   Transfers. Suppose that A in 1992 created an irrevocable trust, with assets of $5,000,000, designating his

niece B as beneficiary of the net income for life,
and the children of B as beneficiaries of principal.
If B had a child or children alive at the creation of
the trust, A has made completed gifts of the entire
corpus of the trust (the present value of the income
interest for life, plus the present value of the
remainder). When B (the income beneficiary) dies
thereafter, her interest simply ceases to exist, and
no part of the trust corpus is a part of her net
probate estate.

Under the Tax Reform Act of 1986 a "Tax on
Certain Generation–Skipping Transfers," a tax
substantially equivalent to the Estate Tax, is imposed at B's death (when what is termed a "taxable
termination" occurs). B is viewed as if she, rather
than A, were the creator of the gift of corpus that
becomes possessory at B's death (B is the "deemed
transferor"). But B's estate is not liable for the
Generation–Skipping Tax. The trustee is personally liable for the payment of the tax, § 2603(a)(2),
and the tax is payable out of the corpus of the trust
(unless otherwise provided in the trust instrument).

A "taxable distribution" (as opposed to a "taxable termination") is demonstrated by the following example. Suppose that A in 1992 had a nephew B, and B had children. A created an irrevocable trust, with assets of $5,000,000, designating
B as beneficiary of the net income for life, and
giving the trustee a power to distribute the corpus
from time to time among B's children during B's
lifetime. Children of B were designated benefi-

ciaries of the principal in default of distribution.
Thereafter the trustee makes a distribution of corpus to the children of B. The distribution is a
"taxable distribution." Section 2612(b). The distributee of the property is personally liable for the
payment of the tax.

A "direct skip" occurs, for example, when the
transferor makes an inter vivos or testamentary
gift to a grandchild, rather than giving to the
transferor's child, who in turn might transfer the
property to his or her child.

Not all generation-skipping transfers are affected by the Generation–Skipping Tax. For example,
suppose that A in 1992 had four children, B, C, D,
and E, and all four of the children of A had
children. A created an irrevocable trust with a
corpus of $1,000,000. By the terms of the trust,
each child of A was designated the beneficiary for
life of the net income from $250,000, and on the
death of such income beneficiary, $250,000 of prin-
cipal was payable to such income beneficiary's children. This generation-skipping trust is unaffected
by the Generation–Skipping Tax because corpus in
its entirety falls within the $1,000,000 lifetime
exemption for each transferor. Section 2631(a).

Where facts invoke the Federal Estate Tax, there
is no "taxable termination" or "taxable distribution" (as the case may be). For example, suppose
that A in 1992 had a niece B, and B had children.
A created an irrevocable trust, designating B as
beneficiary of the net income for life, and giving B

a general power of appointment over the remainder. Children of B were designated beneficiaries of principal in default of appointment. B dies thereafter, never having exercised the power and still possessing the power. The Generation–Skipping Tax does not apply. Under § 2041 of the Estate Tax, possession of the general power of appointment brings the value of the corpus of the trust into B's gross estate for Federal Estate Tax purposes, and therefore no generation-skipping occurs.

Application of the Generation–Skipping Tax does not turn on the use of the trust device. Generation-skipping trust equivalents (such as the legal life estate-and-remainder combination) are within the reach of the tax.

§ 13.21 What is a "Generation"? A generation-skipping trust (or its equivalent) has beneficiaries in two or more generations younger than that of the creator of the trust. If A in 1992 created an irrevocable trust designating his niece B as the beneficiary of the net income for life, and designating B's children C, D, and E as beneficiaries of the remainder, the trust is a generation-skipping trust. If B were A's spouse rather than A's niece, the trust is not a generation-skipping trust because a spouse of the donor is in the same generation as the donor. Section 2651(c)(1). With respect to generation-skipping transfers outside the family, persons not more than 12½ years younger than the donor are in the generation of the donor. Persons more than 12½ years younger than the donor, but not more than 37½ years younger, are in the first younger generation.

INDEX

References are to Pages

ABATEMENT
Defined, 38–39.
Order, 39.

ACCEPTANCE
Gift, 5–6.

ACCUMULATIONS
See Rule Against Accumulations.

ADEMPTION
See also Anti–Lapse Statute; Lapse.
Avoidance, 31.
Defined, 31.

ADMINISTRATION
Estate, 13–15.
Small estate, 16–18.

ADMINISTRATOR
See also Executor.
Appointment, 14–15, 27.
Function, 15–16.
Responsibility, 15–16.

ADOPTION
Generally, 42–43.

ADVANCEMENT
See also Satisfaction.

ADVANCEMENT—Cont'd
Defined, 38.

AGE CONTINGENCIES
Creation, 197–198, 202.

AGENCY
Revocable trust, 169.

ALIENATION
See Restraints On Alienation; Spendthrift Trusts.

ANIMAL
Trust for, 235.

ANNUITY
Annuity trust, 239.
Federal Estate Tax, 324–325.

ANNUITY TRUST
See also Unitrust.
Tax Reform Act, 239.

ANTENUPTIAL AGREEMENT
See Prenuptial Agreement.

ANTI-LAPSE STATUTE
See also Lapse.
Function, 30.
Operation, 41–42.

APPOINTMENT
See Powers of Appointment.

ASSIGNMENT
Beneficial interest, 176–177.
Insurance,
        Generally, 126–127.
    Fire, 130–131.
    Liability, 131.
    Life, 128–130.

ATTACHMENT
Beneficial interest, 176–180.

ATTORNEY GENERAL
Charitable trusts, 236.

BENEFICIARIES' INTERESTS
See Blended Trusts; Discretionary Trusts; Gifts; Spendthrift
    Trusts; Support Trusts.

BEQUEST
See also Devise; Legacy.
Defined, 26.
General, 39.
Specific, 39.

BLENDED TRUSTS
See also Claflin Trusts; Discretionary Trusts; Spendthrift
    Trusts; Support Trusts.
Generally, 179–180.

BODY OF DECEDENT
Disposition, 85.

BOND
Executor, see Executor.
Gift of, 8.
Guardian, see Guardian.
P.O.D., 51.
United States Savings, Co-ownership, 50–51.

BREACH OF EXPRESS TRUST
Self-dealing, 277–278.

BURDEN OF PROOF
Contribution of survivor, 312–313.

CAPACITY
See also Mental Capacity.
Testamentary, 80.

CAPTURE
Appointive property, 217.

CHARITABLE DEDUCTION
Generally, 238–239, 329–331.

CHARITABLE TRUSTS
Generally, 234–241.
Duration, 237–238.
Enforcement, 236.
Tax Reform Act, 239.

CLAFLIN TRUSTS
 See also Blended Trusts; Discretionary Trusts; Spendthrift
      Trusts; Support Trusts
Generally, 178–179.

CLASS GIFTS
 Generally, 198–200.
Anti-lapse statute, 206–207.
Closing class, 198–199.
Drafting, 204–210.
Postponed, 199–200.

CODICIL
 See also Wills.
Defined, 32.

COMMUNITY FOUNDATIONS
Generally, 240–241.

COMMUNITY PROPERTY
 Generally, 22–23, 60–61.
Conflict of laws, 69–72.
Election by surviving spouse, 72–73.
Federal taxation, 68–69.
Life insurance, 64–67.
Management, 67–68.
Separate property, 62–64.
States, 61–62.

COMMUNITY TRUSTS
See Community Foundations.

CONFLICTS OF INTEREST
 See also Loyalty.
Fiduciaries, 277–280.

DEVISE
Defined, 26.

DISCLAIMER
See Renunciation.

DISCRETIONARY TRUSTS
     See also Blended Trusts; Spendthrift Trusts; Support
         Trusts.
   Generally, 177–178.
Clause creating, 178.

DIVORCE
Effect on will substitutes, 58.

DOCTRINE OF WORTHIER TITLE
See Worthier Title Doctrine.

DOWER
Abolition, 26.

DURABLE POWER OF ATTORNEY
Generally, 184–185.

DURATION OF TRUSTS
Generally, 237–238.
Charitable, 237.
Honorary, 235.
Private, 181–184.
Unincorporated association, 237.

DUTIES OF TRUSTEE
Investments, 281–284.
Loyalty, 277–280.
Procuring insurance, 280.

ELECTION BY SURVIVING SPOUSE
Revocable trust, 232–234.
Right, 33–34, 72–73.

EMPLOYEE BENEFIT PLANS
See also Pensions.
Generally, 141–144.

ENFORCEMENT
See Charitable Trusts; Honorary Trusts; Unincorporated Association.

ESTATE TAX
See Federal Estate Tax.

EXCLUSIVE OR EXCLUSIONARY POWERS
Generally, 219–220.

EXECUTION OF WILLS
See Wills.

EXECUTOR
See also Administrator.
Appointment, 14–15, 27.
Exemption from bond, 91.

EXECUTOR—Cont'd
Function, 15.
Nomination, 91.
Powers, 91–92.
Responsibility, 15–16.

EXECUTORY INTERESTS
Generally, 188–189.

FEDERAL ESTATE TAX
Generally, 290–294.
Annuity, 324–325.
Charitable deduction, 329–331.
Contemplation of death, 291–331.
Exemption, 291.
Gross estate, 292, 310–311.
Joint tenancy, 311–316.
Life insurance, 325–326.
Marital deduction, 229–232, 293, 306–310.
Orphan's deduction, 305.
Powers of appointment, 326–329.
Retained life estate, 319–321.
Revocable trust, 317–319.
Survivorship interests, 311–316.
Tenancy by entirety, 313.
Transfer taking effect at death, 321–324.
Transfer within three years of death, 291–292, 316–317.
Unified credit, 291, 295, 299–300.

FEDERAL GIFT TAX
Generally, 290–294.
Charitable deduction, 329–331.
Exclusion, 294, 299–303.
Exemption, 291.
Gift described, 295–299.
Joint tenancy, 313–314.
Marital deduction, 303–305.
Marital property rights, 298–299.
Minors, 302–303.
Powers of appointment, 296, 331.
Revocable trust, 297.
Split gifts, 303–305.
Stock, 297.
Support rights, 298.
Survivorship interests, 311–316.
Unified credit, 291, 295, 299–300.

FEDERAL INCOME TAX
Charitable deduction, 238.

FEE SIMPLE DETERMINABLE
Described, 188–189.

FIDUCIARY
See Administrator; Executor; Guardian; Trustee.

FOREIGN ASSETS
Generally, 23–24.

FUTURE INTERESTS
See also Class Gifts.
Changing, 190–194.
Class gifts, 198–204.
Executory interest, 188.
Possibility of reverter, 188–189.
Powers, see Powers of Appointment.
Remainder, 186–187.
Reversion, 186–187.
Right of entry, 188.
Using, 194–198.

GENERAL LEGACIES
See Bequest.

GENERATION–SKIPPING TAX
Generally, 331–334.
Generation defined, 334.
Taxable distribution, 332–333.
Taxable termination, 332.

GIFT TAX
Federal, see Federal Gift Tax.
State, 53.

GIFTS
Bonds, 8–9.
Causa mortis, 9–10.
Intangibles, 8–10.
Inter vivos, 4.
Lifetime, 4.
Minors, 10.
Personal property, 5–8.
Savings account, 9.
Testamentary, 4.

GROSS ESTATE
See Federal Estate Tax.

GUARDIAN
Exemption from bond, 89–90.
Nomination, 88–89.

GUARDIANSHIP
Generally, 223–228.
Trusteeship as alternative, 90, 223–228.
Trusteeship compared, 223–228.

HEIRS
See also Next of Kin.
Defined, 26.

HONORARY TRUSTS
Generally, 235–238.
Duration, 237.
Enforcement, 237.

ILLEGITIMATE
Generally, 43.

ILLUSORY APPOINTMENTS
Generally, 219–220.

INCORPORATION BY REFERENCE
Generally, 169–171.
Use by lawyers, 2.

INDEMNITY
Insurance, 106.
Trustee's right, 273–277.

INDEPENDENT SIGNIFICANCE
Generally, 172.
Revocable trust, 171–175.

INDESTRUCTIBLE TRUSTS
Generally, 180–184.

INDIVIDUAL RETIREMENT ACCOUNTS
Generally, 228–229.
Non-employed spouse, 229.

INFANTS
See Minors.

INSURANCE
Assignment,
        Generally, 126–127.
    Fire, 130–131.
    Liability, 131.
    Life, 128–130.
Casualty, 105–106.
Fire, 105–106.
Homeowners, 106–107.
Inland marine, 105.
Insurable interest, 114–117.
Liability, 105–107, 113–114.
Life, see Life Insurance.
Marine, 105.
Property, 105–106, 113–114, 130–131.

INSURANCE TRUSTS
Generally, 110, 225.

INTANGIBLE PERSONAL PROPERTY
Gift, 8–10.

INTENT
Requirement,
    Gift, 5.

INTESTATE
Defined, 25.

INTESTATE LAWS
See Descent and Distribution.

INVESTMENTS
Trust, 280–284.

JOINT TENANCY
    See also Tenancy by Entirety.
Defined, 46.
Severability, 48.

KEOGH TRUSTS
Generally, 228.

LAPSE
    See also Anti–Lapse Statute.
Avoidance, 30.
Defined, 30.

LEGACY
   See also Bequest.
Defined, 26.

LIABILITIES OF TRUSTEE, EXECUTOR, OR ADMINISTRATOR
See Contracts of Trustee; Torts; Trustee.

LIFE INSURANCE
   See also Insurance.
Assignment, 126–130.
Cash surrender value, 108.
Change of beneficiary, 124–126.
Collateral for loan, 109.
Federal Estate Tax, 112, 325–326.
Insurable interest, 114–115.
Kinds of policies, 117–120.
Life insured, 107–110.
Lump sum payment, 121.
Paid up, 118.
Proceeds, 18, 110–112, 120–123.
Settlement options, 120–123.
State law, 110–112.
Why buy, 108–110.

LIMITATION
Words of, 190.

LIVING WILL
Generally, 185.

LOYALTY
   See also Conflicts of Interest
Duty, 277–280.

MARITAL DEDUCTION
Federal Estate Tax, 229–232, 293, 306–310.
Federal Gift Tax, 303–305.
Trust, 229–232.

MENTAL CAPACITY
Settlor of trust, 165.
Testator of will, 80, 165.

MINORS
Federal Gift Tax, 302–303.
Gift to, 6, 10.

MORTMAIN ACTS
Generally, 239–240.
Limit testamentary freedom, 35.

NEXT OF KIN
See also Heirs.
Defined, 26.

NOMINEES
Property in name of, 287.

NON–CHARITABLE ASSOCIATIONS
See Unincorporated Association.

ORAL TRUSTS
Generally, 158–163.

ORPHAN'S DEDUCTION
Generally, 305–306.

PAY ON DEATH
Bank account, 56–57.
United States Savings Bond, 51.

PENSIONS
Forced retirement, 146–147.
Government, 141–142.
Health and welfare, 143–144.
Outside probate estate, 19.
Private,
Generally, 141–146.
Funded, 143.
Insured, 143.
Persons covered, 142.
Portability, 144–146.
Trusteed, 142–143.
Vesting, 144–146.
Social security, 133–141.
Veterans, 150–152.

PER CAPITA
See also Per Stirpes.
Avoidance, 85.
Defined, 39–40.

PER STIRPES
See also Per Capita.
Avoidance, 85.

PER STIRPES—Cont'd
Defined, 39–41.

PERPETUITIES, RULE AGAINST
See Rule Against Perpetuities.

PERSONAL PROPERTY
Bank account, 56–57.
United States Savings Bond, 51.
Gift, 5–11.
Intangible, 8–11.
P.O.D., ——.
Tangible, 7–8.
United States Savings Bond, 51.

POSSIBILITY OF REVERTER
See Future Interests.

POUR–OVER WILL
Generally, 171–176.
Use by lawyers, 2.
Use with trust, 171–175.

POWER
See Administrator; Executor; Powers in Trust; Powers of Appointment; Trustee.

POWERS IN TRUST
Generally, 219–220.
Release, 212.

POWERS OF APPOINTMENT
Generally, 210–216.
Anti-lapse statute, 216–217.
Capture, 217.
Exclusive defined, 220.
Federal Estate and Gift Taxes, 326–329.
General defined, 211.
Hotchpot clause, 221–222.
Illusory appointment, 219–220.
In trust, 219–220.
Motivation, 214–216.
Origin, 213–214.
Power in trust, 219–220.
Release, 211–212.
Renunciation, 211–212.
Special, 211.

POWERS OF APPOINTMENT—Cont'd
Terminology, 210–213.
Use by lawyers, 2.

PRENUPTIAL AGREEMENT
Effect on elective share, 34.

PRETERMITTED HEIR
Anticipating, 83.
Statute,
    Function, 83.
    Limits testamentary freedom, 35.

PROBATE
    See also Administration; Wills.
Avoidance, 18–19, 51–52.
Will, 14.

PROOF
See Burden of Proof.

PURCHASE
Words of, 190.

RELEASE
Power of appointment, 211–212.

REMAINDERS
See Future Interests.

REMOTENESS OF VESTING
See Rule Against Perpetuities.

RENUNCIATION
    Generally, 43–44.
Bequest or devise, 296.
Power of appointment, 211–212.

RESTRAINTS ON ALIENATION
Limit testamentary freedom, 35.

RESULTING TRUSTS
Charitable trust fails, 236.

REVERSIONS
See Future Interests.

REVOCATION
Trust, 163–165.

REVOCATION—Cont'd
Will, 35–36.

RIGHT OF ENTRY FOR CONDITION BROKEN
See Future Interests.

RULE AGAINST ACCUMULATIONS
    Generally, 269–270.
Limits testamentary freedom, 35.

RULE AGAINST PERPETUITIES
    Generally, 246–251.
Appointments, 260–261.
Class gifts, 252–257.
Cy pres, 268.
Drafting, 261–267.
Limits testamentary freedom, 35.
Perpetuities period, 251–252.
Powers, 257–259.
Reforming, 267–269.
Uniform statutory rule, 268–269.
Use by lawyers, 2.
Wait and see, 267–268.

RULE IN SHELLEY'S CASE
Generally, 242–246.

SATISFACTION
    See also Advancement.
Avoidance, 38.
Defined, 38.

SAVINGS ACCOUNT
    See also Totten Trusts.
Gift, 9.
Pay on death, 56–57.

SAVINGS BANK TRUSTS
See Totten Trusts.

SETTLEMENT OPTIONS
See Life Insurance.

SHELLEY'S CASE, RULE IN
See Rule in Shelley's Case.

SIMULTANEOUS DEATH
Survivorship interests, 54–56.

SOCIAL SECURITY
Becoming insured, 137–139.
Benefits,
        Generally, 11–12, 139–141.
    Child, 139–140.
    Disability, 138.
    Husband, 139–140.
    Retirement, 139–140.
    Wife, 139–140.
History, 134.
Persons covered, 135.
Portability, 135–136.
Quarters of coverage, 137–138.

SPENDTHRIFT TRUSTS
        See also Blended Trusts; Discretionary Trusts; Support
                Trusts.
    Generally, 176–177.
Clause creating, 177.

SPOUSE
Surviving,
    Provision for, 32–33.
    Right of election, 33–34, 57–58.

STATUTE OF FRAUDS
Generally, 158–163.

STATUTE OF WILLS
Generally, 158–163.

STATUTES
See Mortmain Acts; Predetermitted Heir; Statute of Frauds;
    Statute of Wills.

STOCK
Gift, 8.

SUBSTITUTION, GIFT BY
See Anti–Lapse Statute.

SUPPORT TRUSTS
    See also Blended Trusts; Discretionary Trusts; Spendthrift
            Trusts.
Generally, 179–180.

SURVIVORSHIP, REQUIREMENT
Generally, 36–38.

TAXES
See Federal Estate Tax; Federal Gift Tax; Federal Income Tax.

TENANCY BY ENTIRETY
See also Joint Tenancy.
Defined, 46.
Severability, 49.

TENANTS IN COMMON
Defined, 45–46.

TERMINATION OF TRUST
Generally, 180–184.

TESTATOR
Defined, 25.
Interview with, 79.
Mental capacity, 80, 165.

TORTS
Fiduciary responsibility, 275–277.

TOTTEN TRUSTS
Generally, 56–57.

TRUSTEE
Administrative powers, 284–289.
Contract liability, 271–277.
Duty of loyalty, 277–280.
Investments, 280–284.
Right to exoneration, 273.
Right to indemnity, 272–277.
Right to reimbursement, 273.
Tort liability, 271–277.

TRUSTS
Charitable, see Charitable Trusts.
Community, see Community Foundations.
Duration, 180–184.
Individual retirement accounts, 228–229.
Inter vivos, 155.
Investments, 280–284.
Irrevocable, 163.
Keogh, 228.
Marital deduction, 229–232.
Private,
    Creation, 155–163.
    Requirements, 158–163.

TRUSTS—Cont'd
Q-tip, 307.
Revocable, 163–169, 232–234.
Statute of frauds, 158–163.
Statute of wills, 158–163.
Termination, 180–184.
Testamentary, 155.

UNIFORM PROBATE CODE
Generally, 20.
Survival requirement, 37.
Surviving divorced spouse, 58.
Survivorship interests, 57.

UNINCORPORATED ASSOCIATION
Enforcement of trust of, 237.
Trust for, 237.

UNITRUST
See also Annuity Trust.
Tax Reform Act, 239.

VESTED OR CONTINGENT CONSTRUCTION
See Contingent Remainders.

VETERANS' BENEFITS
Benefits,
Generally, 150–153.
Disability, 152.
Family, 152.
Coverage, 151.

WAIT AND SEE
See Rule Against Perpetuities.

WILLS
Attestation clause, 93–94.
Closing recitation, 92–93.
Codicil, 32.
Dispositive clause, 82–84.
Drafting,
Generally, 75–79.
Caveats, 85–88.
Execution, 2, 95–96.
Freedom of testation, 34–35.
Introductory clause, 79–82.
Limited function, 74–75.

WILLS—Cont'd
Probate, 14.
Revocation, 35–36.
Safeguarding, 99.
Self-proved, 96–99.
Statutory, 99.
Testamentary capacity, 2.
Videotaping execution, 95.

WORKERS' COMPENSATION
Generally, 147–148.
Benefits, 19, 149–150.
History, 147.

WORTHIER TITLE DOCTRINE
Generally, 242–246.
Avoidance, 245.
Use by lawyers, 2.

†